STAR WARS
AGE OF REBELLION

HEROES

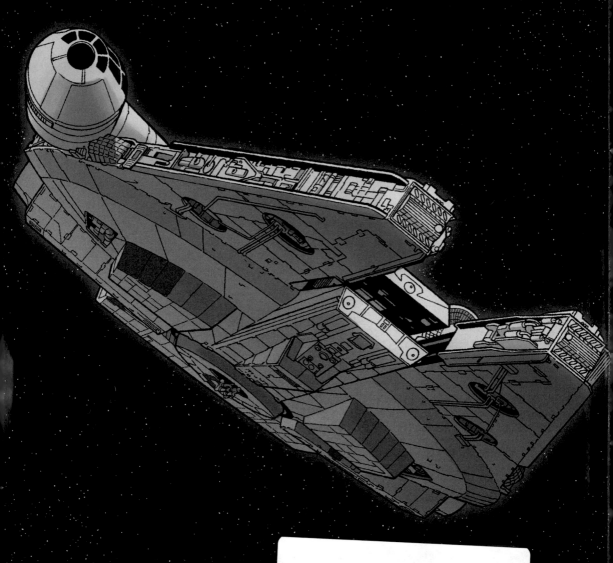

STAR WARS
AGE OF REBELLION

Collection Editor	**JENNIFER GRÜNWALD**	VP Production & Special Projects	**JEFF YOUNGQUIST**
Assistant Editor	**CAITLIN O'CONNELL**	SVP Print, Sales & Marketing	**DAVID GABRIEL**
Associate Managing Editor	**KATERI WOODY**	Director, Licensed Publishing	**SVEN LARSEN**
Editor, Special Projects	**MARK D. BEAZLEY**	Book Designer	**ADAM DEL RE**

STAR WARS: AGE OF REBELLION — HEROES. Contains material originally published in magazine form as STAR WARS: AGE OF REBELLION — HAN SOLO #1, LANDO CALRISSIAN #1, LUKE SKYWALKER #1, PRINCESS LEIA #1 and SPECIAL #1. First printing 2019. ISBN 978-1-302-91708-1. Published by MARVEL WORLDWIDE, INC., a subsidiary of MARVEL ENTERTAINMENT, LLC. OFFICE OF PUBLICATION: 135 West 50th Street, New York, NY 10020. STAR WARS and related text and illustrations are trademarks and/or copyrights, in the United States and other countries, of Lucasfilm Ltd. and/or its affiliates.© & ™ Lucasfilm Ltd. No similarity between any of the names, characters, persons, and/or institutions in this magazine with those of any living or dead person or institution is intended, and any such similarity which may exist is purely coincidental. Marvel and its logos are TM Marvel Characters, Inc. **Printed in Canada.** DAN BUCKLEY, President, Marvel Entertainment; JOHN NEE, Publisher; JOE QUESADA, Chief Creative Officer; TOM BREVOORT, SVP of Publishing; DAVID BOGART, Associate Publisher & SVP of Talent Affairs; DAVID GABRIEL, SVP of Sales & Marketing, Publishing; JEFF YOUNGQUIST, VP of Production & Special Projects; DAN CARR, Executive Director of Publishing Technology; ALEX MORALES, Director of Publishing Operations; DAN EDINGTON, Managing Editor; SUSAN CRESPI, Production Manager; STAN LEE, Chairman Emeritus. For information regarding advertising in Marvel Comics or on Marvel.com, please contact Vit DeBellis, Custom Solutions & Integrated Advertising Manager, at vdebellis@marvel.com. For Marvel subscription inquiries, please call 888-511-5480. **Manufactured between 6/14/2019 and 7/16/2019 by SOLISCO PRINTERS, SCOTT, QC, CANADA.**

10 9 8 7 6 5 4 3 2 1

HEROES

Writer — GREG PAK

PRINCESS LEIA #1
Artists, pp. 1-12 & 20 — CHRIS SPROUSE & KARL STORY
Artists, pp. 13-19 — WILL SLINEY, MARC DEERING & KARL STORY

HAN SOLO #1
Penciler — CHRIS SPROUSE
Inker — KARL STORY

LANDO CALRISSIAN #1
Artist — MATTEO BUFFAGNI

LUKE SKYWALKER #1
Pencilers — CHRIS SPROUSE, SCOTT KOBLISH & STEFANO LANDINI
Inkers — KARL STORY & MARC DEERING

Color Artist — TAMRA BONVILLAIN
Cover Art — TERRY DODSON & RACHEL DODSON

STAR WARS: AGE OF REBELLION SPECIAL #1
"THE TRIAL OF DAGOBAH"
Writer — MARC GUGGENHEIM
Artist — ANDREA BROCCARDO
Color Artist — DONO SÁNCHEZ-ALMARA

"STOLEN VALOR"
Writer/Artist — JON ADAMS
Color Artist — CHRIS O'HALLORAN

Cover Art — GIUSEPPE CAMUNCOLI & GURU-eFX

Letterer — VC'S TRAVIS LANHAM
Assistant Editor — TOM GRONEMAN
Editor — MARK PANICCIA

Editor in Chief — C.B. CEBULSKI
Chief Creative Officer — JOE QUESADA
President — DAN BUCKLEY

For Lucasfilm:
Senior Editor — ROBERT SIMPSON
Creative Director — MICHAEL SIGLAIN
Lucasfilm Story Group — JAMES WAUGH, LELAND CHEE, MATT MARTIN
Lucasfilm Art Department — PHIL SZOSTAK

PRINCESS LEIA

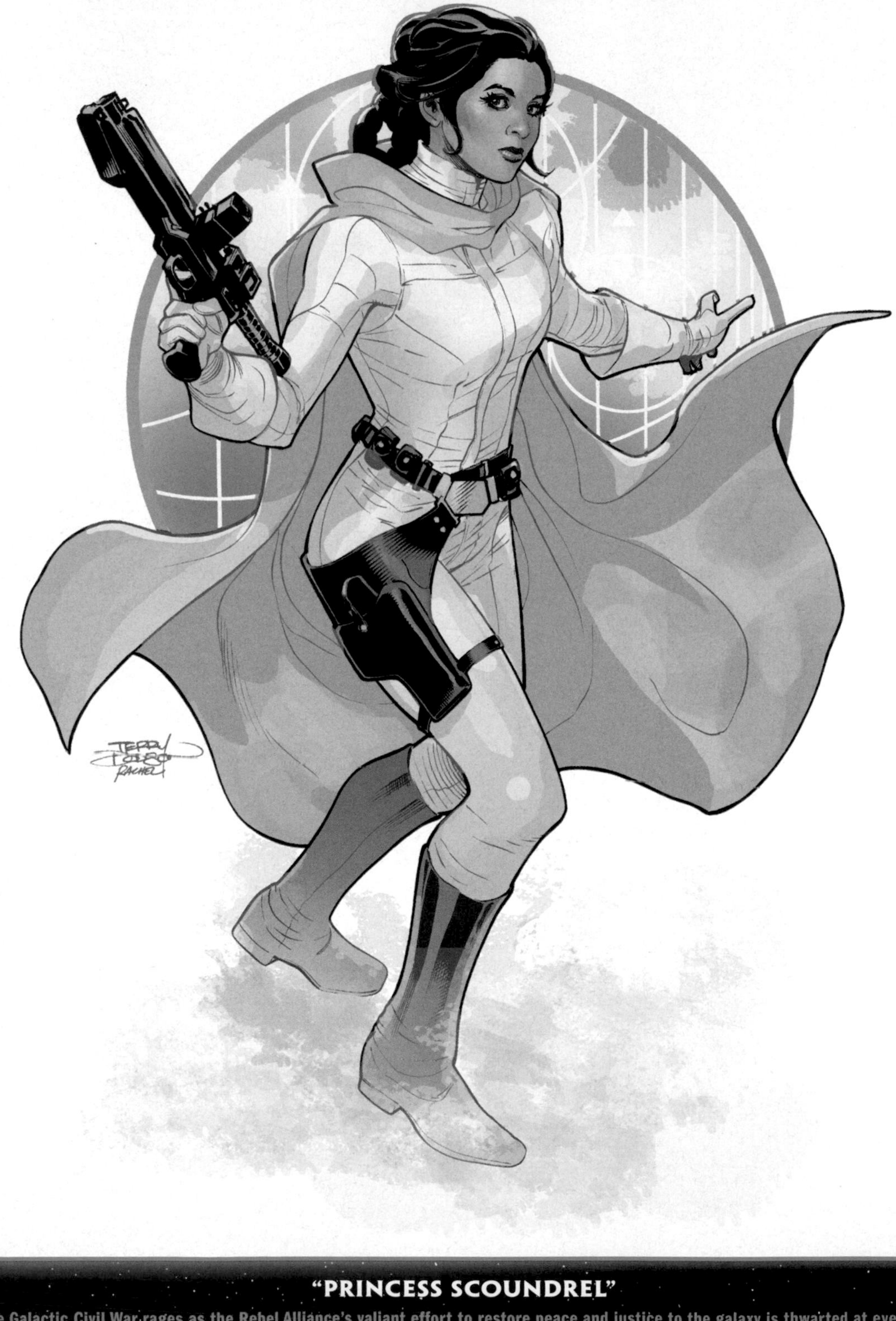

"PRINCESS SCOUNDREL"

The Galactic Civil War rages as the Rebel Alliance's valiant effort to restore peace and justice to the galaxy is thwarted at every turn by the evil Galactic Empire. Princess Leia Organa of Alderaan is one of the Rebellion's most important heroes. She's given years to the war as a skilled diplomat, a military leader and as a symbol of hope for the downtrodden across the galaxy. But now, for love, she'll have to become something new — a scoundrel. . .

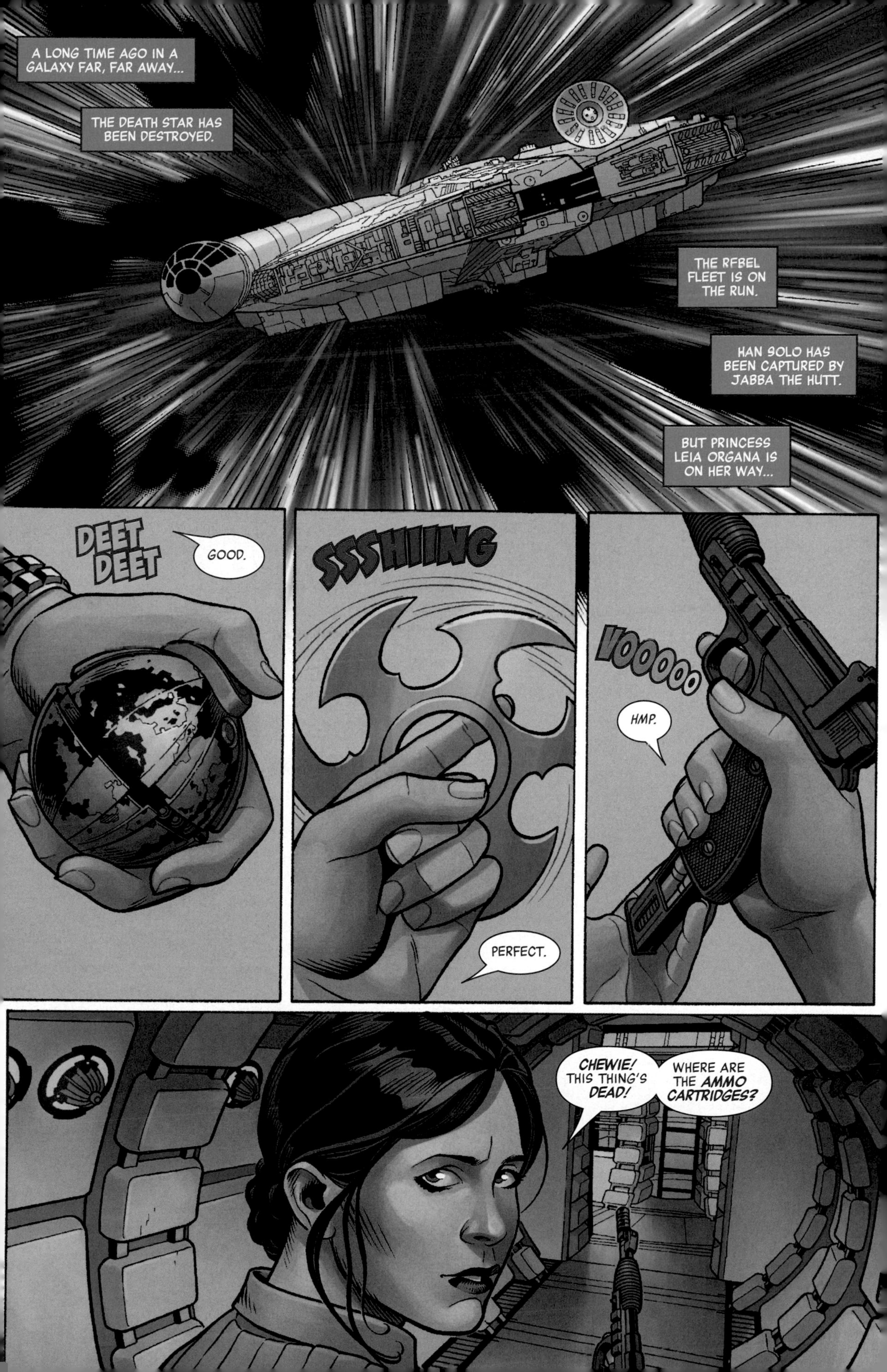
A LONG TIME AGO IN A GALAXY FAR, FAR AWAY...
THE DEATH STAR HAS BEEN DESTROYED.
THE REBEL FLEET IS ON THE RUN.
HAN SOLO HAS BEEN CAPTURED BY JABBA THE HUTT.
BUT PRINCESS LEIA ORGANA IS ON HER WAY...
DEET DEET
GOOD.
SSSHIIING
PERFECT.
VOOOOO
HMP.
CHEWIE! THIS THING'S DEAD!
WHERE ARE THE AMMO CARTRIDGES?

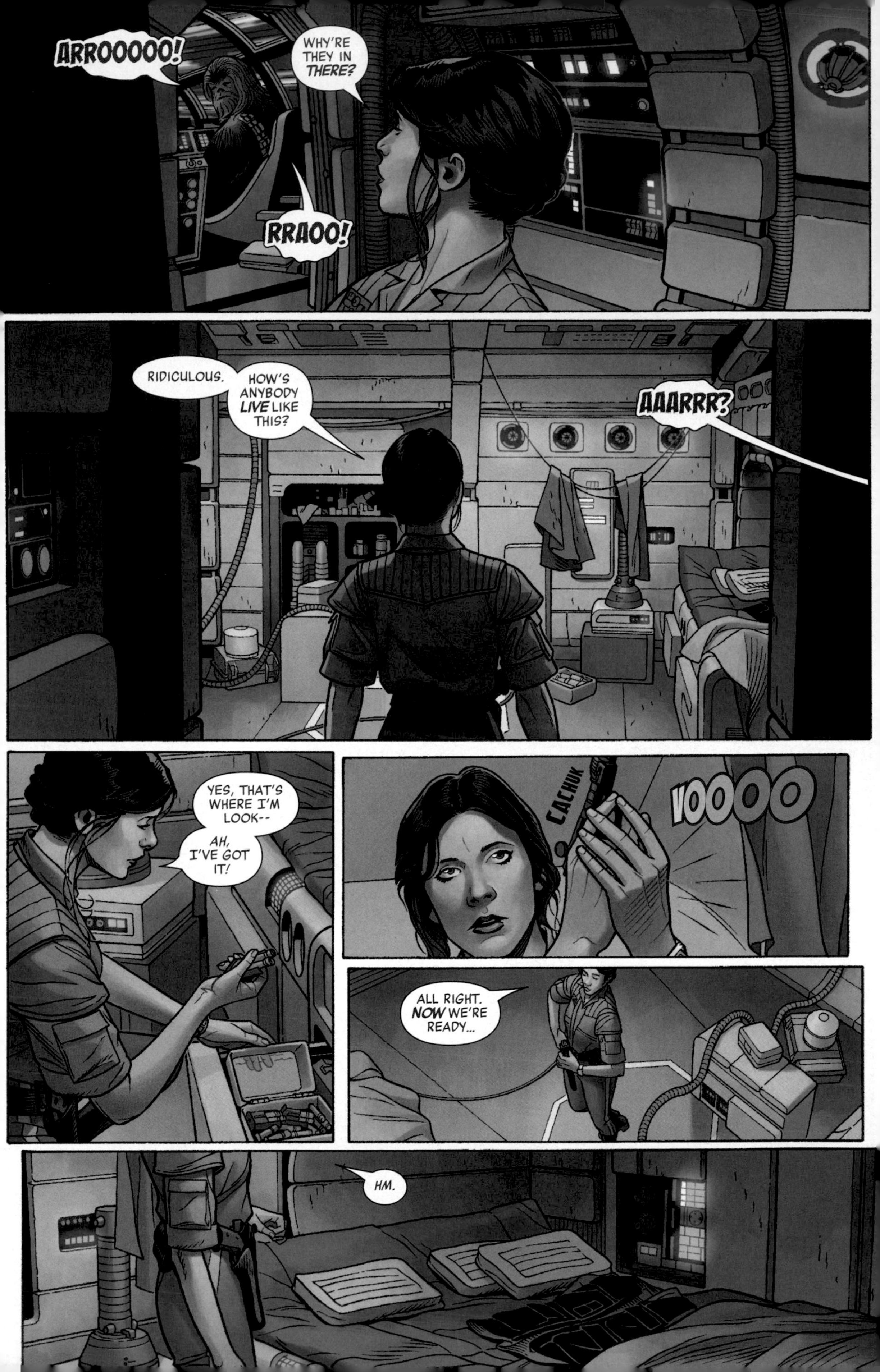
ARROOOOO!
WHY'RE THEY IN THERE?
RRAOO!
RIDICULOUS.
HOW'S ANYBODY LIVE LIKE THIS?
AAARRR?
YES, THAT'S WHERE I'M LOOK--
AH, I'VE GOT IT!
CACHUK
VOOOO
ALL RIGHT. NOW WE'RE READY...
HM.

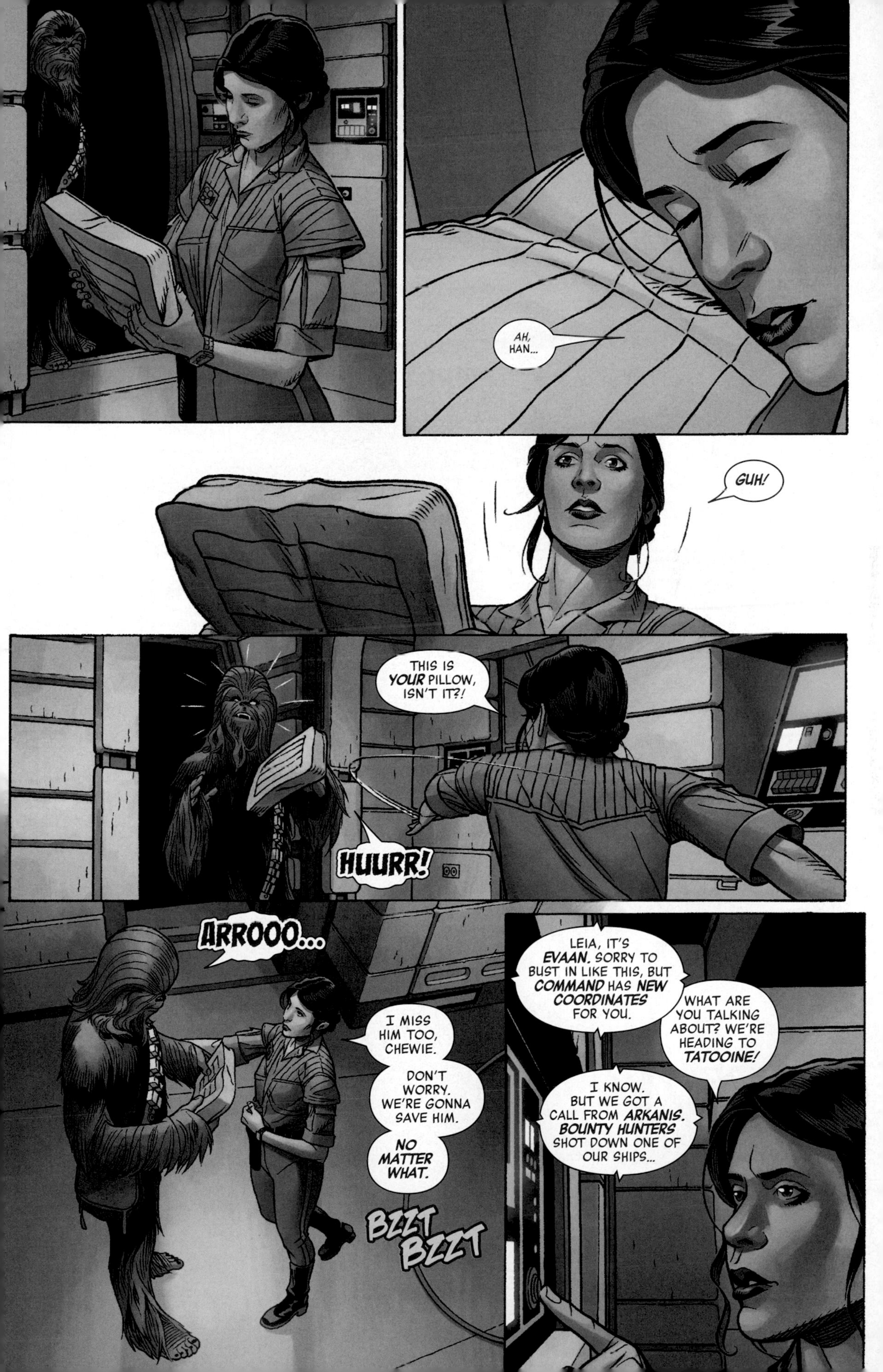
AH, HAN...
GUH!
THIS IS YOUR PILLOW, ISN'T IT?!
HUURR!
ARROOO...
I MISS HIM TOO, CHEWIE.
DON'T WORRY. WE'RE GONNA SAVE HIM.
NO MATTER WHAT.
BZZT BZZT
LEIA, IT'S EVAAN. SORRY TO BUST IN LIKE THIS, BUT COMMAND HAS NEW COORDINATES FOR YOU.
WHAT ARE YOU TALKING ABOUT? WE'RE HEADING TO TATOOINE!
I KNOW. BUT WE GOT A CALL FROM ARKANIS. BOUNTY HUNTERS SHOT DOWN ONE OF OUR SHIPS...

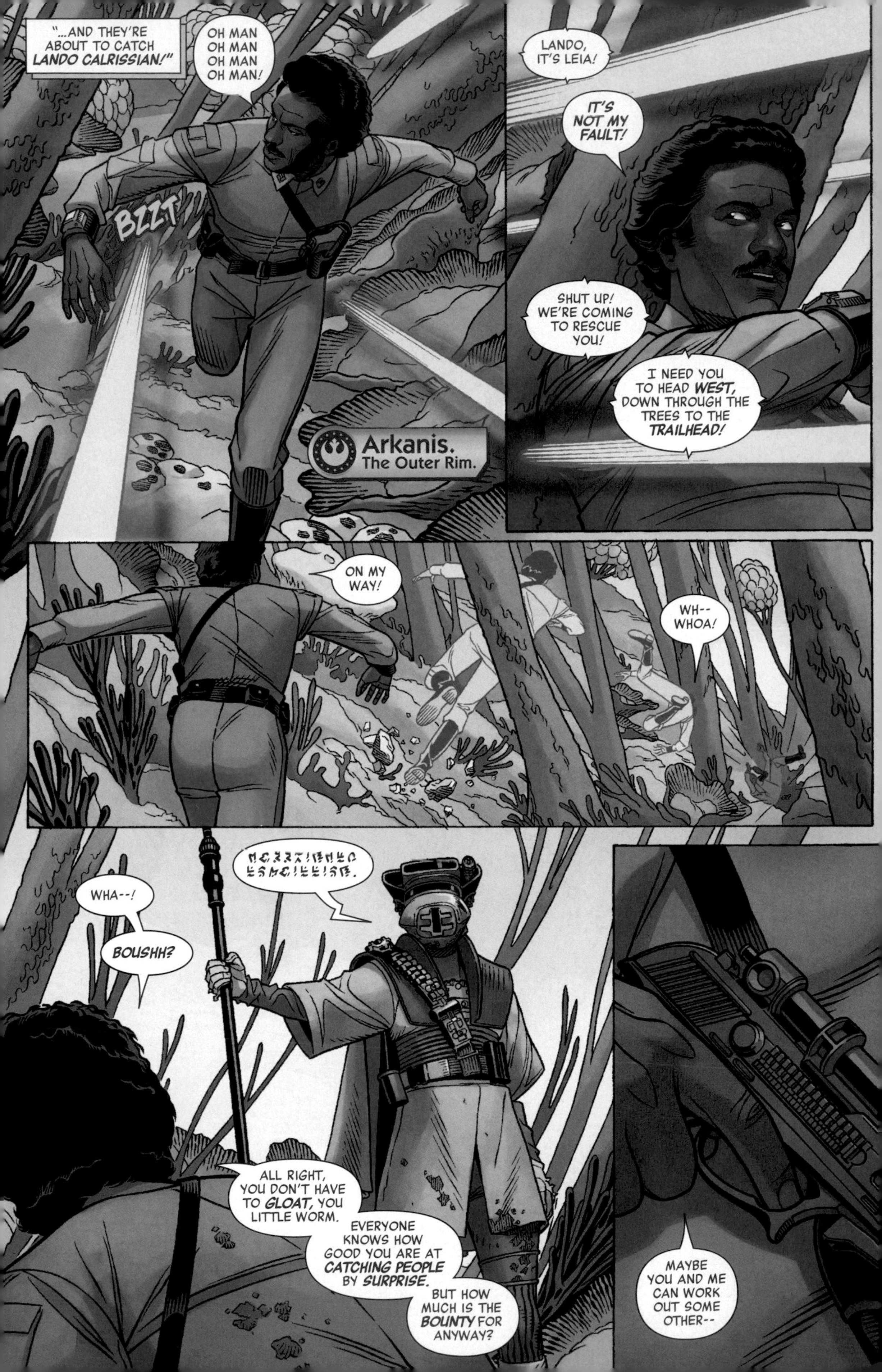
"...AND THEY'RE ABOUT TO CATCH LANDO CALRISSIAN!"
OH MAN OH MAN OH MAN OH MAN!
BZZT
Arkanis. The Outer Rim.
LANDO, IT'S LEIA!
IT'S NOT MY FAULT!
SHUT UP! WE'RE COMING TO RESCUE YOU!
I NEED YOU TO HEAD WEST, DOWN THROUGH THE TREES TO THE TRAILHEAD!
ON MY WAY!
WH-- WHOA!
WHA--!
BOUSHH?
ALL RIGHT, YOU DON'T HAVE TO GLOAT, YOU LITTLE WORM.
EVERYONE KNOWS HOW GOOD YOU ARE AT CATCHING PEOPLE BY SURPRISE.
BUT HOW MUCH IS THE BOUNTY FOR ANYWAY?
MAYBE YOU AND ME CAN WORK OUT SOME OTHER--

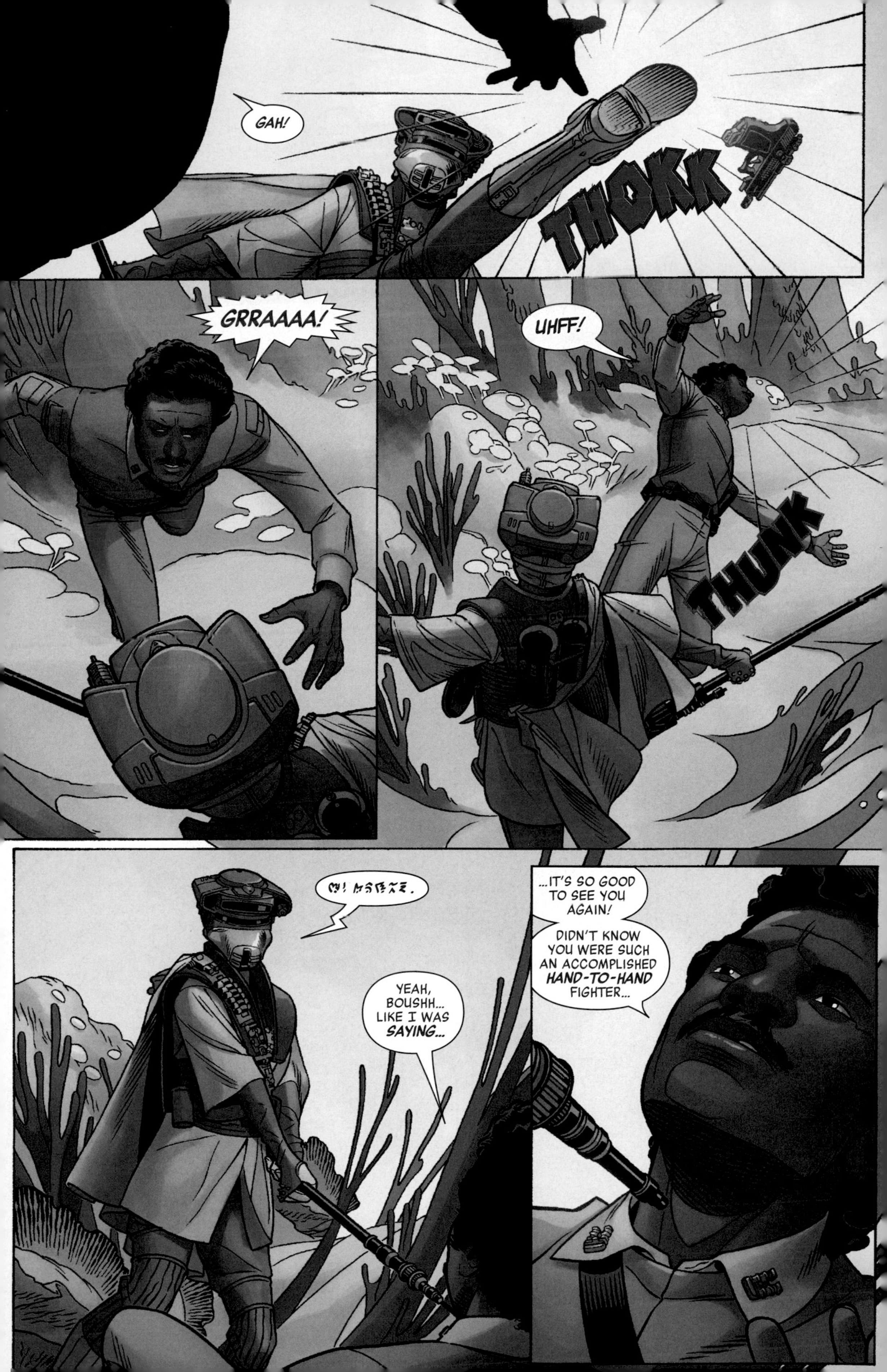
GAH!
THOKK
GRRAAAA!
UHFF!
THUNK
YEAH, BOUSHH... LIKE I WAS *SAYING...*
...IT'S SO GOOD TO SEE YOU AGAIN!
DIDN'T KNOW YOU WERE SUCH AN ACCOMPLISHED *HAND-TO-HAND* FIGHTER...

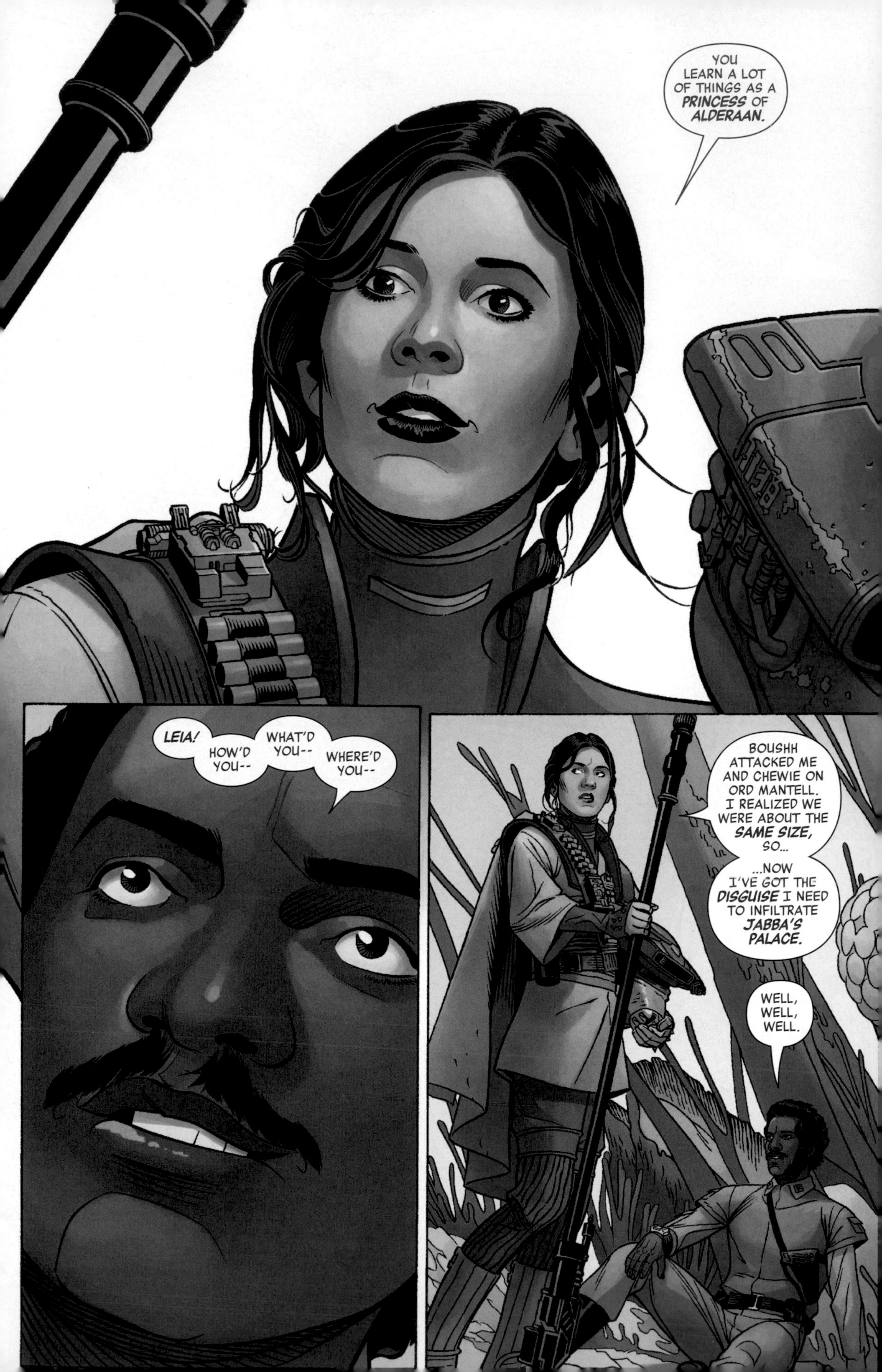
YOU LEARN A LOT OF THINGS AS A PRINCESS OF ALDERAAN.
LEIA!
HOW'D YOU--
WHAT'D YOU--
WHERE'D YOU--
BOUSHH ATTACKED ME AND CHEWIE ON ORD MANTELL. I REALIZED WE WERE ABOUT THE SAME SIZE, SO...
...NOW I'VE GOT THE DISGUISE I NEED TO INFILTRATE JABBA'S PALACE.
WELL, WELL, WELL.

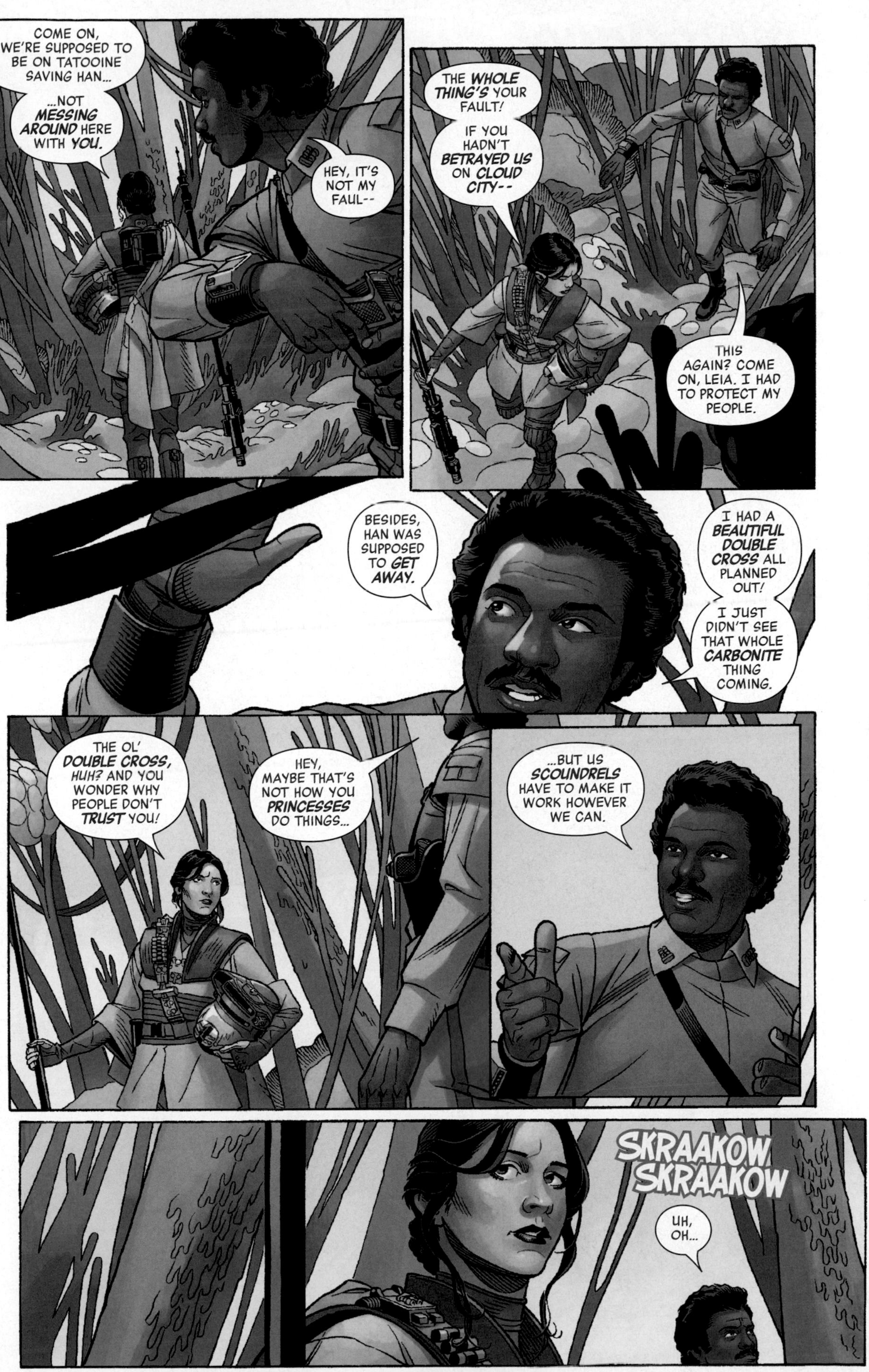
COME ON, WE'RE SUPPOSED TO BE ON TATOOINE SAVING HAN...
...NOT MESSING AROUND HERE WITH YOU.
HEY, IT'S NOT MY FAUL--
THE WHOLE THING'S YOUR FAULT!
IF YOU HADN'T BETRAYED US ON CLOUD CITY--
THIS AGAIN? COME ON, LEIA. I HAD TO PROTECT MY PEOPLE.
BESIDES, HAN WAS SUPPOSED TO GET AWAY.
I HAD A BEAUTIFUL DOUBLE CROSS ALL PLANNED OUT!
I JUST DIDN'T SEE THAT WHOLE CARBONITE THING COMING.
THE OL' DOUBLE CROSS, HUH? AND YOU WONDER WHY PEOPLE DON'T TRUST YOU!
HEY, MAYBE THAT'S NOT HOW YOU PRINCESSES DO THINGS...
...BUT US SCOUNDRELS HAVE TO MAKE IT WORK HOWEVER WE CAN.
SKRAAKOW SKRAAKOW
UH, OH...

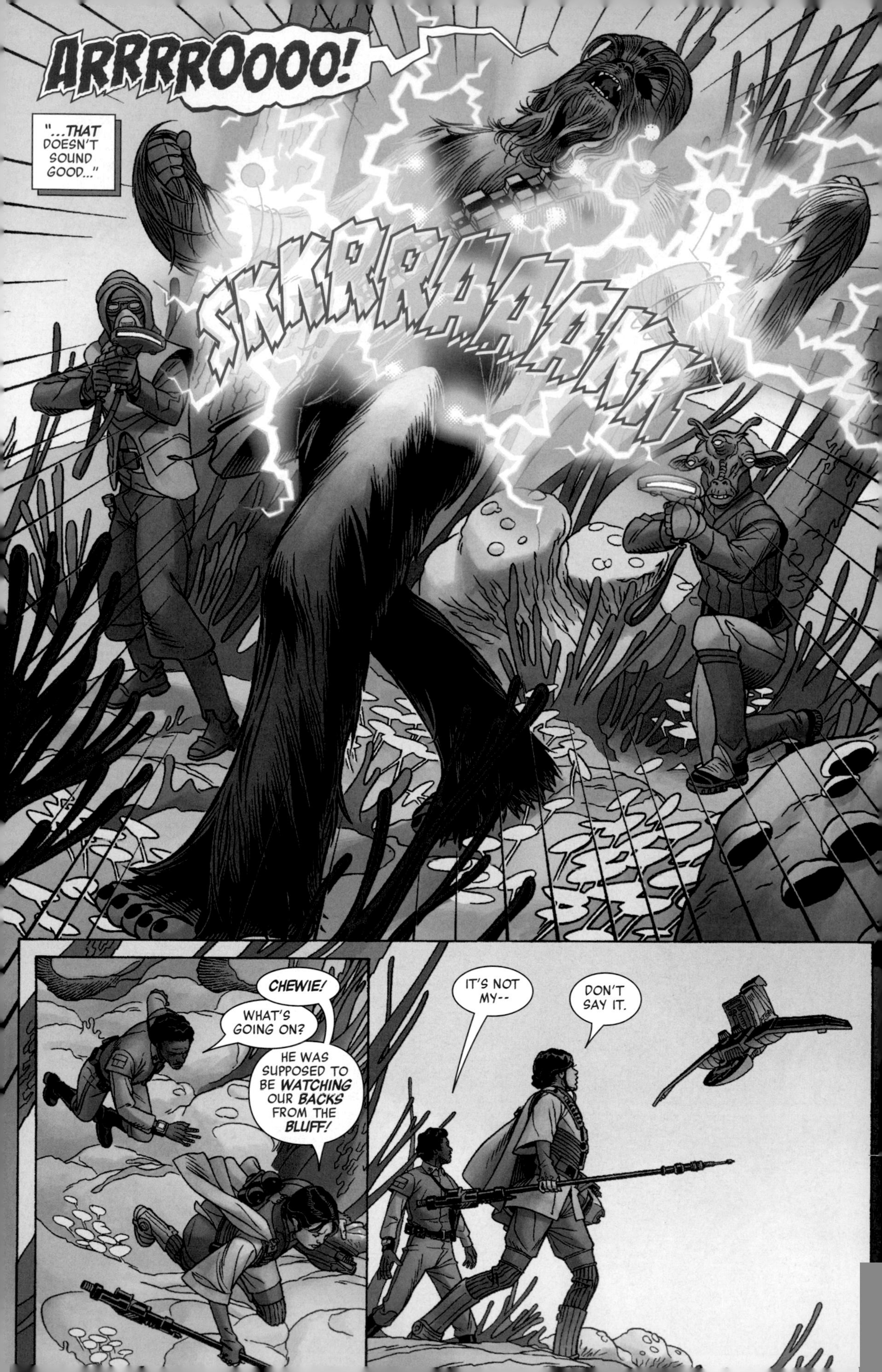
ARRRROOOO!
"...THAT DOESN'T SOUND GOOD..."
SKKRRAAAAK!
CHEWIE!
WHAT'S GOING ON?
HE WAS SUPPOSED TO BE WATCHING OUR BACKS FROM THE BLUFF!
IT'S NOT MY--
DON'T SAY IT.

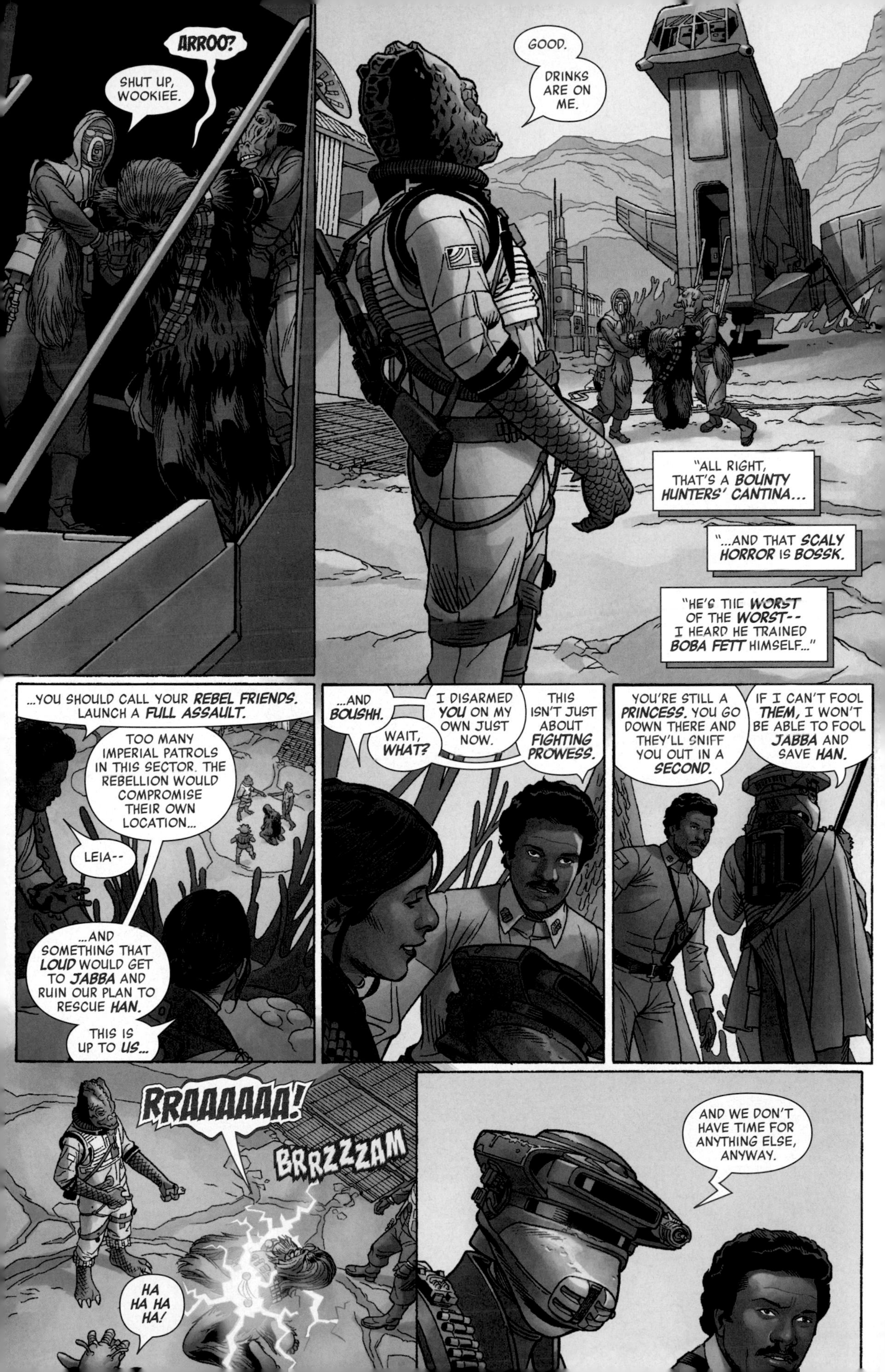
SHUT UP, WOOKIEE.
ARROO?
GOOD.
DRINKS ARE ON ME.
"ALL RIGHT, THAT'S A BOUNTY HUNTERS' CANTINA...
"...AND THAT SCALY HORROR IS BOSSK.
"HE'S THE WORST OF THE WORST-- I HEARD HE TRAINED BOBA FETT HIMSELF..."
...YOU SHOULD CALL YOUR REBEL FRIENDS. LAUNCH A FULL ASSAULT.
TOO MANY IMPERIAL PATROLS IN THIS SECTOR. THE REBELLION WOULD COMPROMISE THEIR OWN LOCATION...
LEIA--
...AND SOMETHING THAT LOUD WOULD GET TO JABBA AND RUIN OUR PLAN TO RESCUE HAN.
THIS IS UP TO US...
...AND BOUSHH.
WAIT, WHAT?
I DISARMED YOU ON MY OWN JUST NOW.
THIS ISN'T JUST ABOUT FIGHTING PROWESS.
YOU'RE STILL A PRINCESS. YOU GO DOWN THERE AND THEY'LL SNIFF YOU OUT IN A SECOND.
IF I CAN'T FOOL THEM, I WON'T BE ABLE TO FOOL JABBA AND SAVE HAN.
RRAAAAAA!
BRRZZZAM
HA HA HA HA!
AND WE DON'T HAVE TIME FOR ANYTHING ELSE, ANYWAY.

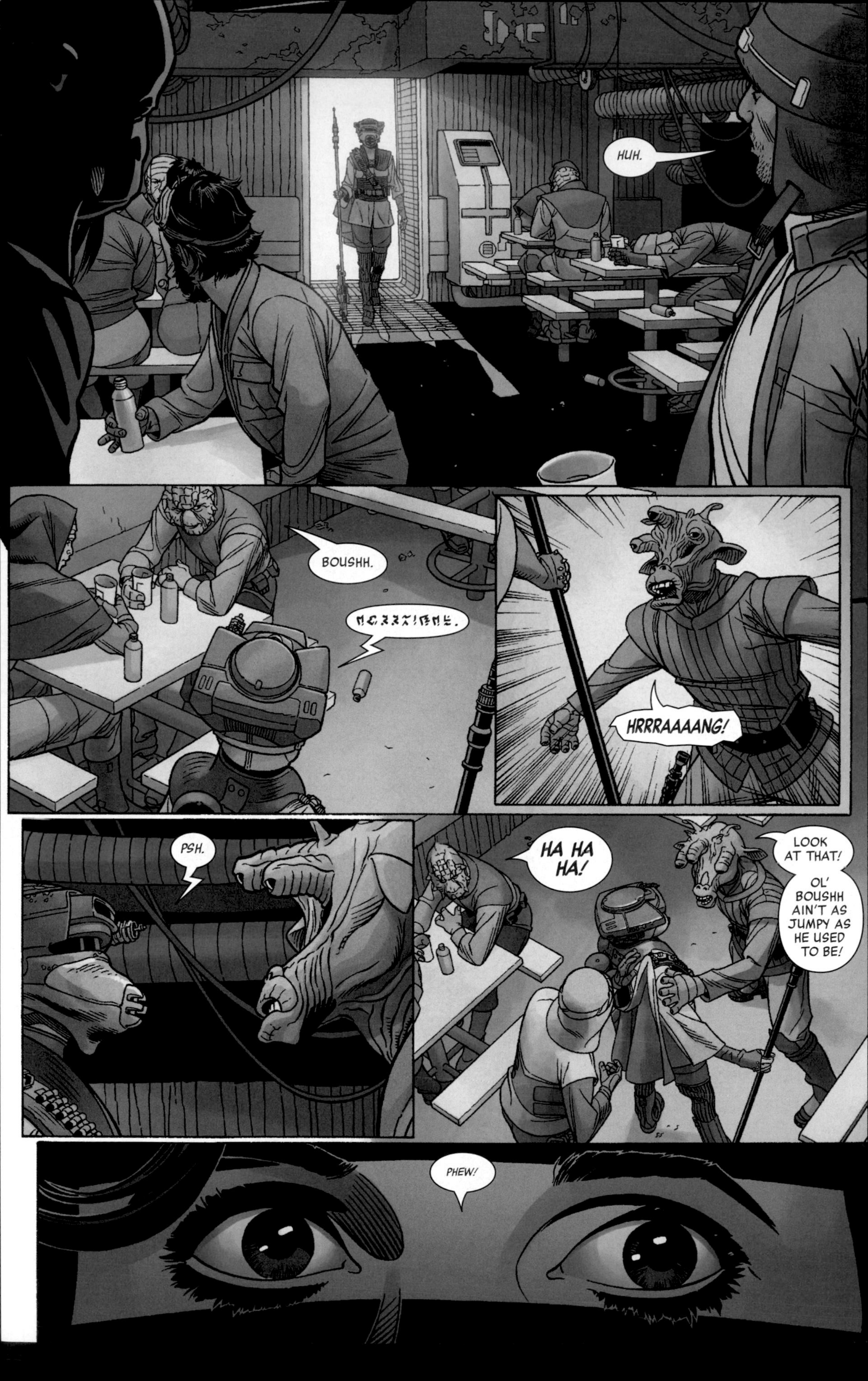
HUH.
BOUSHH.
HRRRAAAANG!
PSH.
HA HA HA!
LOOK AT THAT!
OL' BOUSHH AIN'T AS JUMPY AS HE USED TO BE!
PHEW!

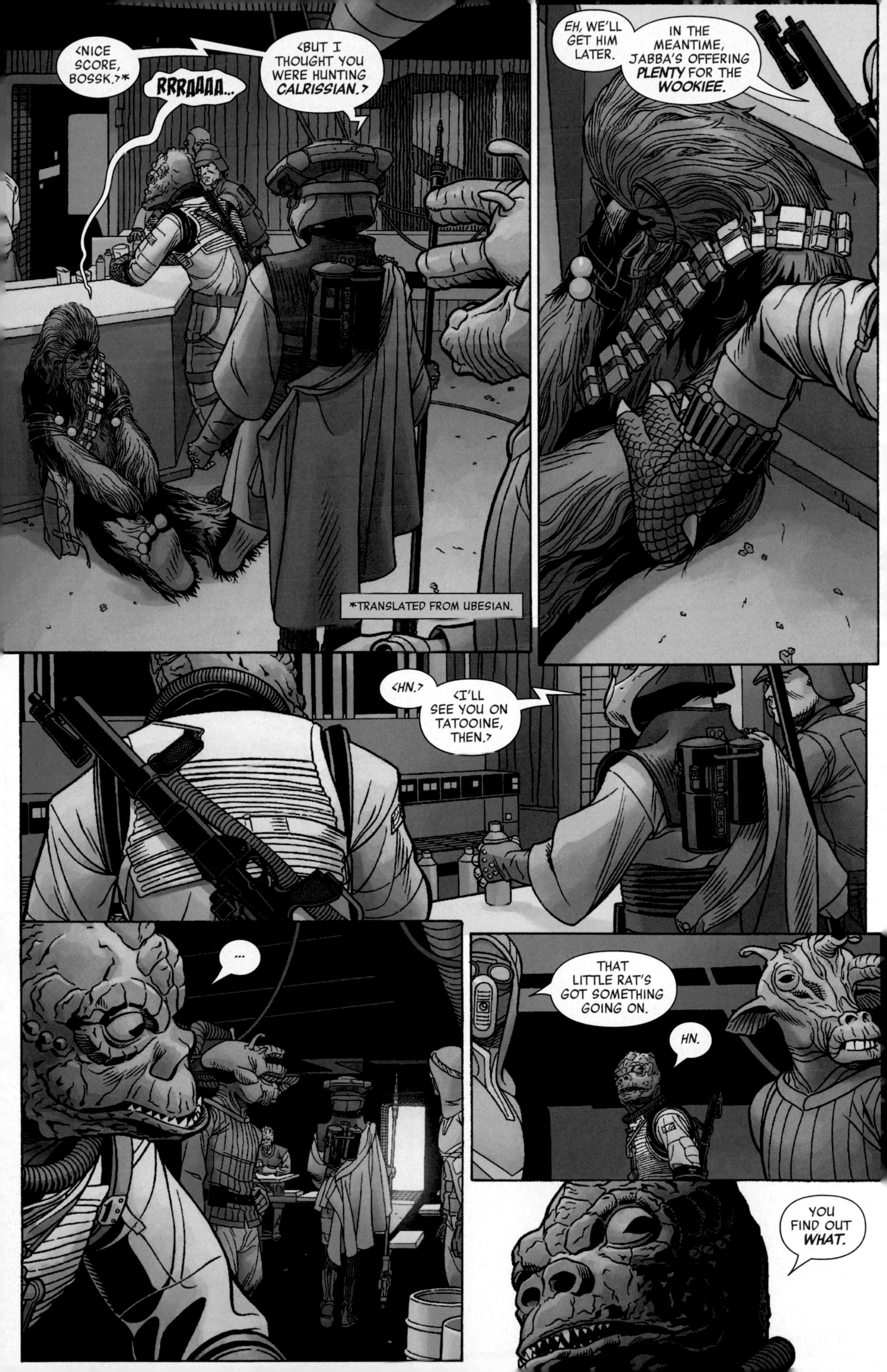

<NICE SCORE, BOSSK.>*
<BUT I THOUGHT YOU WERE HUNTING CALRISSIAN.>
RRRAAAA...
*TRANSLATED FROM UBESIAN.
EH, WE'LL GET HIM LATER.
IN THE MEANTIME, JABBA'S OFFERING PLENTY FOR THE WOOKIEE.
<HN.>
<I'LL SEE YOU ON TATOOINE, THEN.>
...
THAT LITTLE RAT'S GOT SOMETHING GOING ON.
HN.
YOU FIND OUT WHAT.

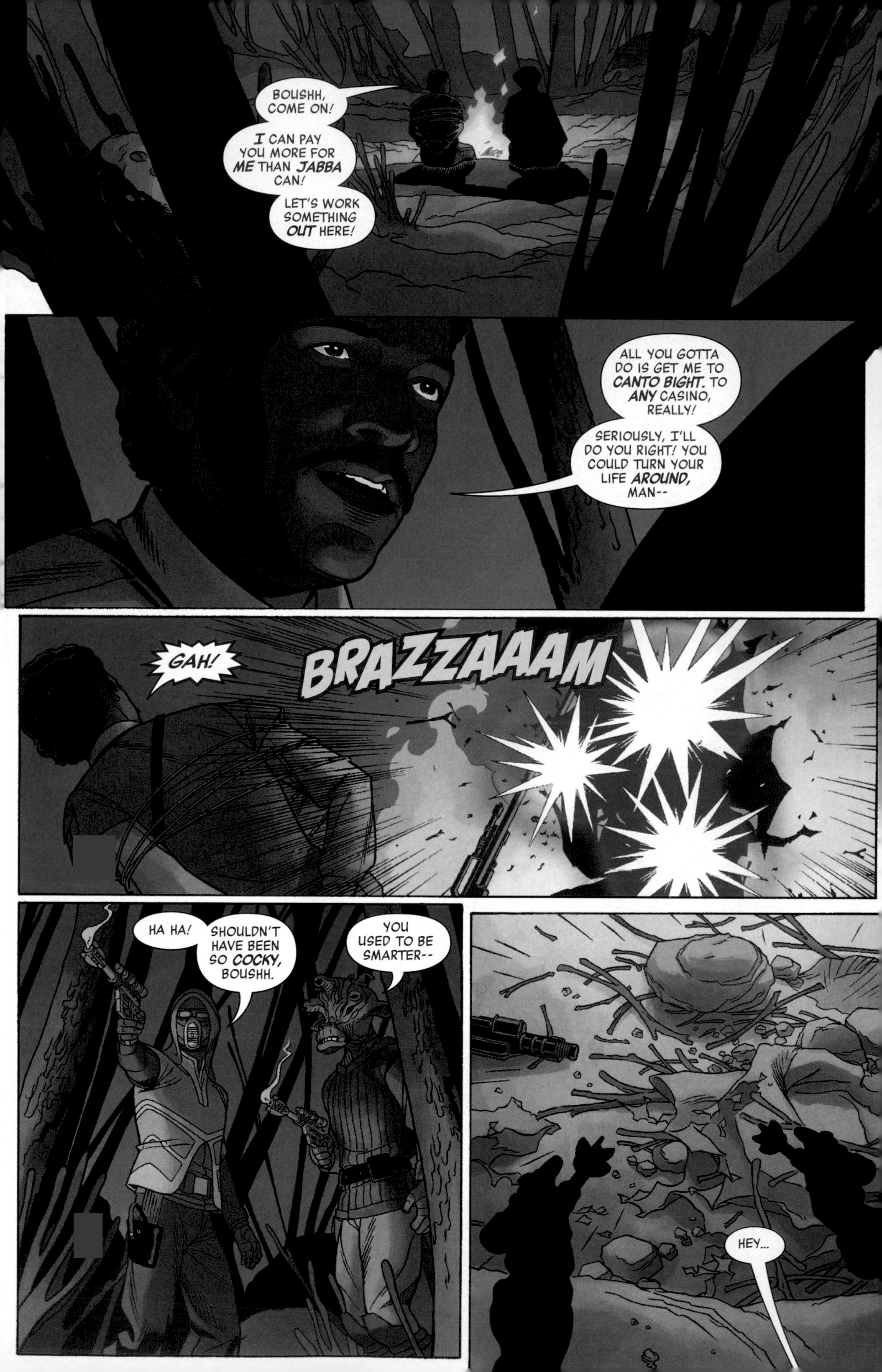
BOUSHH, COME ON!
I CAN PAY YOU MORE FOR ME THAN JABBA CAN!
LET'S WORK SOMETHING OUT HERE!
ALL YOU GOTTA DO IS GET ME TO CANTO BIGHT. TO ANY CASINO, REALLY!
SERIOUSLY, I'LL DO YOU RIGHT! YOU COULD TURN YOUR LIFE AROUND, MAN--
GAH!
BRAZZAAAM
HA HA!
SHOULDN'T HAVE BEEN SO COCKY, BOUSHH.
YOU USED TO BE SMARTER--
HEY...

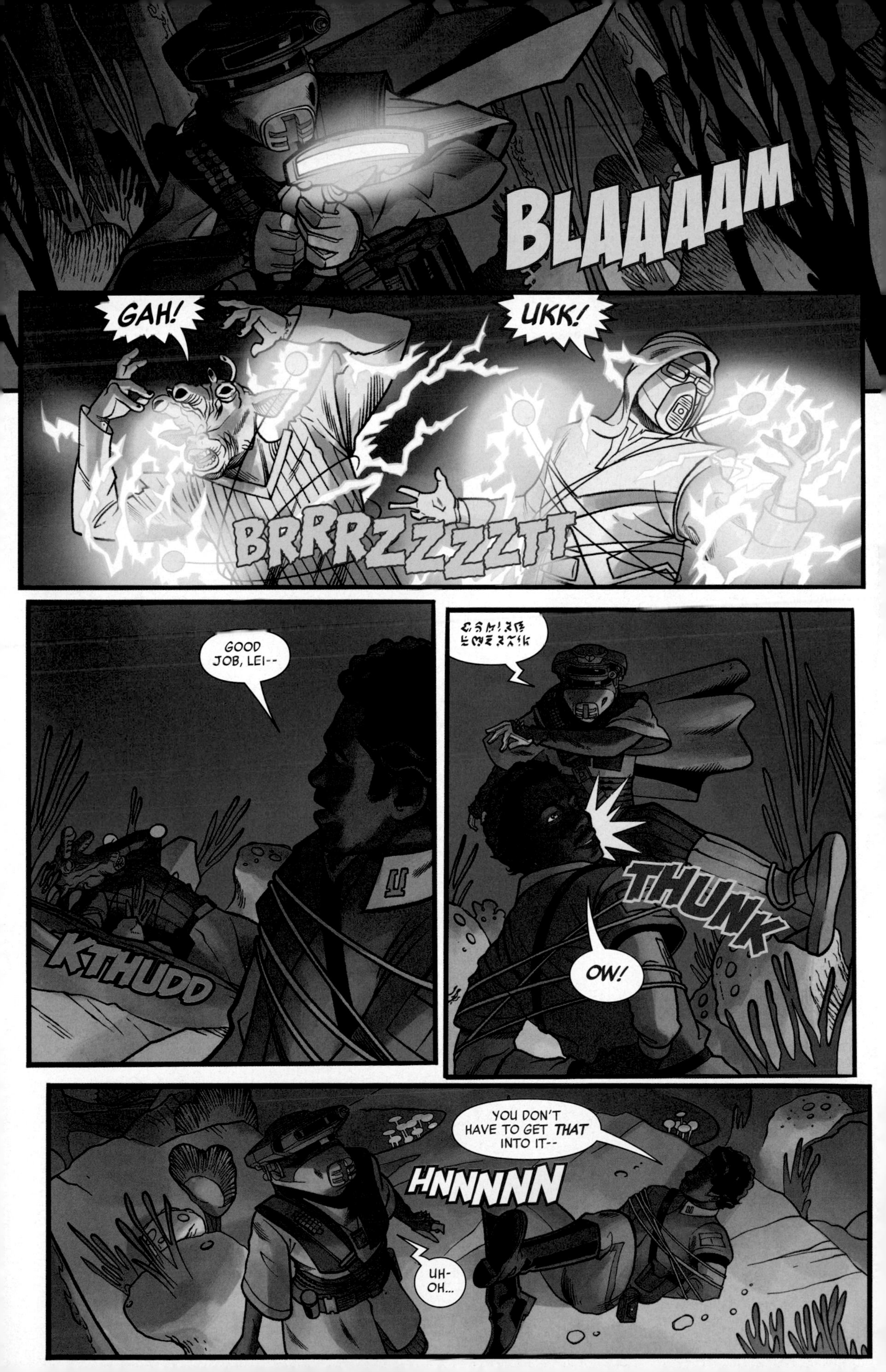

BLAAAAM
GAH!
UKK!
BRRRZZZZTT
GOOD JOB, LEI--
KTHUDD
THUNK
OW!
YOU DON'T HAVE TO GET *THAT* INTO IT--
HNNNNN
UH-OH...

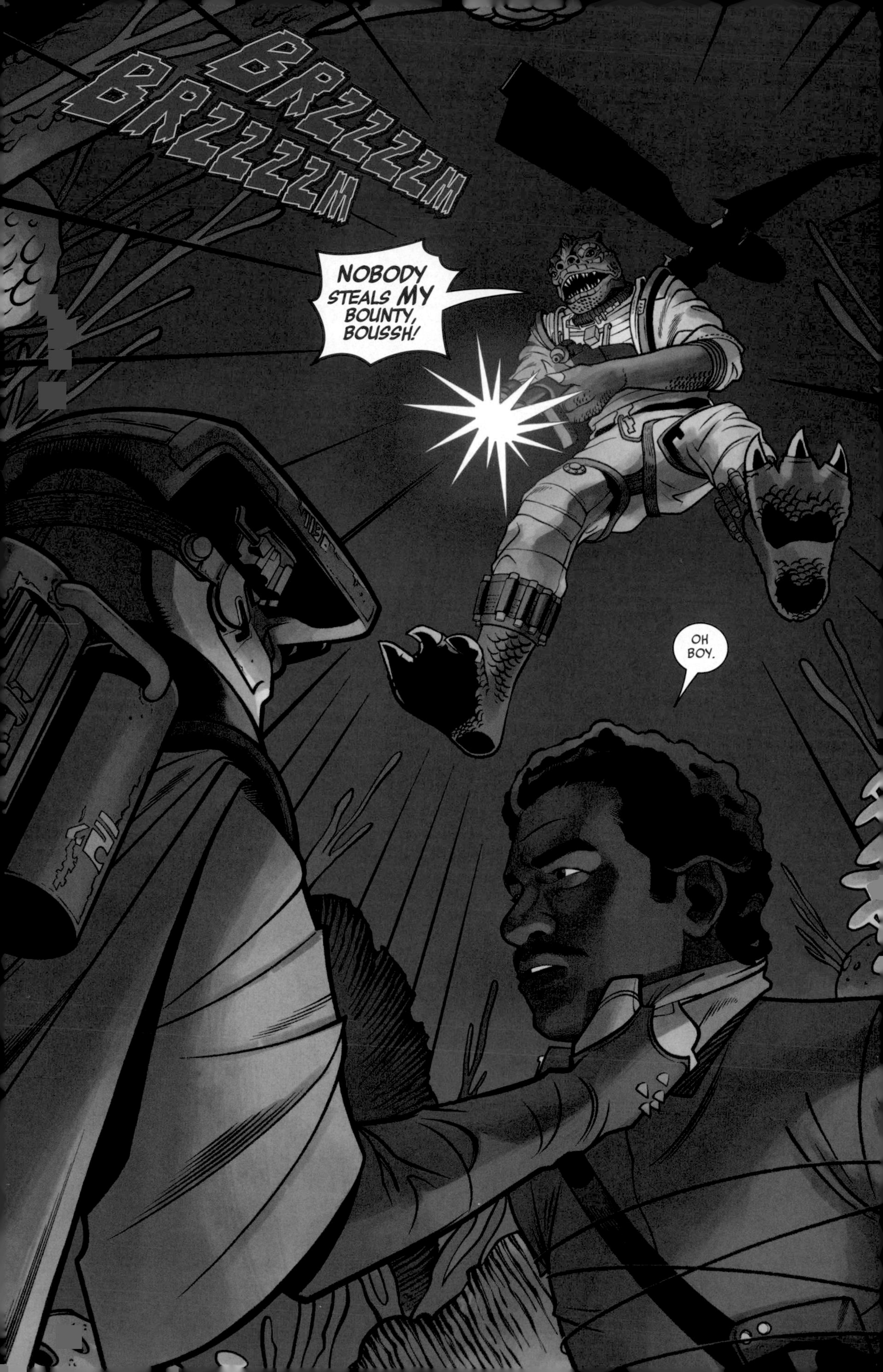
BRZZZZZM
BRZZZZZM
NOBODY STEALS MY BOUNTY, BOUSSH!
OH BOY.

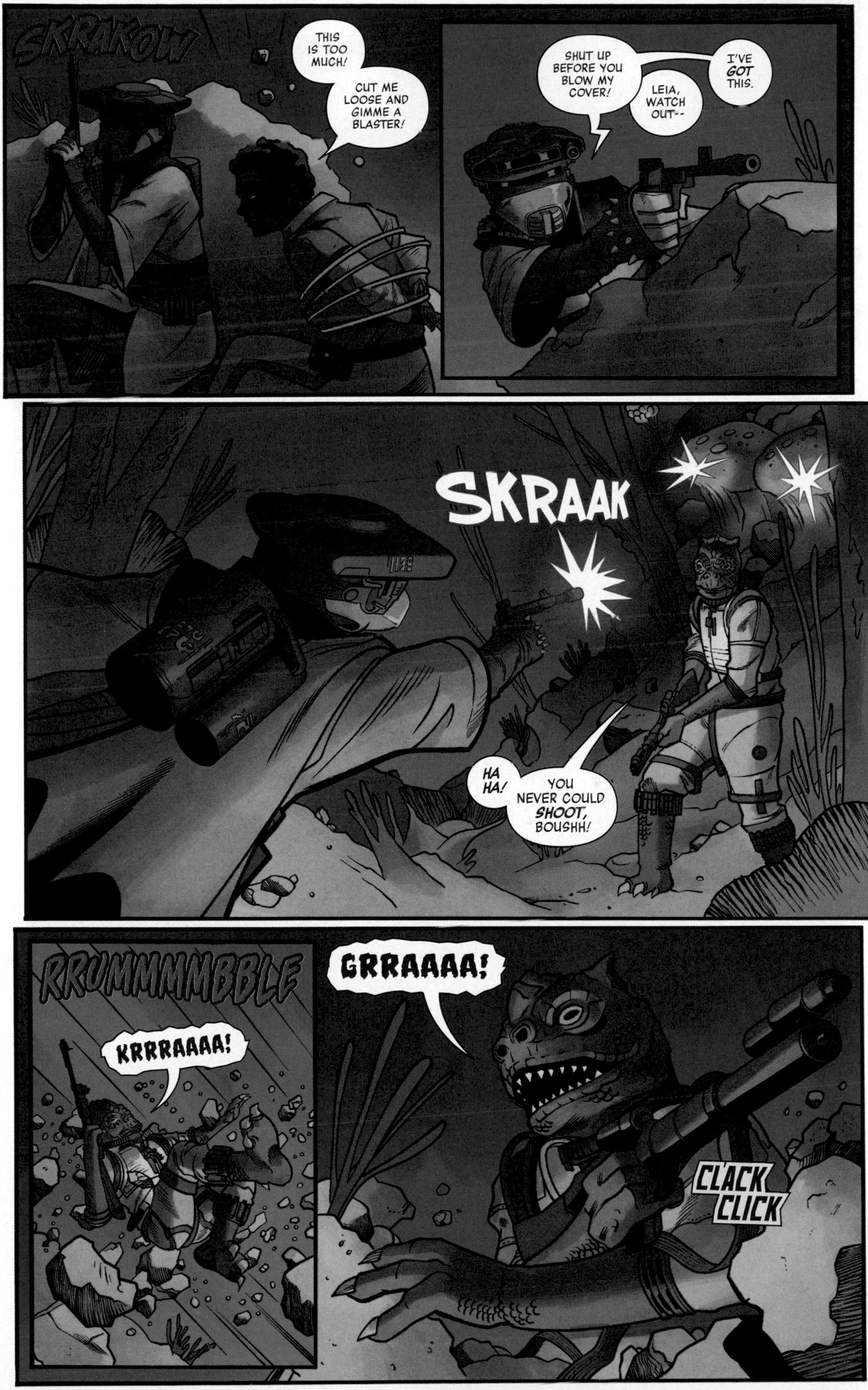

SKRAKOW
THIS IS TOO MUCH!
CUT ME LOOSE AND GIMME A BLASTER!
SHUT UP BEFORE YOU BLOW MY COVER!
I'VE GOT THIS.
LEIA, WATCH OUT--
SKRAAK
HA HA!
YOU NEVER COULD SHOOT, BOUSHH!
RRUMMMMBBLE
KRRRAAAA!
GRRAAAA!
CLACK CLICK

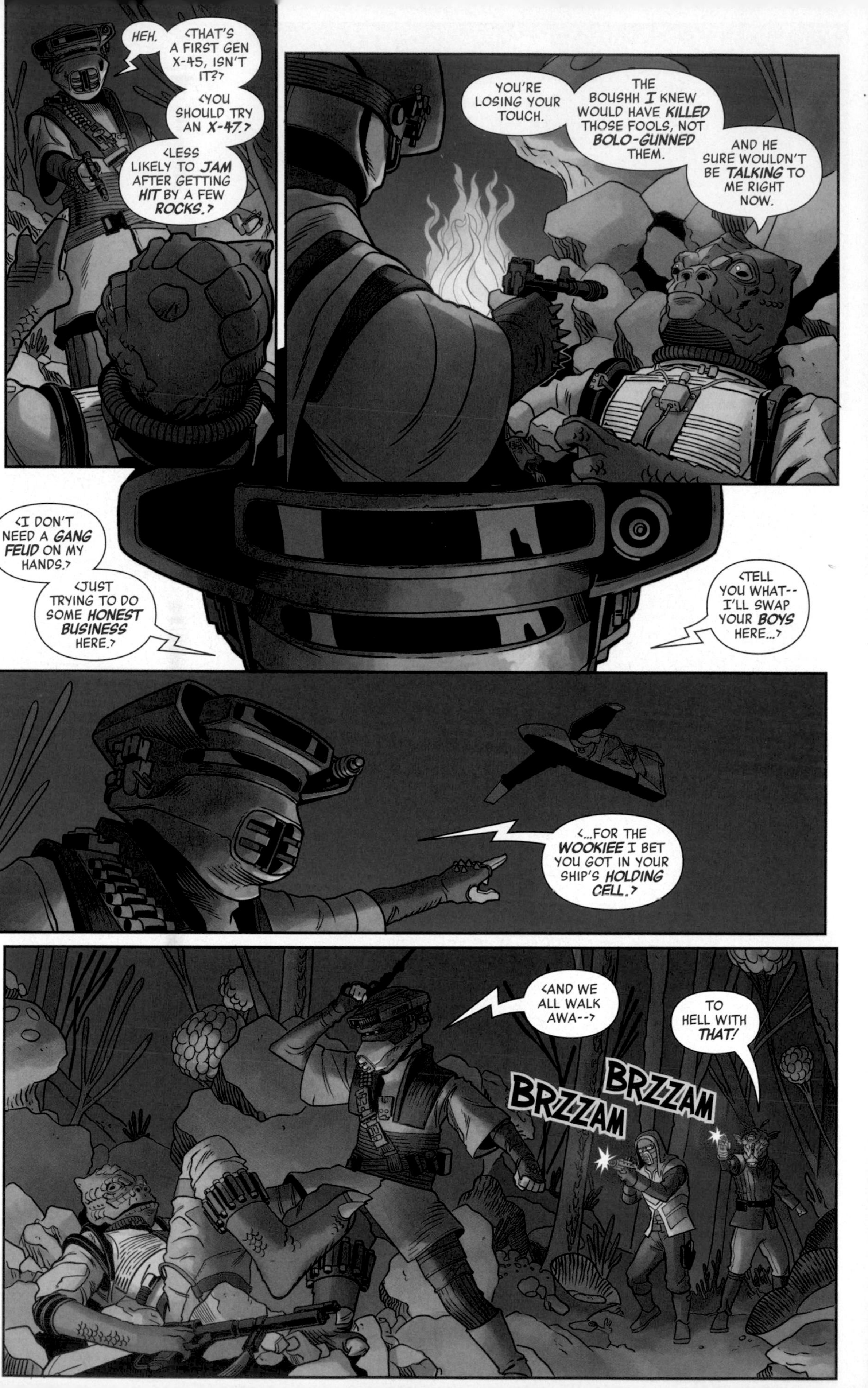
HEH.
<THAT'S A FIRST GEN X-45, ISN'T IT?>
<YOU SHOULD TRY AN X-47.>
<LESS LIKELY TO JAM AFTER GETTING HIT BY A FEW ROCKS.>
YOU'RE LOSING YOUR TOUCH.
THE BOUSHH I KNEW WOULD HAVE KILLED THOSE FOOLS, NOT BOLO-GUNNED THEM.
AND HE SURE WOULDN'T BE TALKING TO ME RIGHT NOW.
<I DON'T NEED A GANG FEUD ON MY HANDS.>
<JUST TRYING TO DO SOME HONEST BUSINESS HERE.>
<TELL YOU WHAT--I'LL SWAP YOUR BOYS HERE...>
<...FOR THE WOOKIEE I BET YOU GOT IN YOUR SHIP'S HOLDING CELL.>
<AND WE ALL WALK AWA-->
TO HELL WITH THAT!
BRZZAM
BRZZAM

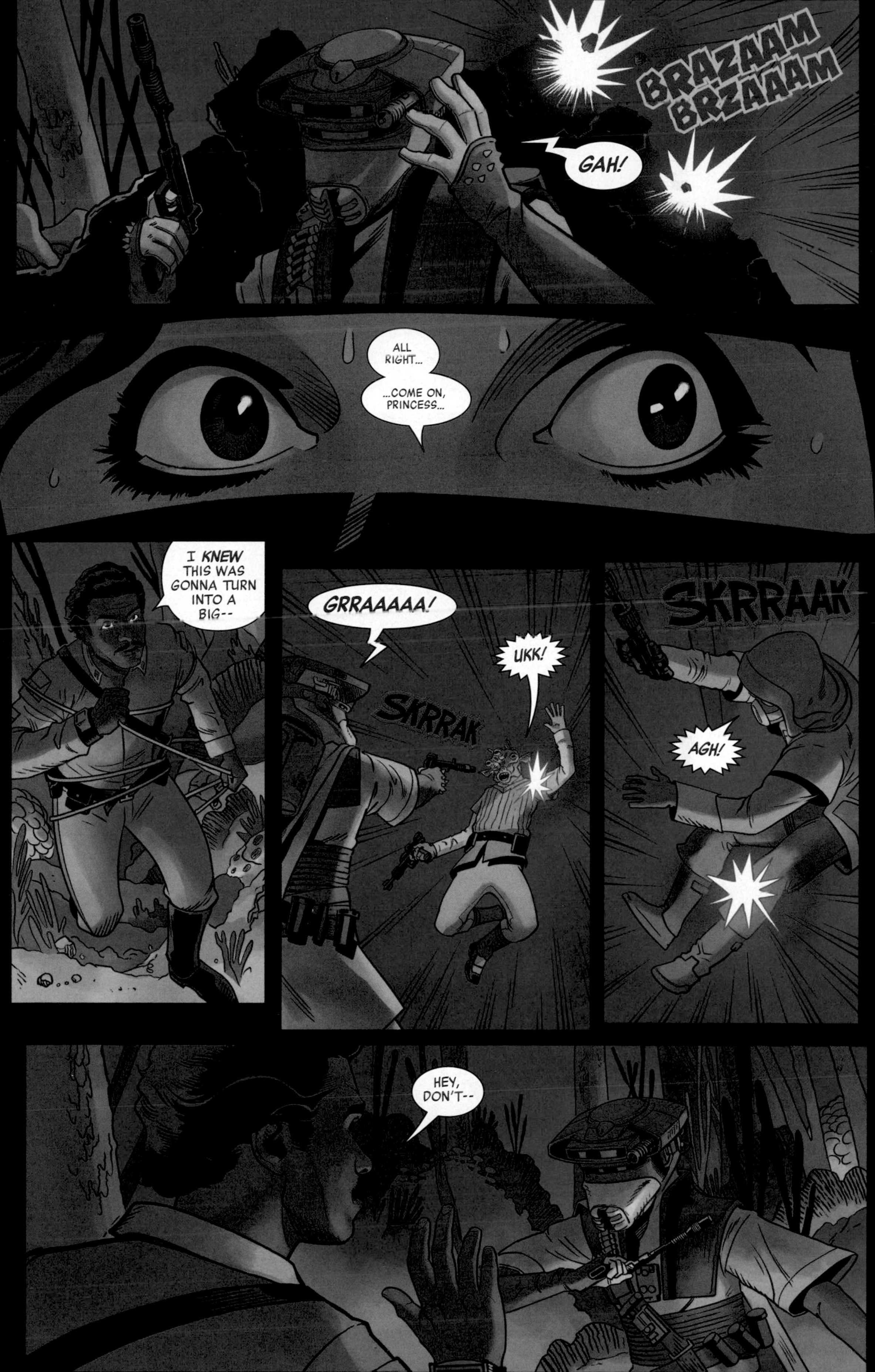
BRAZAAM
BRZAAAM
GAH!
ALL RIGHT...
...COME ON, PRINCESS...
I KNEW THIS WAS GONNA TURN INTO A BIG--
GRRAAAAA!
UKK!
SKRRAK
SKRRAAK
AGH!
HEY, DON'T--

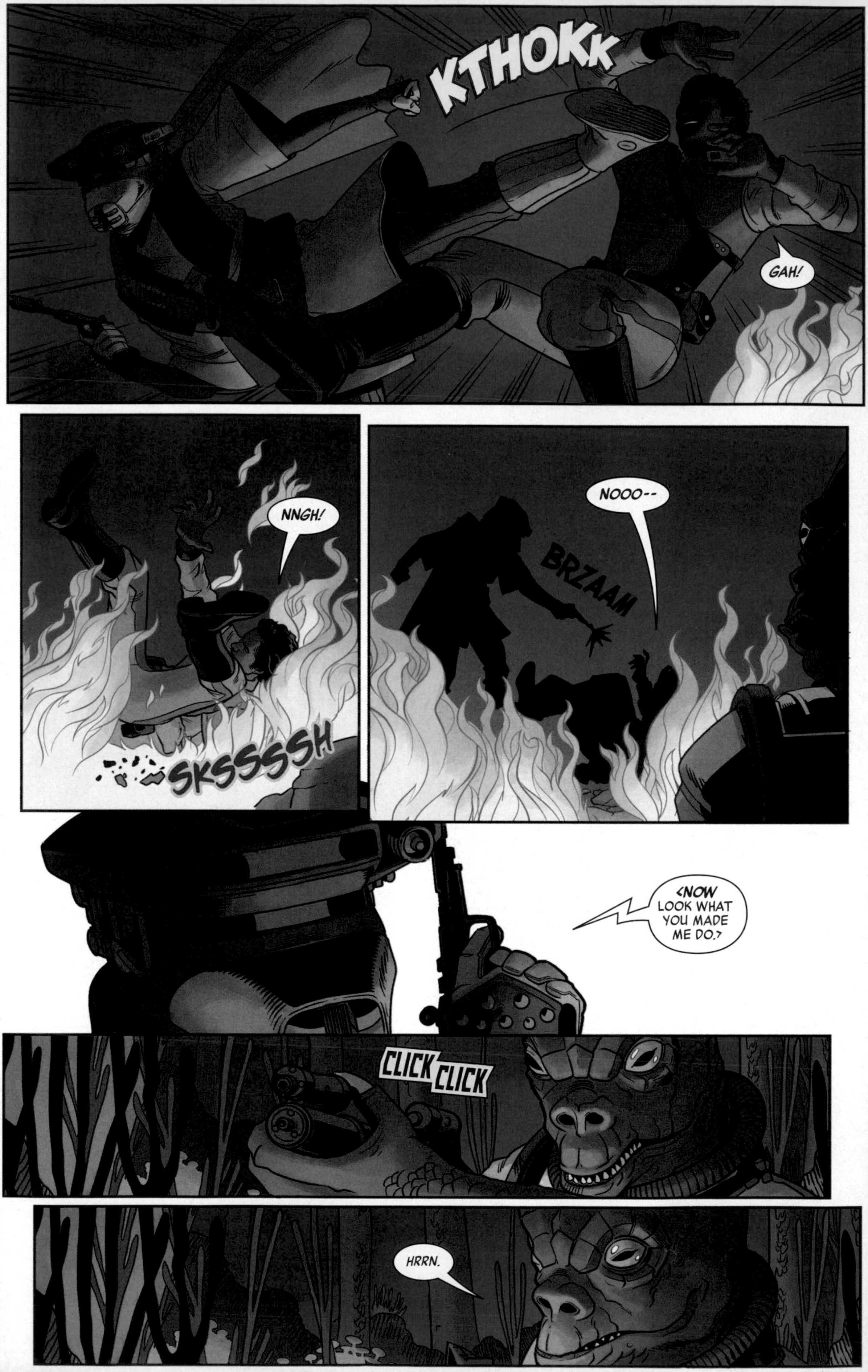
KTHOKK
GAH!
NNGH!
SKSSSSH
NOOO--
BRZAAM
<NOW LOOK WHAT YOU MADE ME DO.>
CLICK CLICK
HRRN.

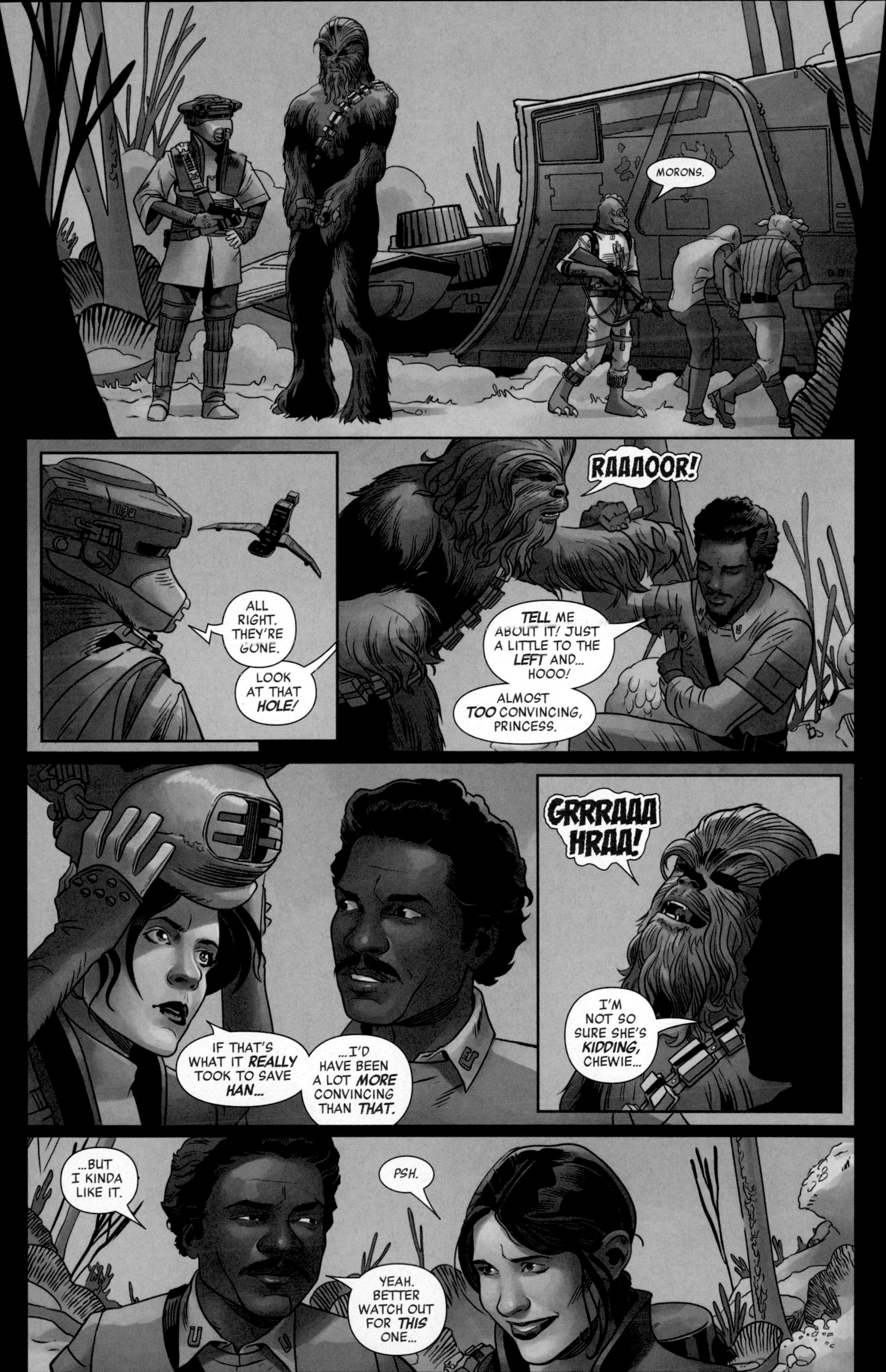

MORONS.
ALL RIGHT. THEY'RE GONE.
LOOK AT THAT HOLE!
RAAAOOR!
TELL ME ABOUT IT! JUST A LITTLE TO THE LEFT AND... HOOO!
ALMOST TOO CONVINCING, PRINCESS.
IF THAT'S WHAT IT REALLY TOOK TO SAVE HAN...
...I'D HAVE BEEN A LOT MORE CONVINCING THAN THAT.
GRRRAAA HRAA!
I'M NOT SO SURE SHE'S KIDDING, CHEWIE...
...BUT I KINDA LIKE IT.
PSH.
YEAH. BETTER WATCH OUT FOR THIS ONE...

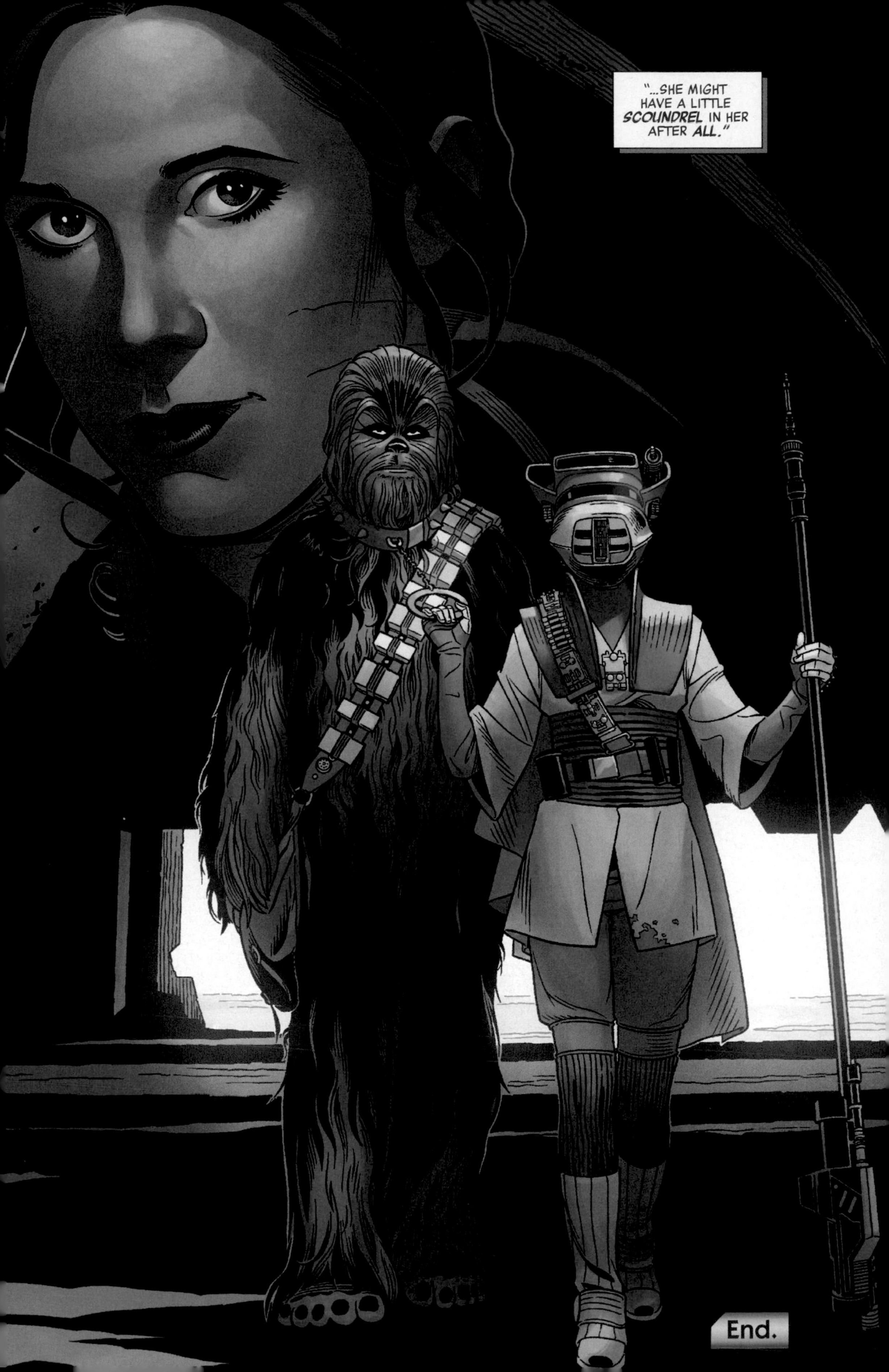
"...SHE MIGHT HAVE A LITTLE SCOUNDREL IN HER AFTER ALL."
End.

AGE OF REBELLION
Princess Leia – Our Princess, Our Hero
By Bria LaVorgna

I cried twice for Carrie Fisher after she died. The first time was on a plane when I turned on my phone and saw she'd passed away. The second time was in a giant convention hall, surrounded by hundreds of fellow *Star Wars* fans, many of who were also shedding more than a few tears.

I knew before I even walked into *Star Wars* Celebration Orlando on that Thursday morning, dressed as Princess Leia in one of her outfits from the comics, that it was going to be an emotional event. After all, it's a convention dedicated entirely to *Star Wars* and we were marking the 40th anniversary of the galaxy far, far away starting with the opening panel where actors and creatives from across the saga celebrated the franchise and what it's meant to them and the world. Toward the end, Kathleen Kennedy and George Lucas took the stage to share some of their memories of Carrie Fisher before introducing Fisher's daughter, Billie Lourd, who delivered a moving tribute to both her mother and the character.

"Nothing about her was a performance," Lourd said. "She loved you, she loved these movies." A short,

poignant yet humorous video about Carrie and Leia and the influence they've had on the world followed, bringing tears to the eyes of many (including me) as the montage of Leia saying the "Help me, Obi-Wan Kenobi" speech over the years started. And then the lights went up to reveal John Williams and the Orlando Philharmonic Orchestra playing the opening notes of Leia's theme. At that point, there wasn't a dry eye left in the house. It was a beautifully moving, cathartic moment made all the more magical by how we got to share it. In that instant, *Star Wars* fandom was one as we both mourned and celebrated our princess together.

Princess Leia Organa is an inspiration in both our galaxy and hers, sparking love and loyalty from those who encounter her and even begrudging respect from some of her enemies. Never afraid to speak her mind, she was *the* original strong female character, paving the way for so many others, not just in *Star Wars* but in different franchises across the world. She redefined what we thought a hero and a princess were supposed to be and taught us that a woman could be both of those things at the same time. Just like her mother Padmé, would decades after

the Original Trilogy, Leia showed us that while the princess may need a rescue sometimes, she could also be the hero and do the rescuing. "She wore a dress through the whole thing," said George Lucas during the Celebration Orlando panel, "but she was the toughest one in the group."

Despite her parents' well-meaning efforts to keep her safe and away from the war, Leia became a member of the Rebel Alliance at the tender age of 16 years old, with their support. By that time, both Bail and Breha Organa were deeply entrenched in the Rebellion, constantly searching for ways to fight back against the Empire without putting Alderaan in the crosshairs. They raised their daughter to always help others, to do what was right and to always remember she had a responsibility to the people of Alderaan. It should've come as no surprise to them that she'd insist on joining the fight too, especially given that she was the biological daughter of Padmé Amidala. Mere years later, she became one of the Rebellion's leaders, promoted to the rank of general after the Empire decimated the fleet.

Leia is the sort of person who takes the myriad of punches that

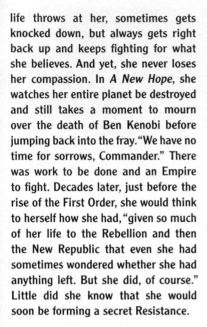

life throws at her, sometimes gets knocked down, but always gets right back up and keeps fighting for what she believes. And yet, she never loses her compassion. In *A New Hope*, she watches her entire planet be destroyed and still takes a moment to mourn over the death of Ben Kenobi before jumping back into the fray. "We have no time for sorrows, Commander." There was work to be done and an Empire to fight. Decades later, just before the rise of the First Order, she would think to herself how she had, "given so much of her life to the Rebellion and then the New Republic that even she had sometimes wondered whether she had anything left. But she did, of course." Little did she know that she would soon be forming a secret Resistance.

There was more to her than just her work for the Rebellion and the Resistance and her enduring service to her fellow Alderaanian survivors, even if they were defining factors and duty always came first. The same Death Star that took everything from her also brought her Han Solo and Luke Skywalker. It brought Leia more family into her life even though she didn't initially realize they were her future husband and secret twin brother respectively. While they certainly didn't beat the Empire single-handedly,

their friendship greatly contributed to bringing about its end. After the war, Luke and Leia decided to conceal that Darth Vader was their biological father, a fact that would rear its angry head decades later and in more ways than one. Her relationships with Han and their son Ben were complicated to say the least, made even more so after Ben fell to the dark side like his grandfather before him and became Kylo Ren, but she still held on to hope. Rebellions are built on hope and so, beneath the sharp retorts and an unending reservoir of stubborn bravery, was Leia Organa.

While dozens have contributed to making the character of Leia what she is, none of it would have been possible without Carrie Fisher, who embodied everything the princess stood for and understood what this character would mean to the world right from the start. "Because she's not a victim, the princess," Fisher said in French in an interview from 1977. "She's strong, and it's good." And she never forgot that or let others forget. Years later, in an interview shortly before her death, Fisher said, "She can do anything. She can do what she can do and do what she can't."

"My mom used to say she never knew where Princess Leia ended and Carrie

Fisher began," said Lourd during her Celebration Orlando tribute. For many fans, it's hard not to feel the same way. We know there are significant differences between the two women and yet they have become so entwined in our hearts and minds, perhaps more so than any other *Star Wars* character, that it is impossible to separate them. We don't yet know how Leia's story will continue without Carrie Fisher or how it will ultimately conclude, but the ending isn't what truly matters. We've seen and taken so much inspiration from her life, and generations to come will continue to do so. Women and girls will keep donning that double-bunned hairdo for Halloween and at conventions and we'll all keep asking ourselves, "What would Leia do?" because she's a role model and someone each of us should strive to be more like.

To us, she's royalty.

References:
Starwars.com
Star Wars: Leia, Princess of Alderaan
STAR WARS #55
Star Wars: Bloodline, pg. 17
The Hollywood Reporter
ABC News

HAN SOLO

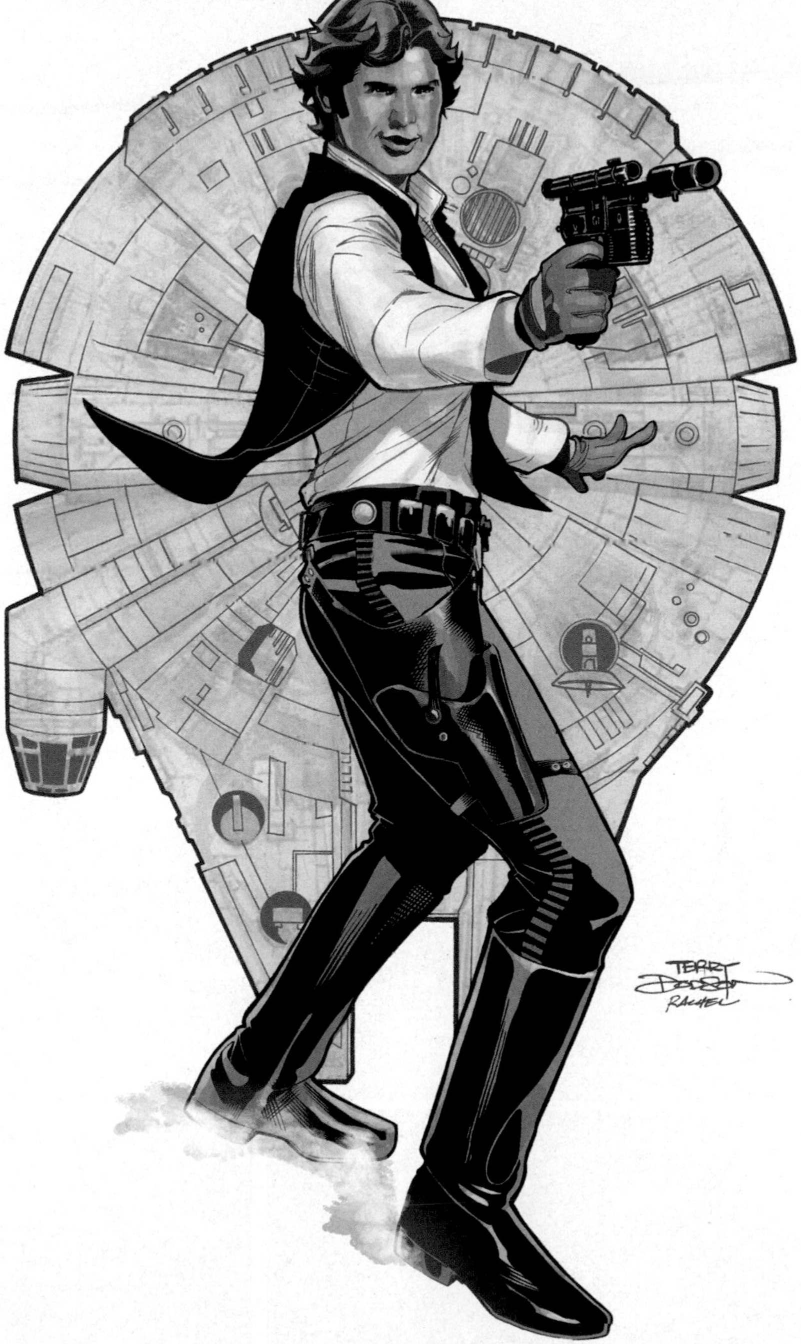
TERRY DODSON
RACHEL

“RUNNING FROM THE REBELLION”

The heroic Rebel Alliance has recently won its first victory against the evil Galactic Empire...thanks to the infamous smuggler Han Solo and his Wookiee companion, Chewbacca. At least, that’s the way HE sees it! It’s time to

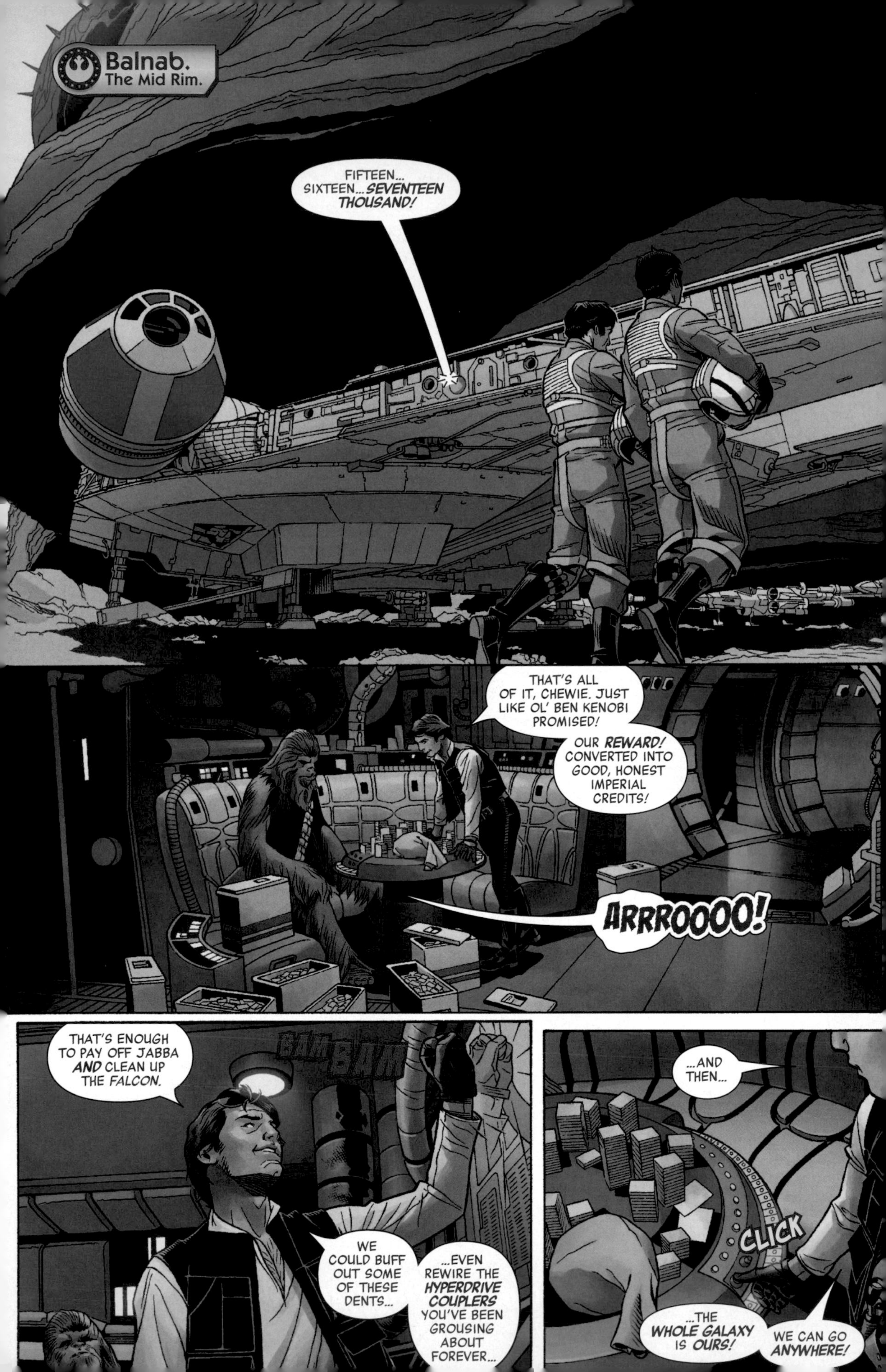
Balnab.
The Mid Rim.
FIFTEEN... SIXTEEN... SEVENTEEN THOUSAND!
THAT'S ALL OF IT, CHEWIE. JUST LIKE OL' BEN KENOBI PROMISED!
OUR REWARD! CONVERTED INTO GOOD, HONEST IMPERIAL CREDITS!
ARRROOOO!
THAT'S ENOUGH TO PAY OFF JABBA AND CLEAN UP THE FALCON.
WE COULD BUFF OUT SOME OF THESE DENTS...
...EVEN REWIRE THE HYPERDRIVE COUPLERS YOU'VE BEEN GROUSING ABOUT FOREVER...
...AND THEN...
CLICK
...THE WHOLE GALAXY IS OURS!
WE CAN GO ANYWHERE!

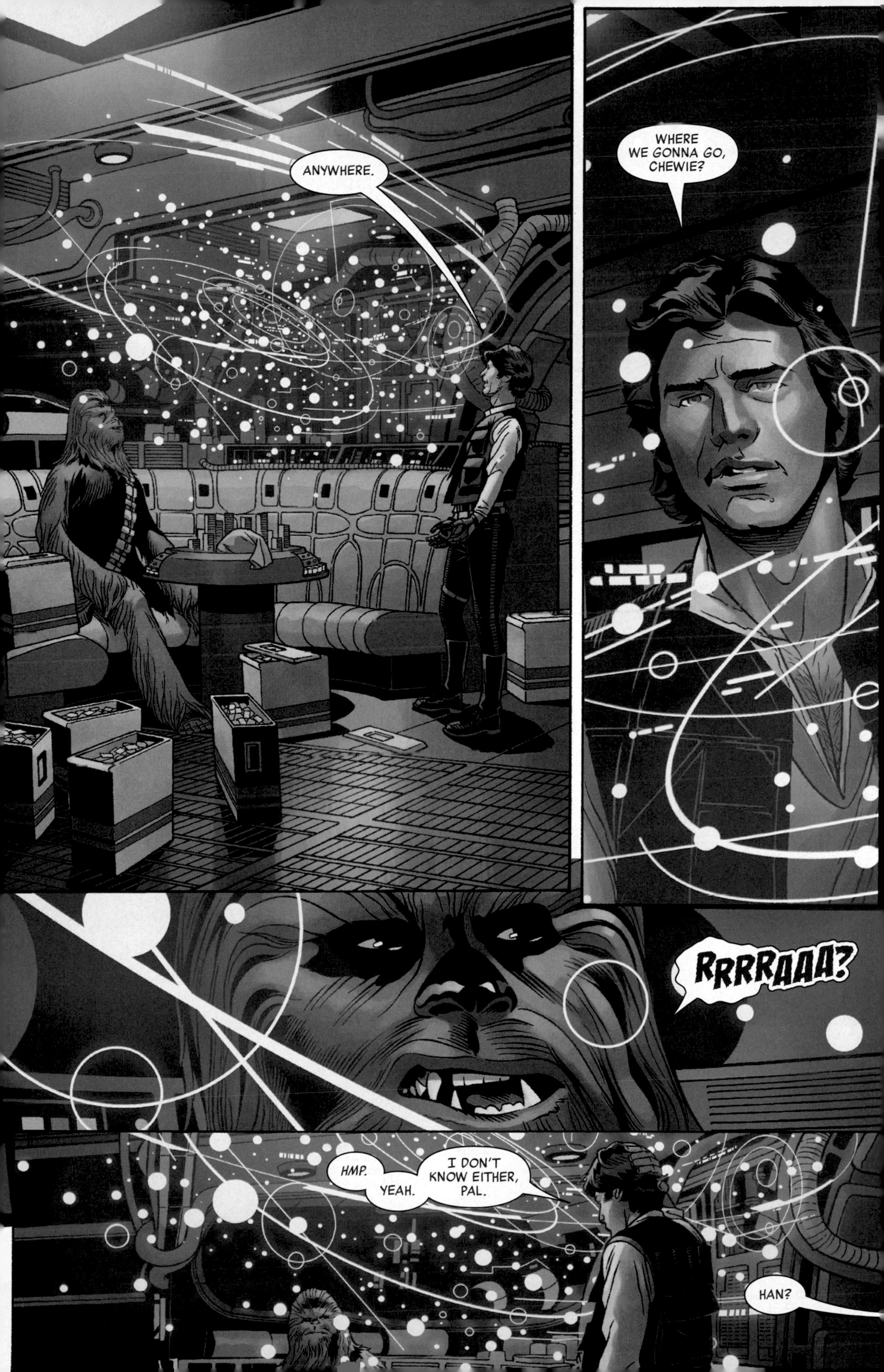
WHERE WE GONNA GO, CHEWIE?
ANYWHERE.
RRRRAAA?
I DON'T KNOW EITHER, PAL.
YEAH.
HMP.
HAN?

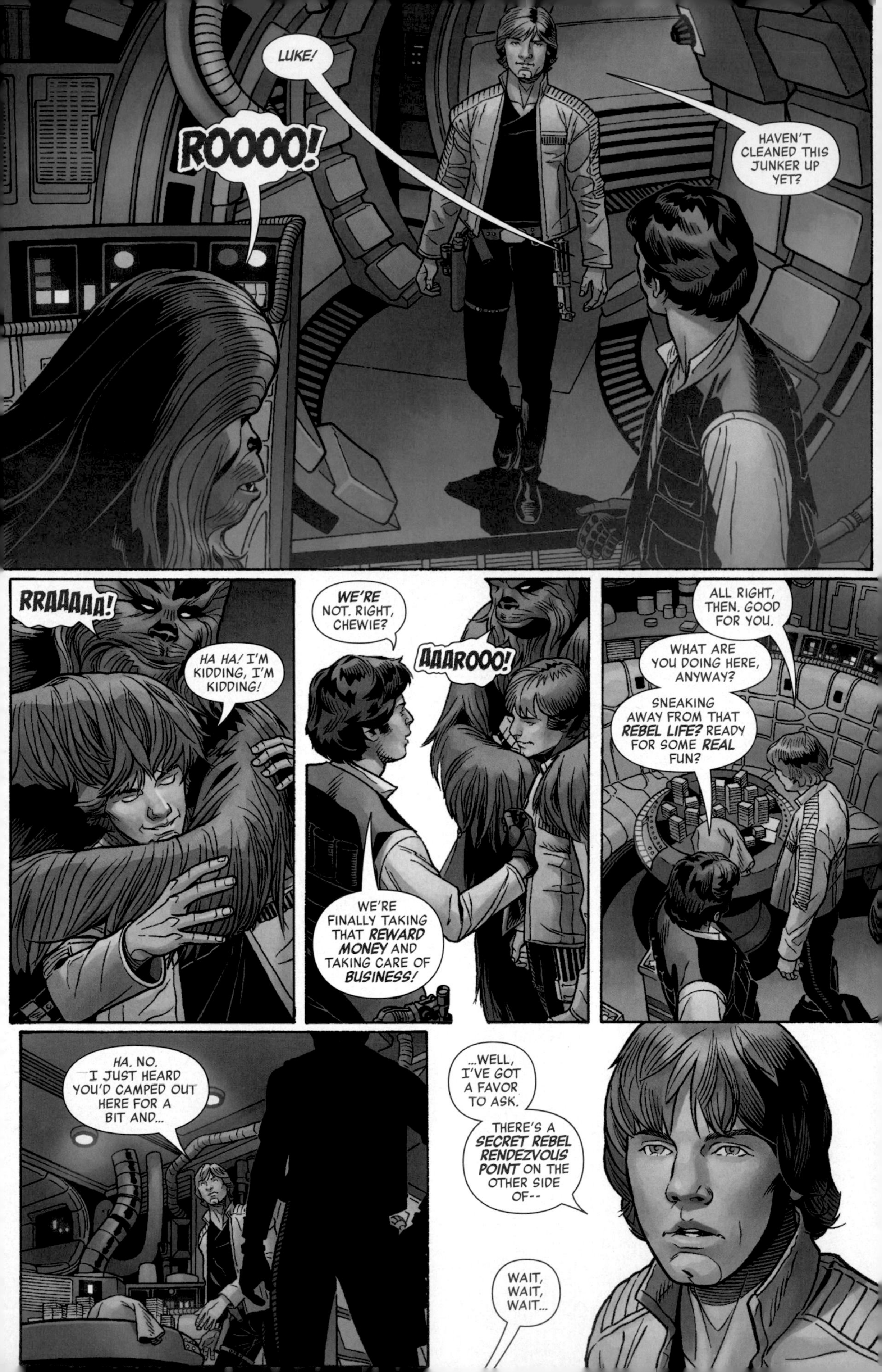
LUKE!
ROOOO!
HAVEN'T CLEANED THIS JUNKER UP YET?
RRAAAAAA!
HA HA! I'M KIDDING, I'M KIDDING!
WE'RE NOT. RIGHT, CHEWIE?
AAAROOO!
WE'RE FINALLY TAKING THAT REWARD MONEY AND TAKING CARE OF BUSINESS!
ALL RIGHT, THEN. GOOD FOR YOU.
WHAT ARE YOU DOING HERE, ANYWAY?
SNEAKING AWAY FROM THAT REBEL LIFE? READY FOR SOME REAL FUN?
HA. NO. I JUST HEARD YOU'D CAMPED OUT HERE FOR A BIT AND...
...WELL, I'VE GOT A FAVOR TO ASK.
THERE'S A SECRET REBEL RENDEZVOUS POINT ON THE OTHER SIDE OF--
WAIT, WAIT, WAIT...

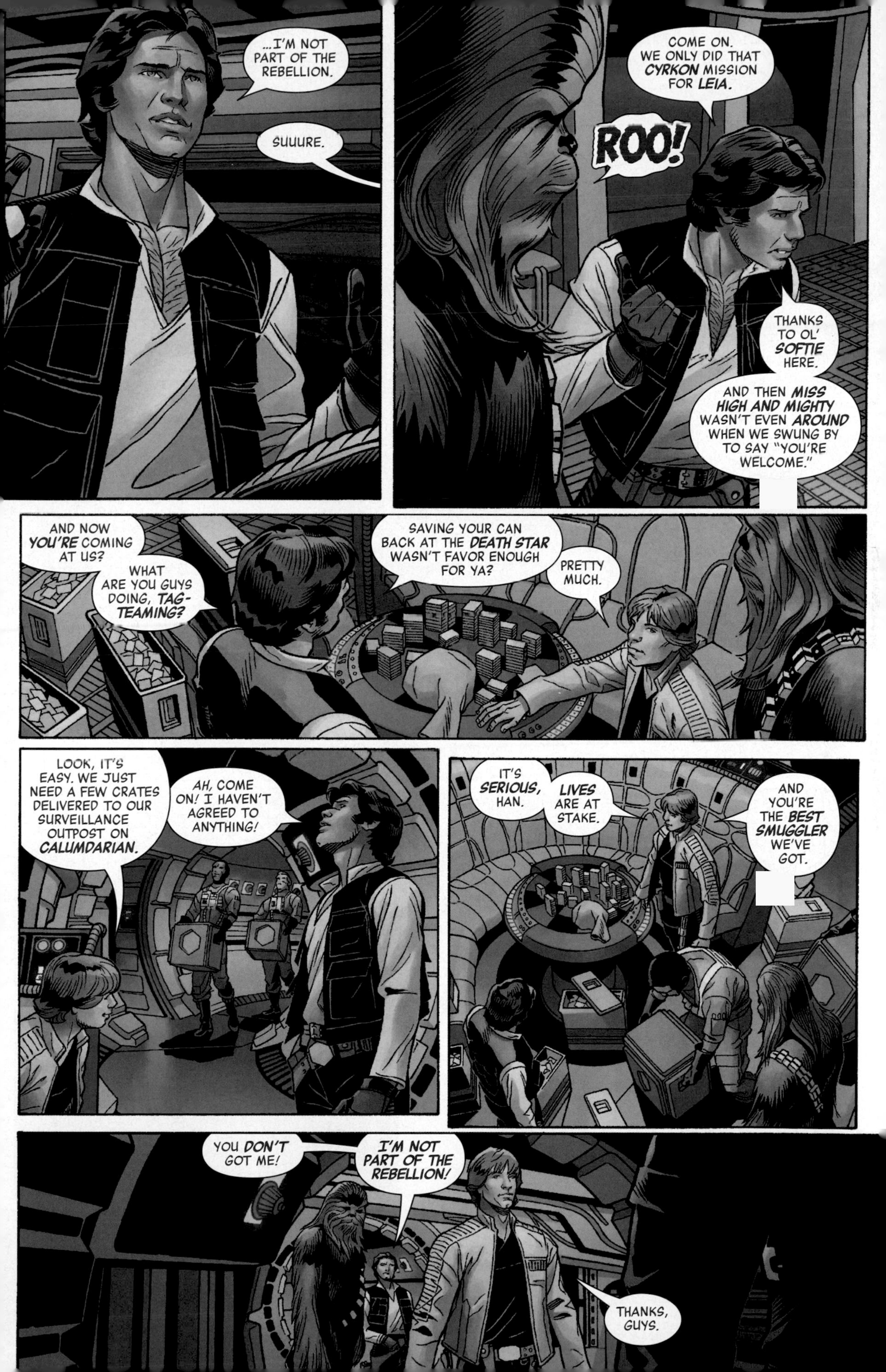
...I'M NOT PART OF THE REBELLION.
SUUURE.
COME ON. WE ONLY DID THAT CYRKON MISSION FOR LEIA.
ROO!
THANKS TO OL' SOFTIE HERE.
AND THEN MISS HIGH AND MIGHTY WASN'T EVEN AROUND WHEN WE SWUNG BY TO SAY "YOU'RE WELCOME."
AND NOW YOU'RE COMING AT US?
WHAT ARE YOU GUYS DOING, TAG-TEAMING?
SAVING YOUR CAN BACK AT THE DEATH STAR WASN'T FAVOR ENOUGH FOR YA?
PRETTY MUCH.
LOOK, IT'S EASY. WE JUST NEED A FEW CRATES DELIVERED TO OUR SURVEILLANCE OUTPOST ON CALUMDARIAN.
AH, COME ON! I HAVEN'T AGREED TO ANYTHING!
IT'S SERIOUS, HAN.
LIVES ARE AT STAKE.
AND YOU'RE THE BEST SMUGGLER WE'VE GOT.
YOU DON'T GOT ME!
I'M NOT PART OF THE REBELLION!
THANKS, GUYS.

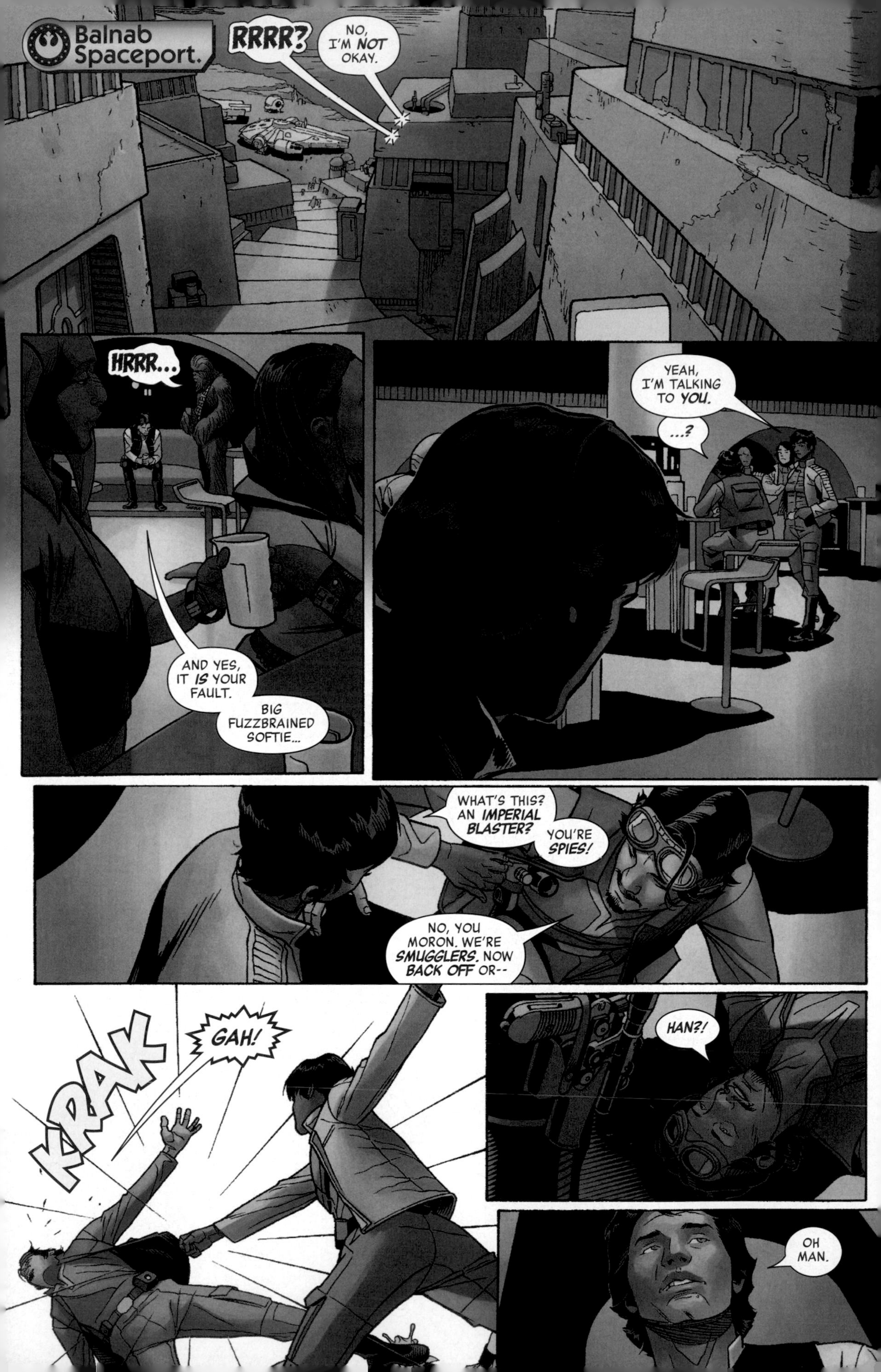
Balnab Spaceport.
RRRR?
NO, I'M NOT OKAY.
HRRR...
AND YES, IT IS YOUR FAULT.
BIG FUZZBRAINED SOFTIE...
YEAH, I'M TALKING TO YOU.
...?
WHAT'S THIS? AN IMPERIAL BLASTER?
YOU'RE SPIES!
NO, YOU MORON. WE'RE SMUGGLERS. NOW BACK OFF OR--
KRAK
GAH!
HAN?!
OH MAN.

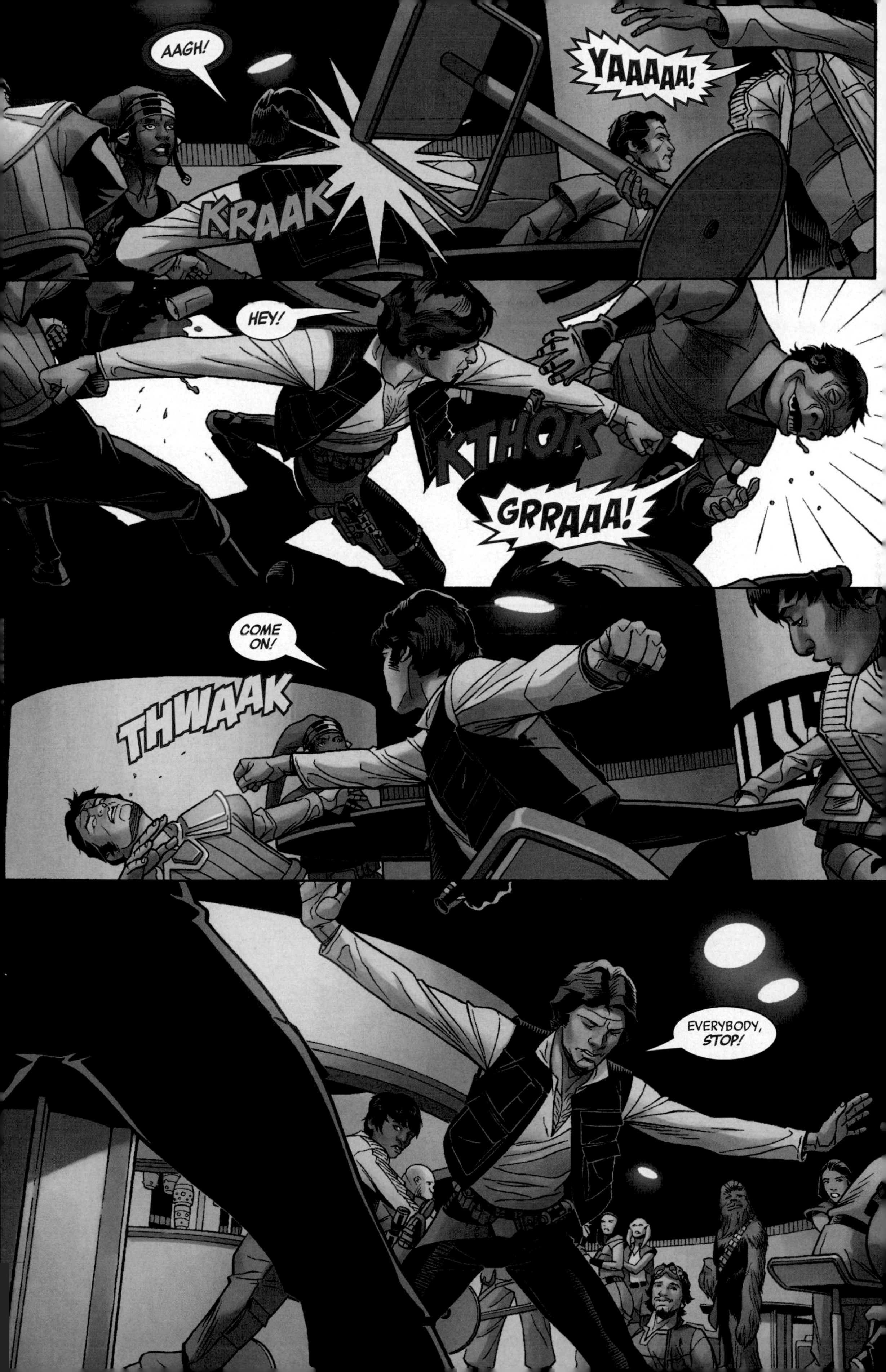
AAGH!
KRAAK
YAAAAA!
HEY!
KTHOK
GRRAAA!
COME ON!
THWAAK
EVERYBODY, STOP!

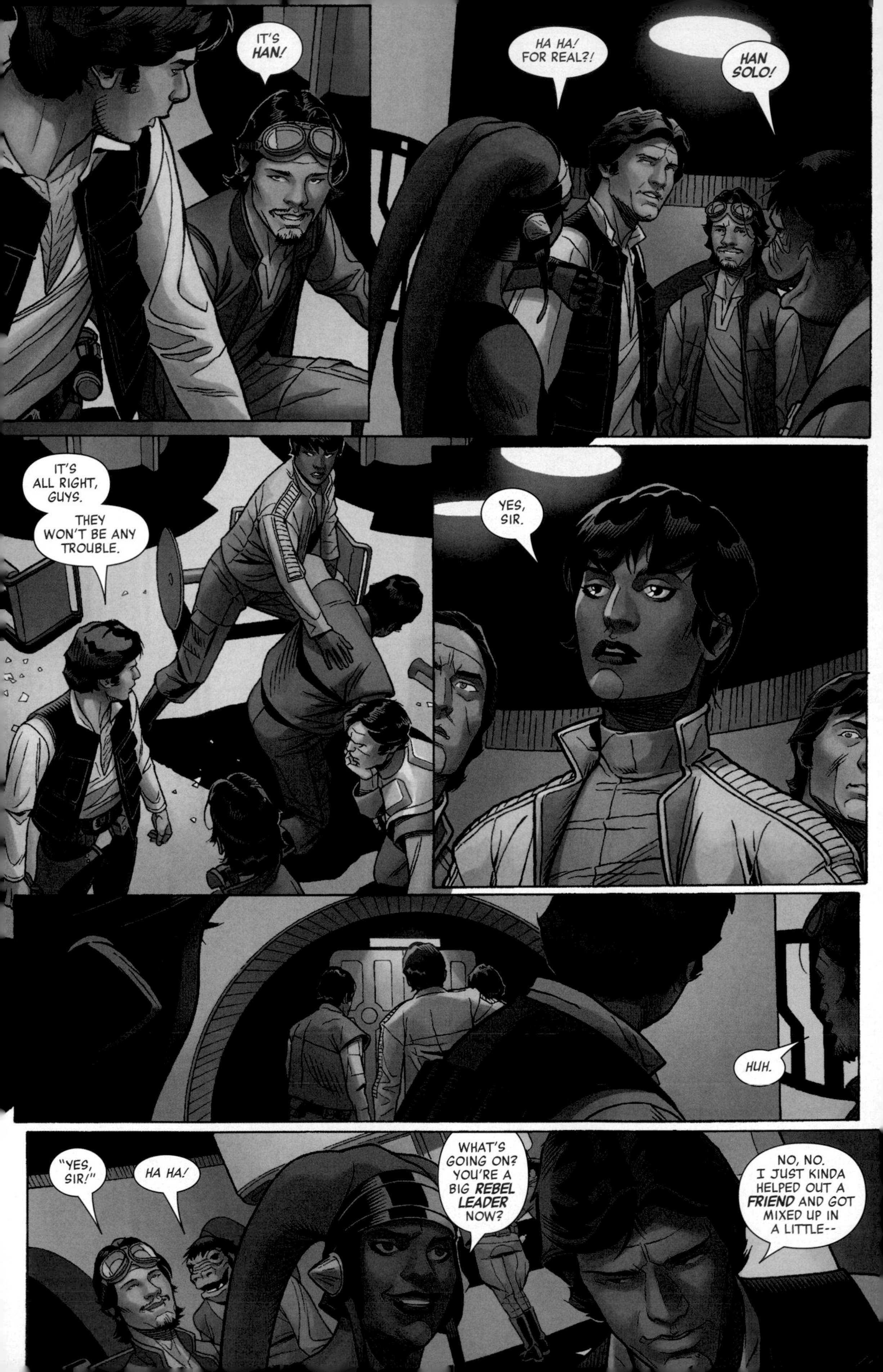
IT'S HAN!
HA HA! FOR REAL?!
HAN SOLO!
IT'S ALL RIGHT, GUYS.
THEY WON'T BE ANY TROUBLE.
YES, SIR.
HUH.
"YES, SIR!"
HA HA!
WHAT'S GOING ON? YOU'RE A BIG REBEL LEADER NOW?
NO, NO. I JUST KINDA HELPED OUT A FRIEND AND GOT MIXED UP IN A LITTLE--

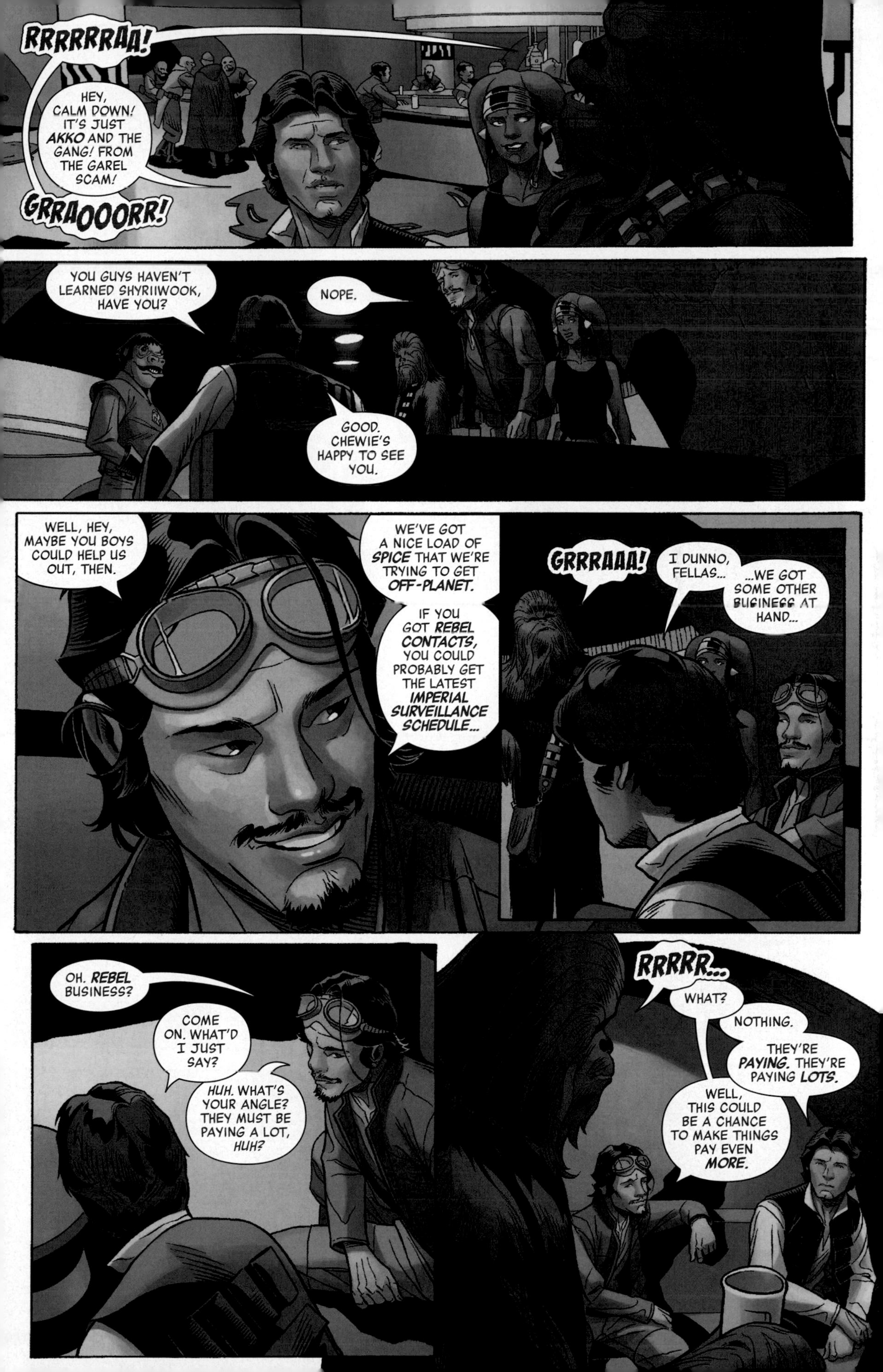
RRRRRRAA!
HEY, CALM DOWN! IT'S JUST AKKO AND THE GANG! FROM THE GAREL SCAM!
GRRAOOORR!
YOU GUYS HAVEN'T LEARNED SHYRIIWOOK, HAVE YOU?
NOPE.
GOOD. CHEWIE'S HAPPY TO SEE YOU.
WELL, HEY, MAYBE YOU BOYS COULD HELP US OUT, THEN.
WE'VE GOT A NICE LOAD OF SPICE THAT WE'RE TRYING TO GET OFF-PLANET.
IF YOU GOT REBEL CONTACTS, YOU COULD PROBABLY GET THE LATEST IMPERIAL SURVEILLANCE SCHEDULE...
GRRRAAA!
I DUNNO, FELLAS...
...WE GOT SOME OTHER BUSINESS AT HAND...
OH. REBEL BUSINESS?
COME ON. WHAT'D I JUST SAY?
HUH. WHAT'S YOUR ANGLE? THEY MUST BE PAYING A LOT, HUH?
RRRRR...
WHAT?
NOTHING.
THEY'RE PAYING. THEY'RE PAYING LOTS.
WELL, THIS COULD BE A CHANCE TO MAKE THINGS PAY EVEN MORE.

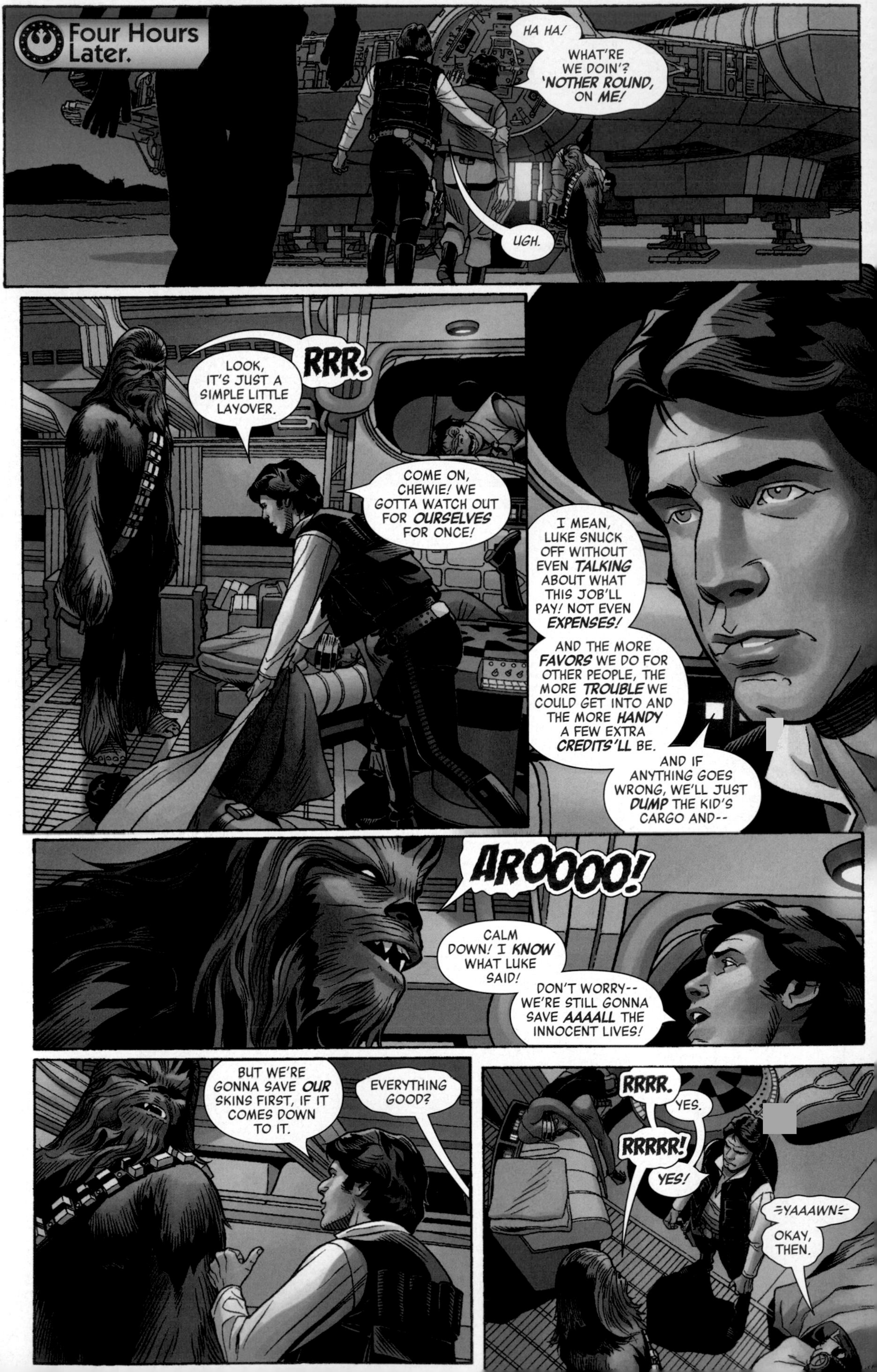

Four Hours Later.
HA HA!
WHAT'RE WE DOIN'? 'NOTHER ROUND, ON ME!
UGH.
LOOK, IT'S JUST A SIMPLE LITTLE LAYOVER.
RRR.
COME ON, CHEWIE! WE GOTTA WATCH OUT FOR OURSELVES FOR ONCE!
I MEAN, LUKE SNUCK OFF WITHOUT EVEN TALKING ABOUT WHAT THIS JOB'LL PAY! NOT EVEN EXPENSES!
AND THE MORE FAVORS WE DO FOR OTHER PEOPLE, THE MORE TROUBLE WE COULD GET INTO AND THE MORE HANDY A FEW EXTRA CREDITS'LL BE.
AND IF ANYTHING GOES WRONG, WE'LL JUST DUMP THE KID'S CARGO AND--
AROOOOO!
CALM DOWN! I KNOW WHAT LUKE SAID!
DON'T WORRY-- WE'RE STILL GONNA SAVE AAAALL THE INNOCENT LIVES!
BUT WE'RE GONNA SAVE OUR SKINS FIRST, IF IT COMES DOWN TO IT.
EVERYTHING GOOD?
RRRR.
YES.
RRRRR!
YES!
=YAAAWN=
OKAY, THEN.

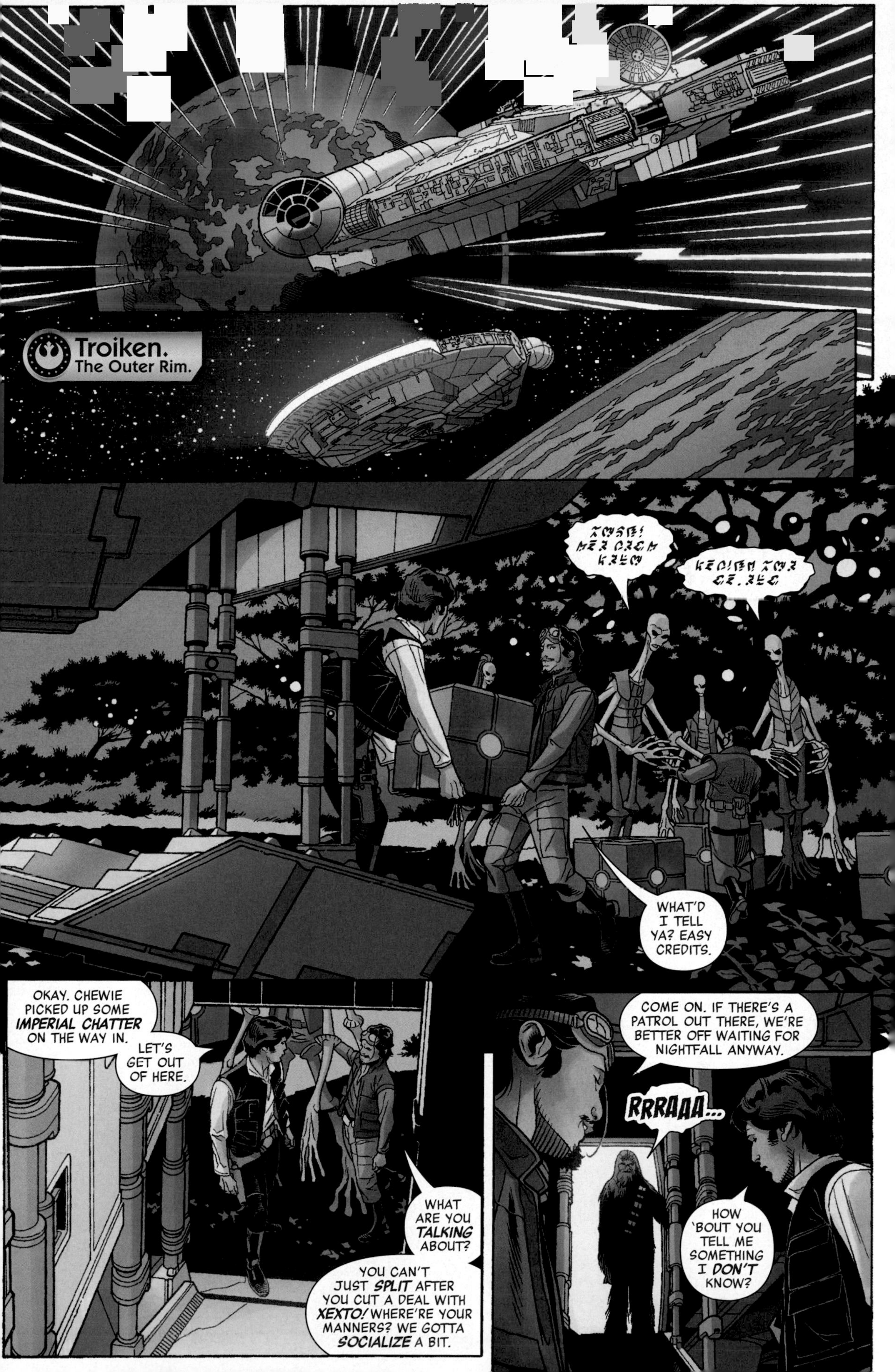
Troiken.
The Outer Rim.
WHAT'D I TELL YA? EASY CREDITS.
OKAY. CHEWIE PICKED UP SOME **IMPERIAL CHATTER** ON THE WAY IN.
LET'S GET OUT OF HERE.
WHAT ARE YOU **TALKING** ABOUT?
YOU CAN'T JUST **SPLIT** AFTER YOU CUT A DEAL WITH **XEXTO!** WHERE'RE YOUR MANNERS? WE GOTTA **SOCIALIZE** A BIT.
COME ON. IF THERE'S A PATROL OUT THERE, WE'RE BETTER OFF WAITING FOR NIGHTFALL ANYWAY.
RRRAAA...
HOW 'BOUT YOU TELL ME SOMETHING I **DON'T** KNOW?

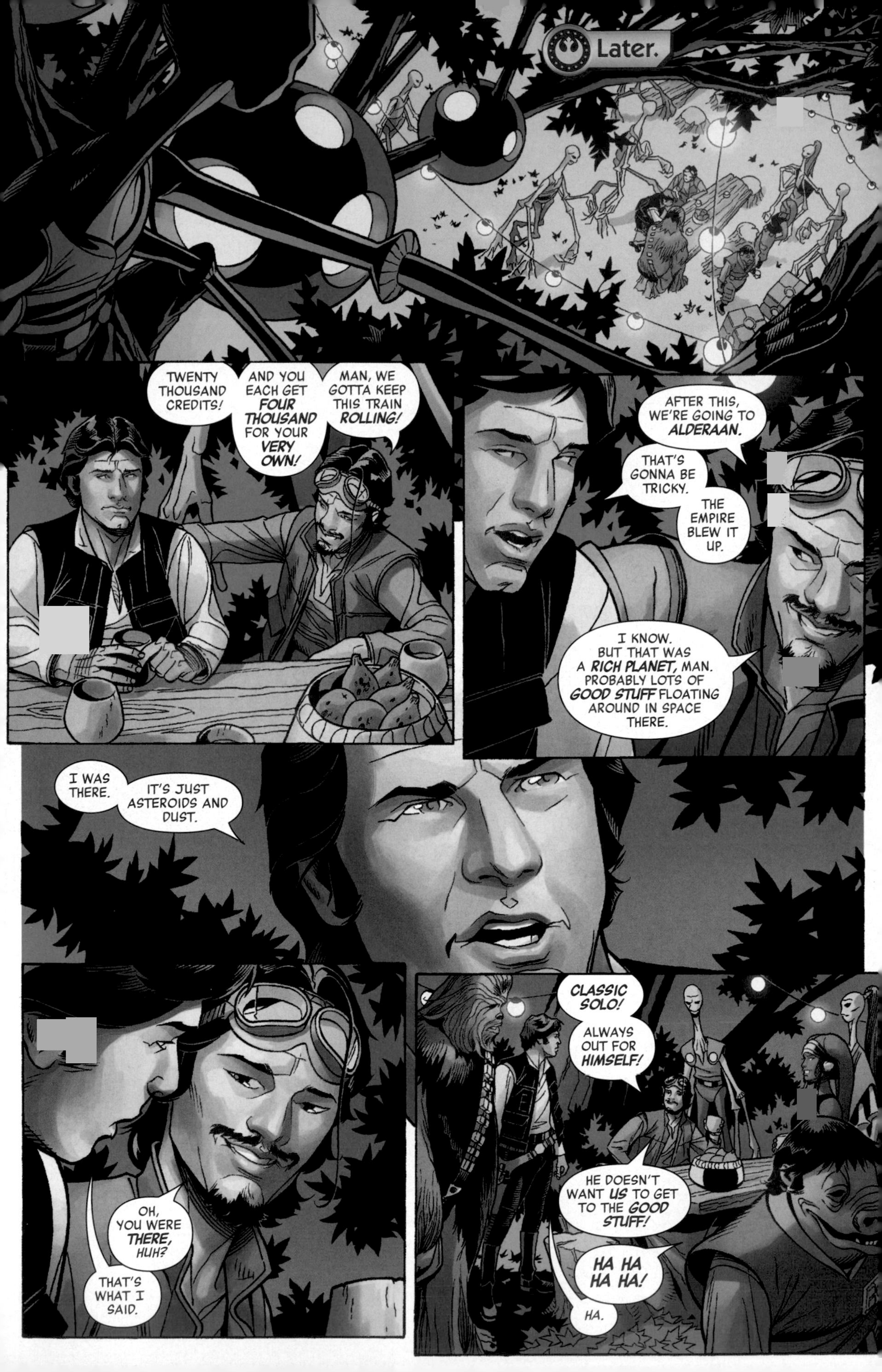
Later.
TWENTY THOUSAND CREDITS!
AND YOU EACH GET FOUR THOUSAND FOR YOUR VERY OWN!
MAN, WE GOTTA KEEP THIS TRAIN ROLLING!
AFTER THIS, WE'RE GOING TO ALDERAAN.
THAT'S GONNA BE TRICKY.
THE EMPIRE BLEW IT UP.
I KNOW. BUT THAT WAS A RICH PLANET, MAN. PROBABLY LOTS OF GOOD STUFF FLOATING AROUND IN SPACE THERE.
I WAS THERE.
IT'S JUST ASTEROIDS AND DUST.
OH, YOU WERE THERE, HUH?
THAT'S WHAT I SAID.
CLASSIC SOLO!
ALWAYS OUT FOR HIMSELF!
HE DOESN'T WANT US TO GET TO THE GOOD STUFF!
HA HA HA HA!
HA.

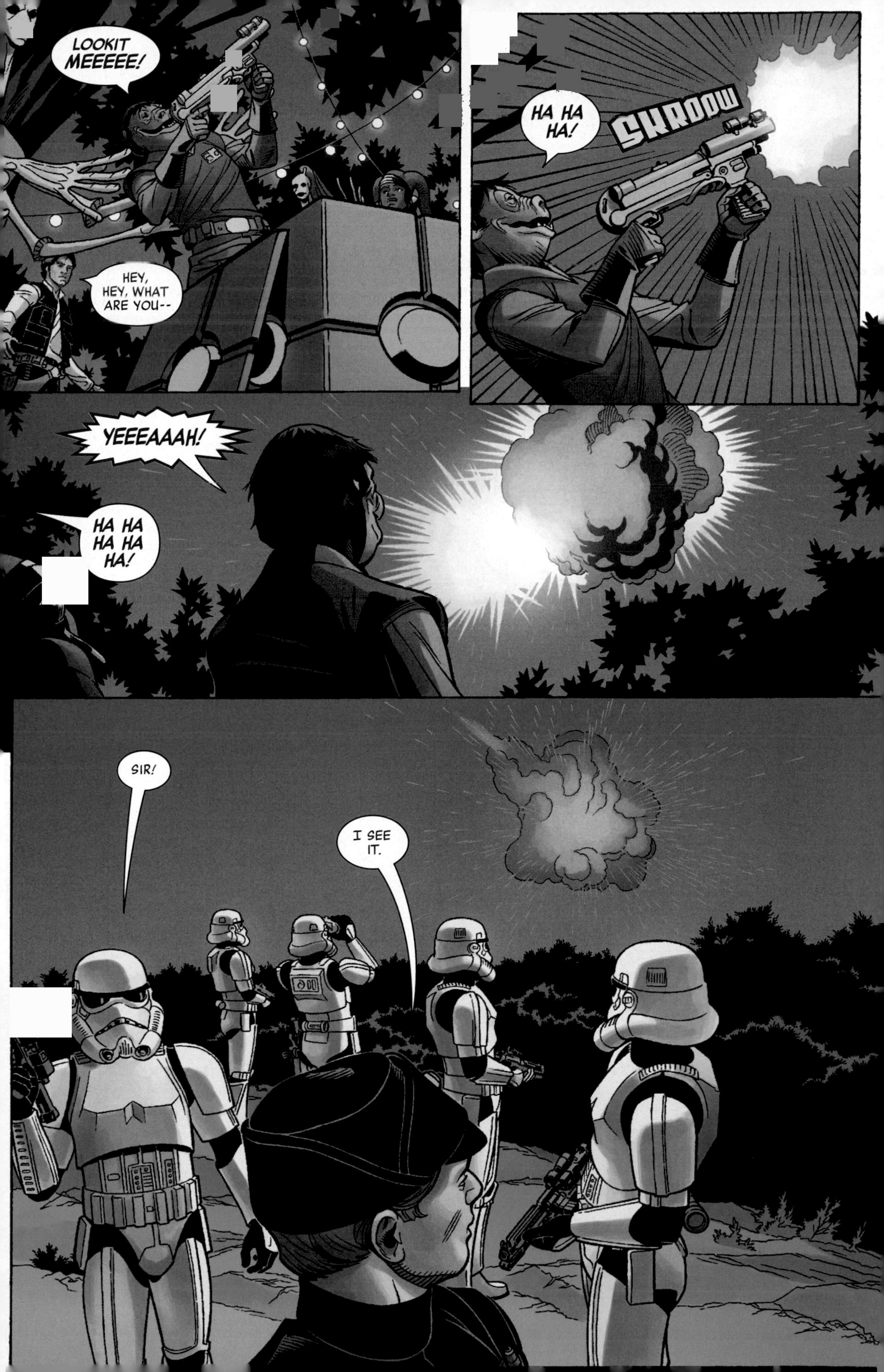

LOOKIT MEEEEE!
HEY, HEY, WHAT ARE YOU--
HA HA HA!
SKROOW
YEEEAAAH!
HA HA HA HA HA!
SIR!
I SEE IT.

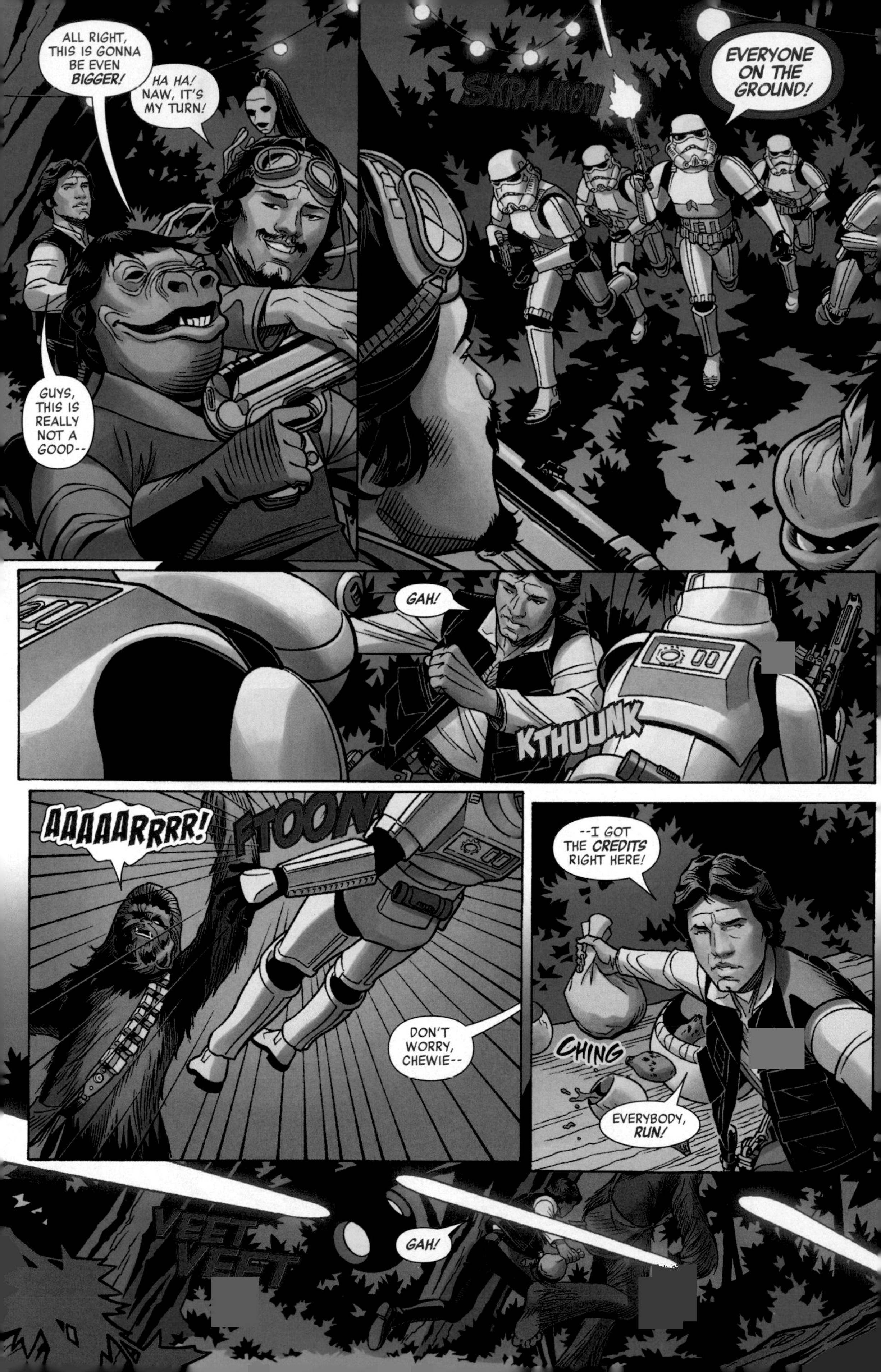
ALL RIGHT, THIS IS GONNA BE EVEN BIGGER!
HA HA! NAW, IT'S MY TURN!
GUYS, THIS IS REALLY NOT A GOOD--
SKRAAKOW
EVERYONE ON THE GROUND!
GAH!
KTHUUNK
AAAAARRRR!
FTOON
DON'T WORRY, CHEWIE--
--I GOT THE CREDITS RIGHT HERE!
CHING
EVERYBODY, RUN!
VEET VEET
GAH!

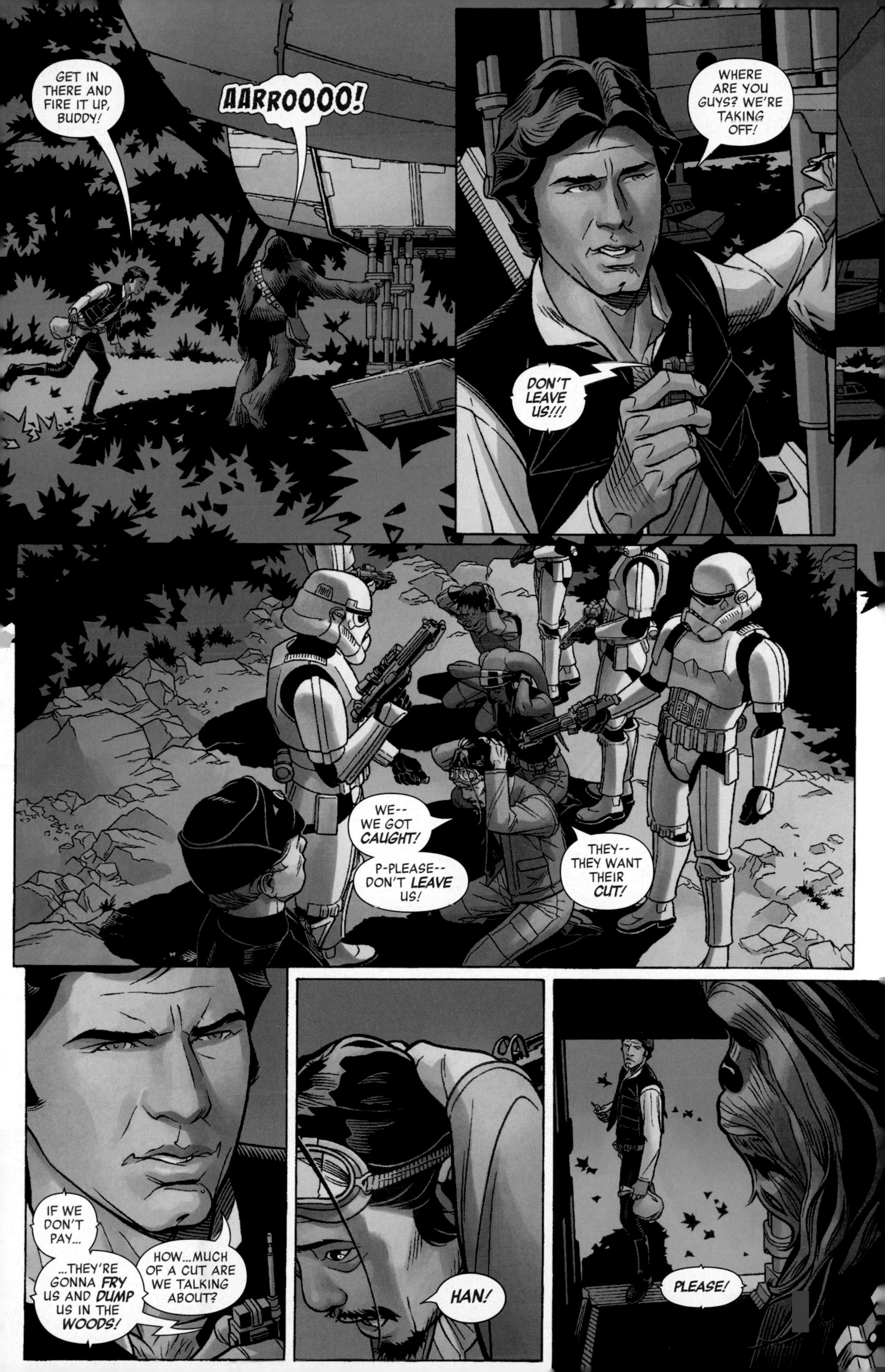
GET IN THERE AND FIRE IT UP, BUDDY!
AARROOOO!
WHERE ARE YOU GUYS? WE'RE TAKING OFF!
DON'T LEAVE US!!!
WE-- WE GOT CAUGHT!
P-PLEASE-- DON'T LEAVE US!
THEY-- THEY WANT THEIR CUT!
IF WE DON'T PAY...
...THEY'RE GONNA FRY US AND DUMP US IN THE WOODS!
HOW...MUCH OF A CUT ARE WE TALKING ABOUT?
HAN!
PLEASE!

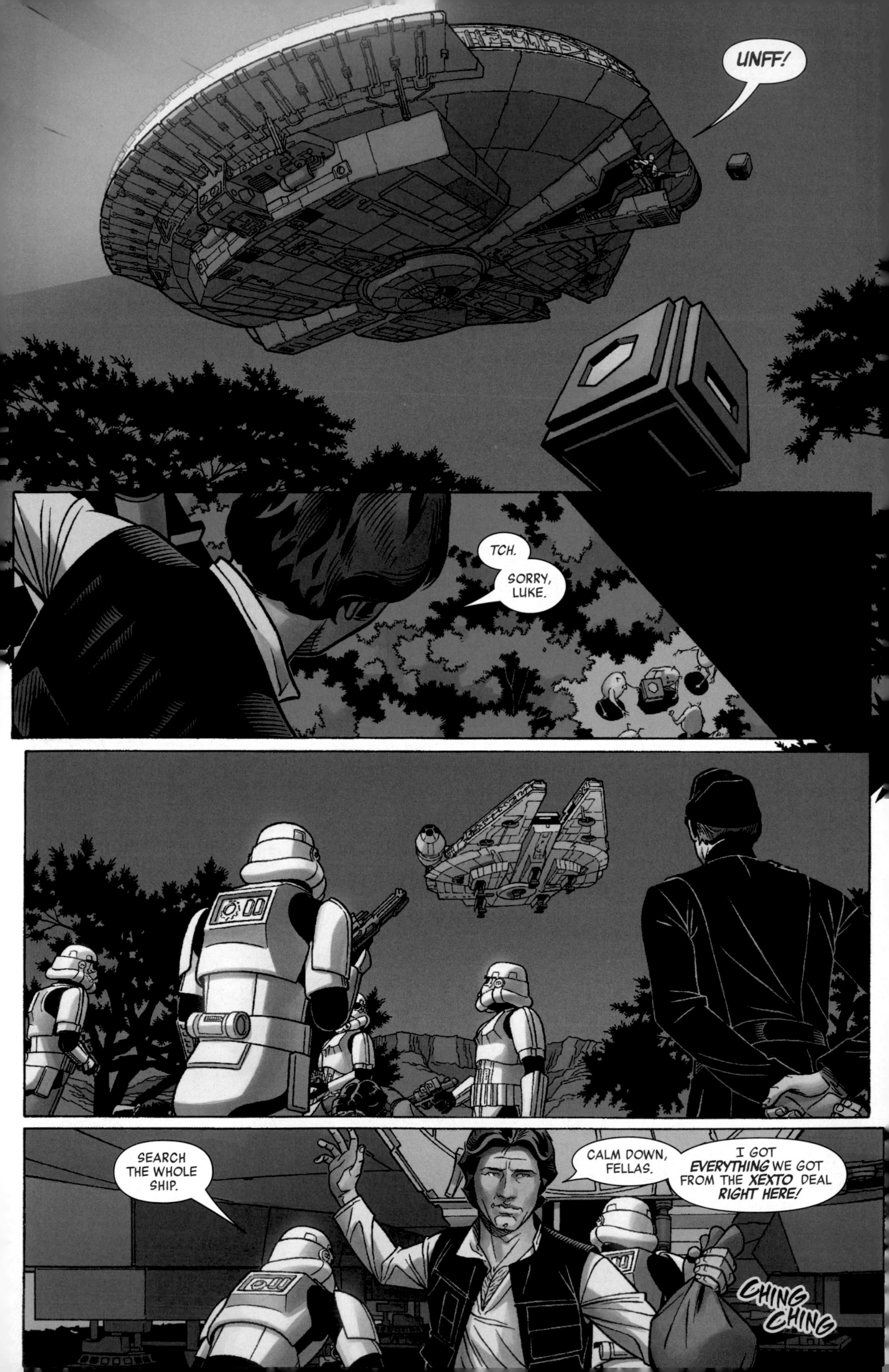

UNFF!
TCH.
SORRY, LUKE.
SEARCH THE WHOLE SHIP.
CALM DOWN, FELLAS.
I GOT EVERYTHING WE GOT FROM THE XEXTO DEAL RIGHT HERE!
CHING CHING

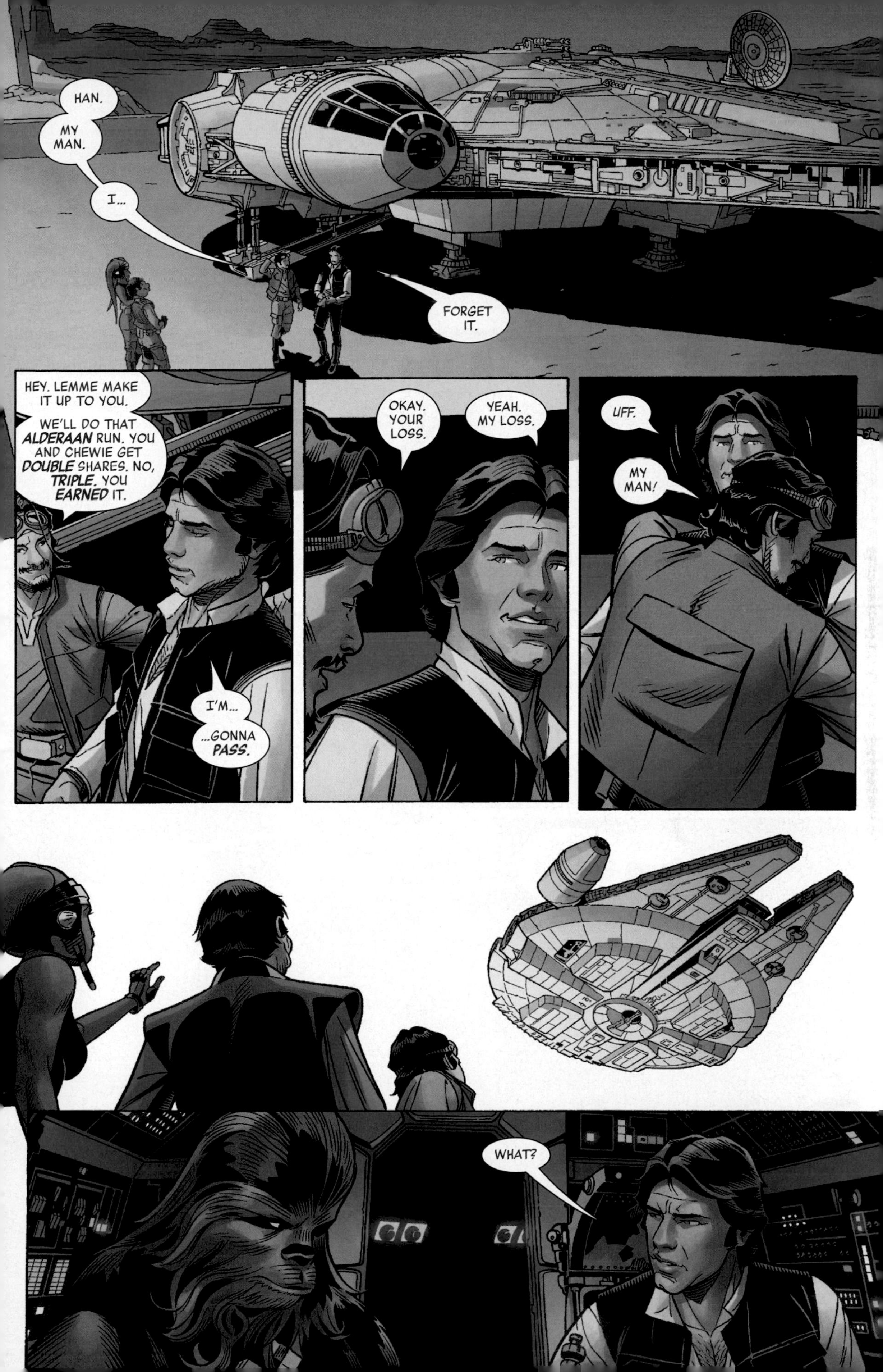
HAN.
MY MAN.
I...
FORGET IT.
HEY. LEMME MAKE IT UP TO YOU.
WE'LL DO THAT ALDERAAN RUN. YOU AND CHEWIE GET DOUBLE SHARES. NO, TRIPLE. YOU EARNED IT.
I'M...
...GONNA PASS.
OKAY. YOUR LOSS.
YEAH. MY LOSS.
UFF.
MY MAN!
WHAT?

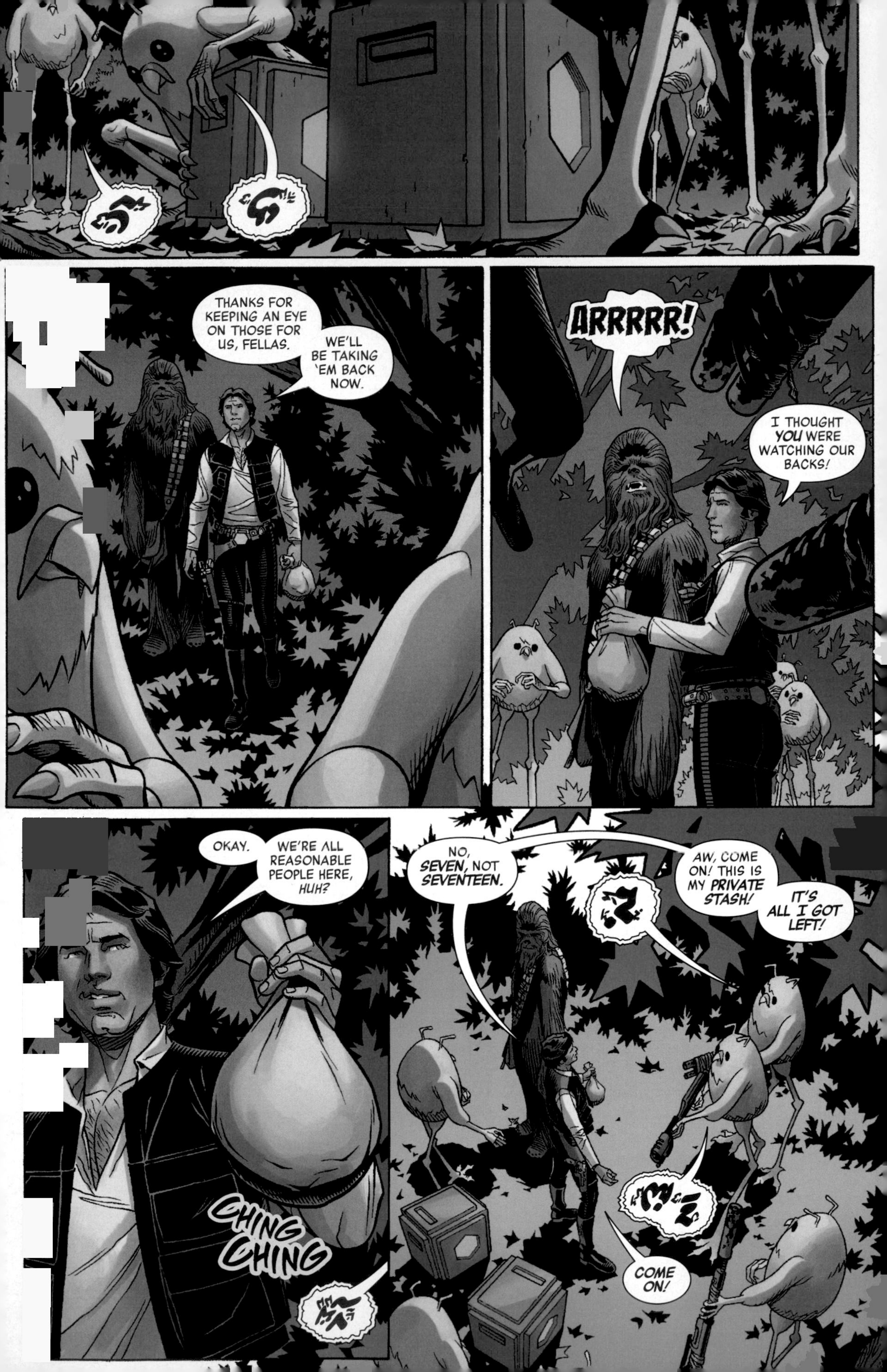
THANKS FOR KEEPING AN EYE ON THOSE FOR US, FELLAS.
WE'LL BE TAKING 'EM BACK NOW.
ARRRRR!
I THOUGHT YOU WERE WATCHING OUR BACKS!
OKAY.
WE'RE ALL REASONABLE PEOPLE HERE, HUH?
CHING CHING
NO, SEVEN, NOT SEVENTEEN.
AW, COME ON! THIS IS MY PRIVATE STASH!
IT'S ALL I GOT LEFT!
COME ON!

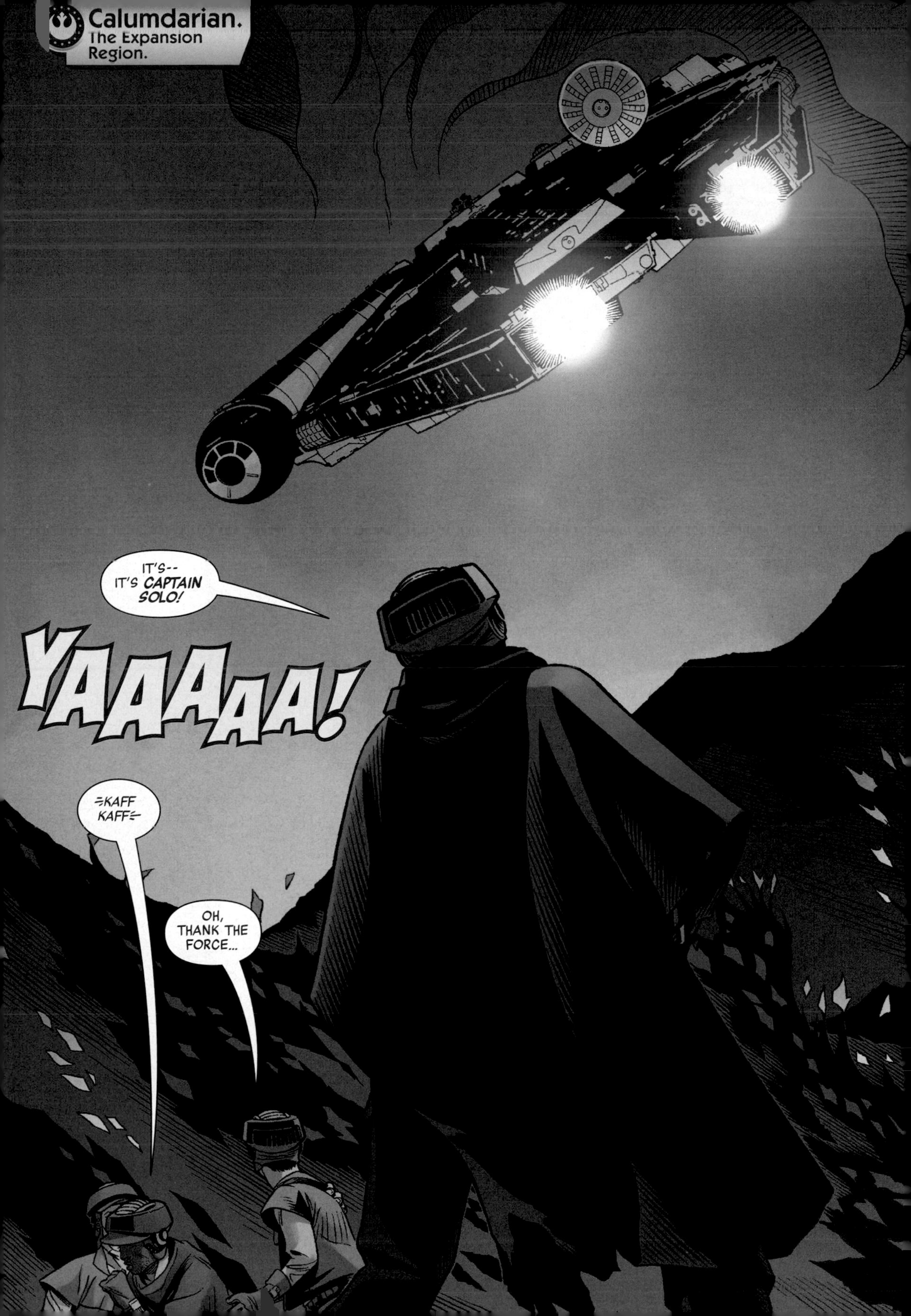

Calumdarian. The Expansion Region.
IT'S-- IT'S CAPTAIN SOLO!
YAAAAA!
KAFF KAFF
OH, THANK THE FORCE...

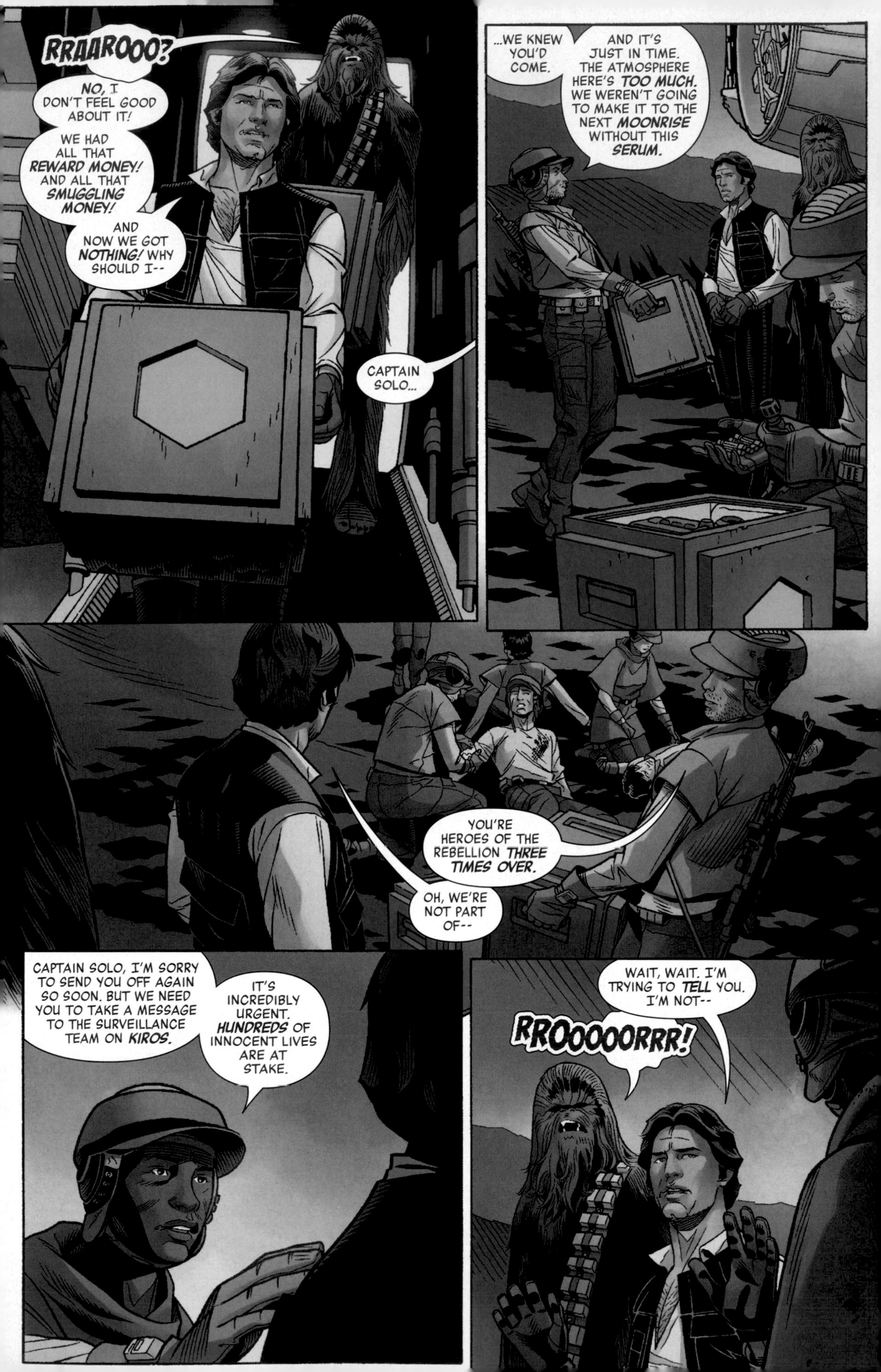
RRAAROOO?
NO, I DON'T FEEL GOOD ABOUT IT!
WE HAD ALL THAT REWARD MONEY! AND ALL THAT SMUGGLING MONEY!
AND NOW WE GOT NOTHING! WHY SHOULD I--
CAPTAIN SOLO...
...WE KNEW YOU'D COME.
AND IT'S JUST IN TIME. THE ATMOSPHERE HERE'S TOO MUCH. WE WEREN'T GOING TO MAKE IT TO THE NEXT MOONRISE WITHOUT THIS SERUM.
YOU'RE HEROES OF THE REBELLION THREE TIMES OVER.
OH, WE'RE NOT PART OF--
CAPTAIN SOLO, I'M SORRY TO SEND YOU OFF AGAIN SO SOON. BUT WE NEED YOU TO TAKE A MESSAGE TO THE SURVEILLANCE TEAM ON KIROS.
IT'S INCREDIBLY URGENT. HUNDREDS OF INNOCENT LIVES ARE AT STAKE.
WAIT, WAIT. I'M TRYING TO TELL YOU. I'M NOT--
RROOOOORRR!

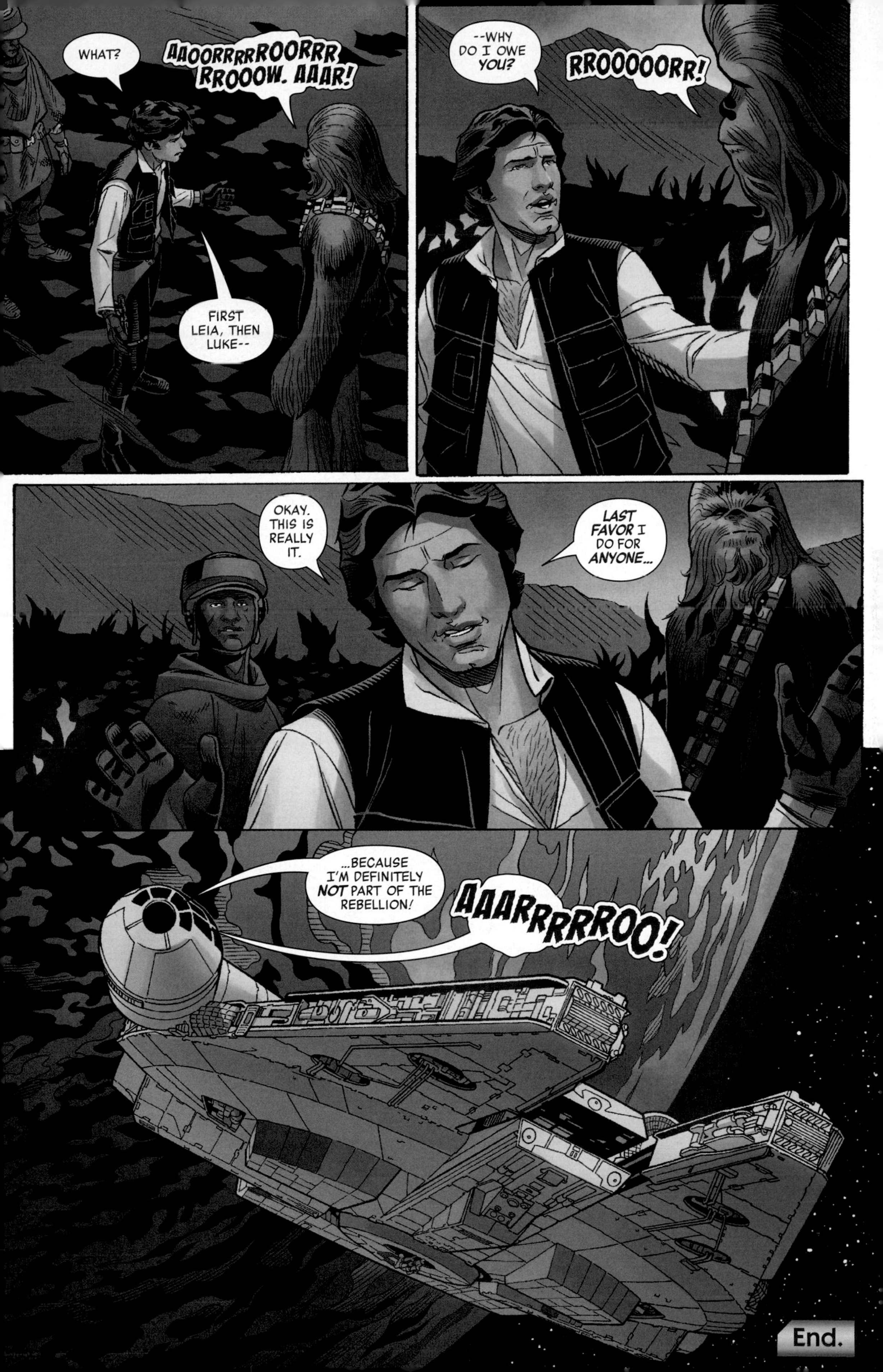
WHAT?
AAOORRRRROORRR RROOOW. AAAR!
FIRST LEIA, THEN LUKE--
--WHY DO I OWE YOU?
RROOOOORR!
OKAY. THIS IS REALLY IT.
LAST FAVOR I DO FOR ANYONE...
...BECAUSE I'M DEFINITELY NOT PART OF THE REBELLION!
AAARRRRROO!
End.

A SOLO FLIGHT

Han Solo traveled the stars—but kept his feet planted firmly on the ground

By Glenn Greenberg

"Kid, I've flown from one side of this galaxy to the other. I've seen a lot of strange stuff. But I've never seen anything to make me believe there's one all-powerful 'Force' controlling everything. There's no mystical energy field that controls *my* destiny. It's all a lot of simple tricks and nonsense."

So says Han Solo, captain of the *Millennium Falcon*, as young Luke Skywalker begins his Jedi training with Ben Kenobi in 1977's *Star Wars*. Solo's skepticism cannot be swayed. Moments later, when Luke is wearing a helmet that renders him sightless and he manages to deflect a practice remote's laser blasts with his lightsaber, Solo dismisses it as mere luck.

For many audience members who watched the movie in its initial release, Solo, to a certain degree, represented their point of view. They didn't quite know what to make of this newfangled space saga from George Lucas featuring bickering robots, Sand People, Jawas and, especially, a mysterious unseen Force. So naturally, they related to Han—the character who actively questioned the more out-there aspects of the story.

UNIVERSAL APPEAL

It's important to note that before *Star Wars* hit theaters, cinematic science fiction was in a somewhat fallow period. The major Hollywood studios had been mostly shying away from sci-fi, considering it too much of a financial risk—

1976's *Logan's Run* being a rare exception. It had been a while since movie audiences had been asked to buy into concepts as imaginative and as fantastical as those in *Star Wars*.

"My character was both useful in advancing the story but also useful to the audience in providing a more contemporary reference—he was the cynic," Harrison Ford, who played Solo, told *Rolling Stone* in December 2015.

This element was essential to the film's success, according to Mark Hamill, who played Luke. "One of the crucial things that I think gave us an advantage," he told this writer in 2017, "was the fact that the Han Solo character acted as a surrogate for the more cynical members of the audience who would be resistant to this kind of storytelling." Since Han, ultimately, went along for the ride, those audience members felt they could too.

THE PATH OF HAN

Much of Han's relatability came from Ford's fun-filled, down-to-earth (if you will) performance, which contrasted perfectly with the earnest innocence of Hamill's Luke, the serene dignity of Sir Alec Guinness' Ben Kenobi and the sharp, no-nonsense idealism of Carrie Fisher's Princess Leia.

Ford himself has said that when playing Han, "I intentionally keep my interpretation simple." That straightforward, practical approach fueled the vision he had for Han's fate in 1983's

Return of the Jedi. "I desperately wanted to die in *Jedi*," Ford said at the time. "I thought it would give the myth some body, that Han Solo, in fact, really had no place to go—he's got no momma, he's got no poppa. He's got no story. He would have best served the situation by giving it the weight of sacrifice, but that was the one thing I was unable to convince George of."

Of course, Han not only survived in *Return of the Jedi*, he returned 32 years later in *The Force Awakens*—now as something of a believer. "It's true," Solo tells Rey and Finn. "The Force, the Jedi, all of it. It's all true." As Ford reflected in *Rolling Stone*, "I didn't have the imagination to recognize the potential in the future for the character."

And while *The Force Awakens* gave Han the powerful send-off that Ford had pushed for decades earlier, audiences would soon learn, courtesy of 2018's *Solo: A Star Wars Story*, that there were more stories to be told about the beloved Corellian smuggler.

Sources

- The Making of Return of the Jedi, *edited by John Phillip Peecher, Del Rey, 1983*
- *Glenn Greenberg interview with Mark Hamill, April 2017*
- *Rolling Stone, December 2015*

LANDO CALRISSIAN

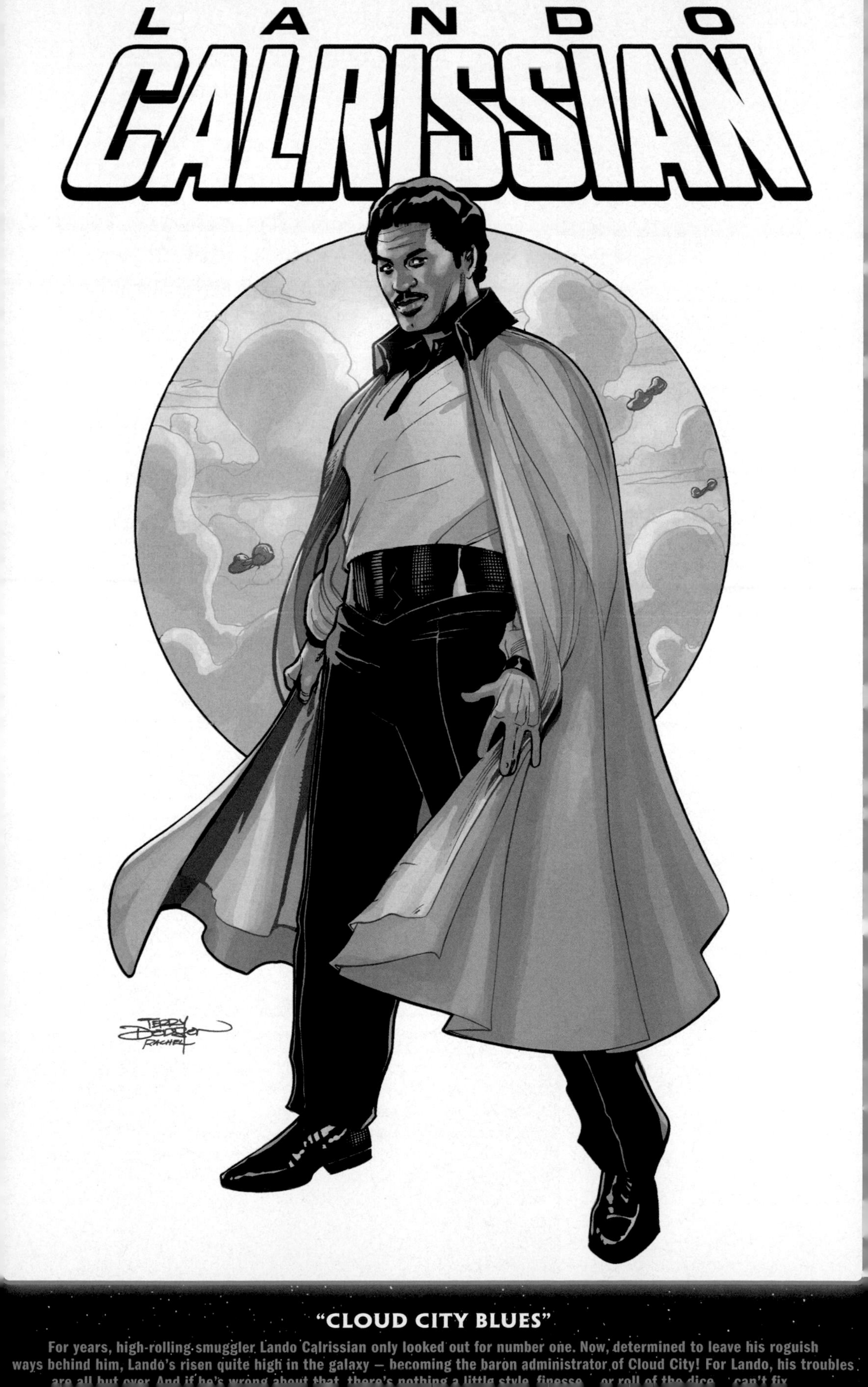

"CLOUD CITY BLUES"

For years, high-rolling smuggler Lando Calrissian only looked out for number one. Now, determined to leave his roguish ways behind him, Lando's risen quite high in the galaxy — becoming the baron administrator of Cloud City! For Lando, his troubles are all but over. And if he's wrong about that, there's nothing a little style, finesse... or roll of the dice... can't fix.

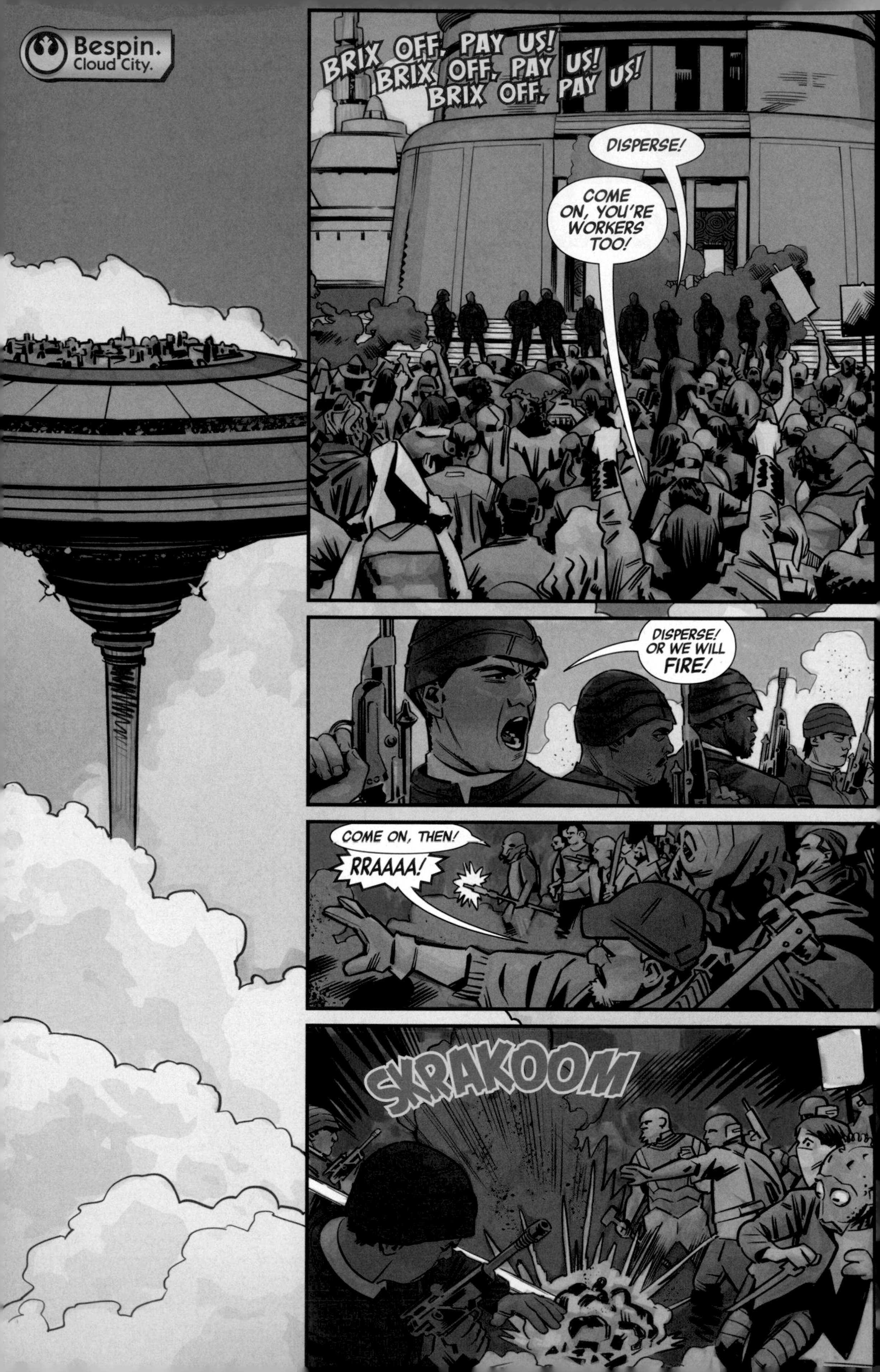
Bespin.
Cloud City.
BRIX OFF, PAY US!
BRIX OFF, PAY US!
BRIX OFF, PAY US!
DISPERSE!
COME ON, YOU'RE WORKERS TOO!
DISPERSE! OR WE WILL FIRE!
COME ON, THEN!
RRAAAA!
SKRAKOOM

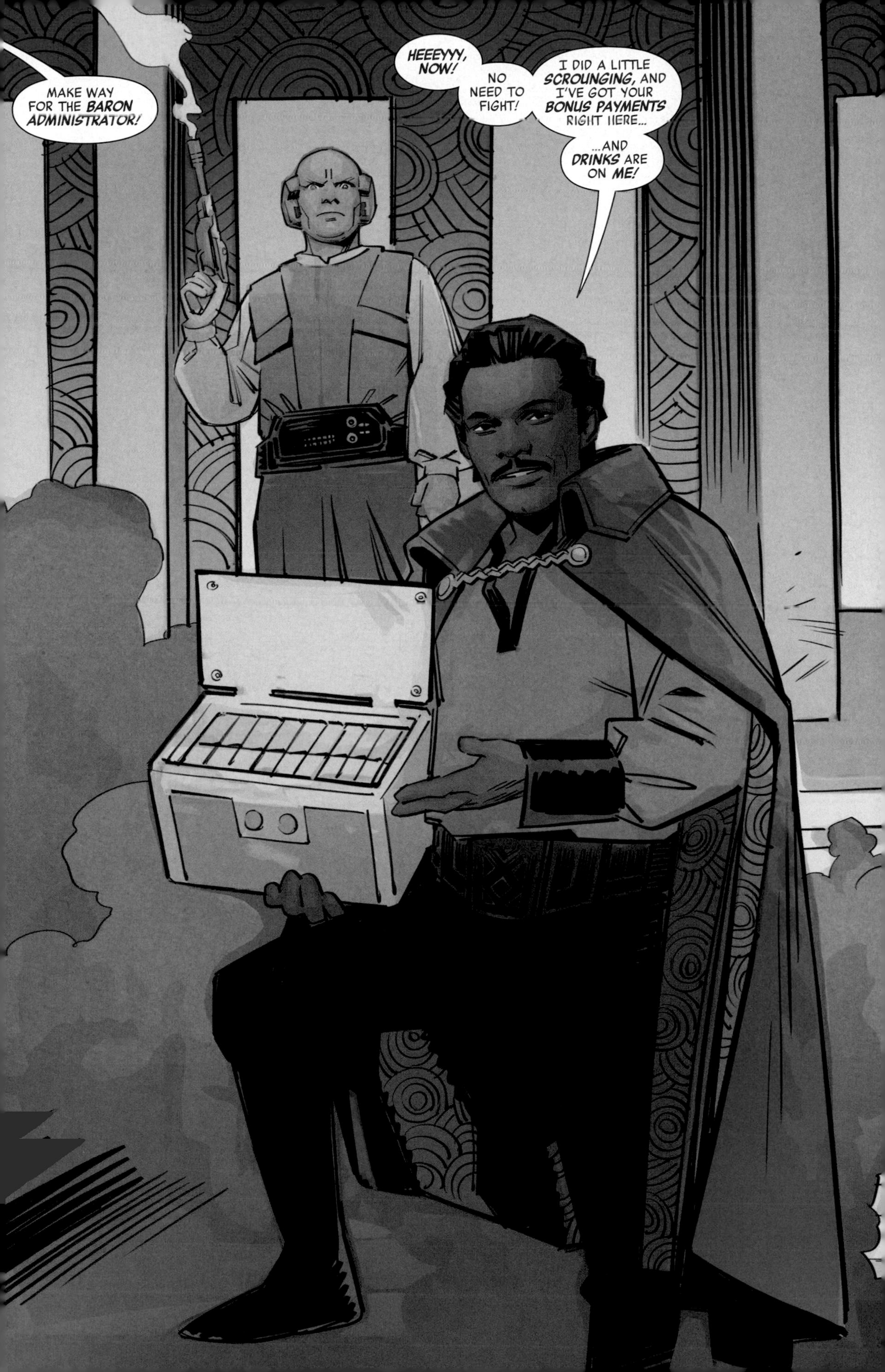
MAKE WAY FOR THE BARON ADMINISTRATOR!
HEEEYYY, NOW!
NO NEED TO FIGHT!
I DID A LITTLE SCROUNGING, AND I'VE GOT YOUR BONUS PAYMENTS RIGHT HERE...
...AND DRINKS ARE ON ME!

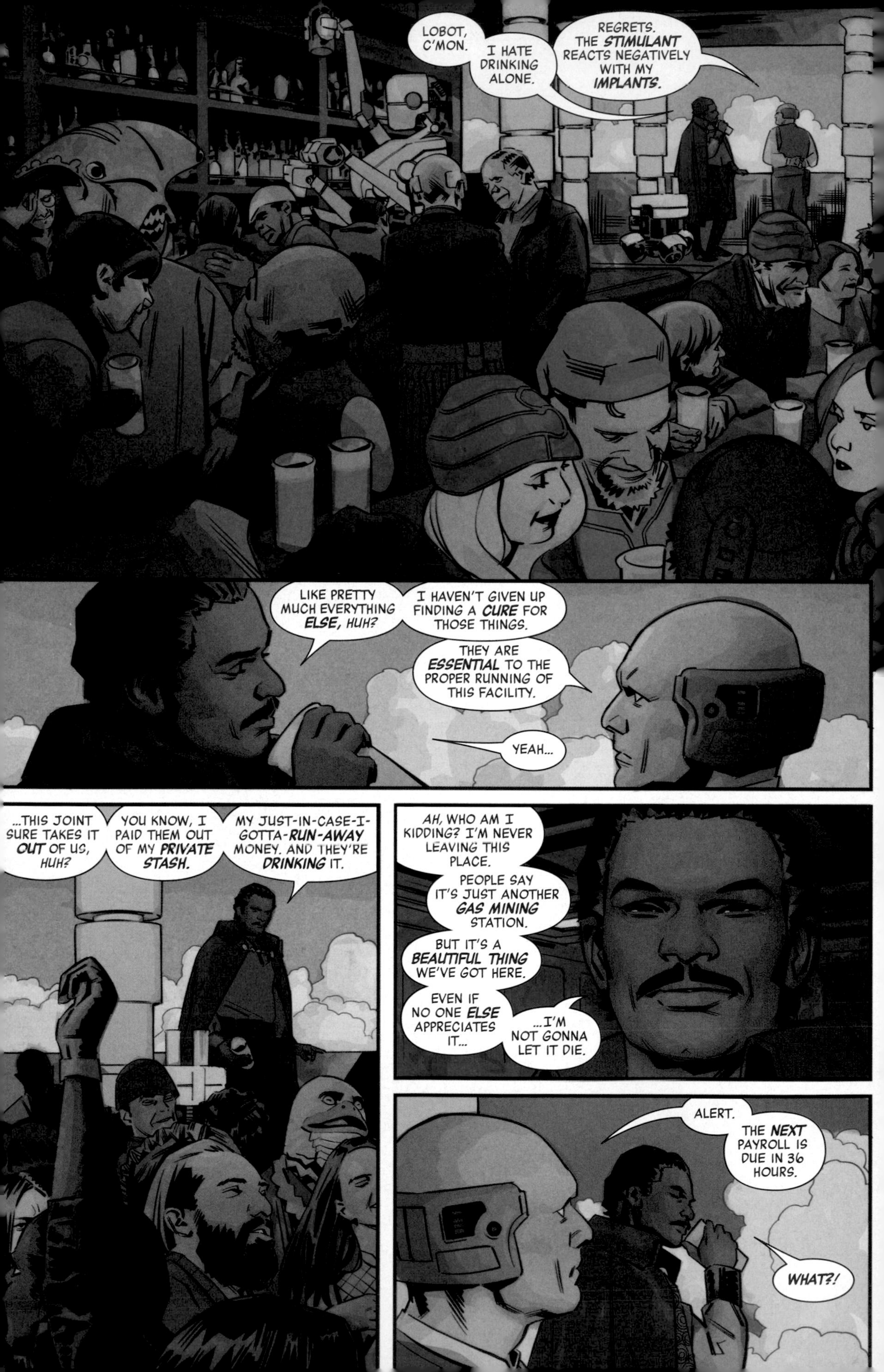
LOBOT, C'MON.
I HATE DRINKING ALONE.
REGRETS. THE STIMULANT REACTS NEGATIVELY WITH MY IMPLANTS.
LIKE PRETTY MUCH EVERYTHING ELSE, HUH?
I HAVEN'T GIVEN UP FINDING A CURE FOR THOSE THINGS.
THEY ARE ESSENTIAL TO THE PROPER RUNNING OF THIS FACILITY.
YEAH...
...THIS JOINT SURE TAKES IT OUT OF US, HUH?
YOU KNOW, I PAID THEM OUT OF MY PRIVATE STASH.
MY JUST-IN-CASE-I-GOTTA-RUN-AWAY MONEY. AND THEY'RE DRINKING IT.
AH, WHO AM I KIDDING? I'M NEVER LEAVING THIS PLACE.
PEOPLE SAY IT'S JUST ANOTHER GAS MINING STATION.
BUT IT'S A BEAUTIFUL THING WE'VE GOT HERE.
EVEN IF NO ONE ELSE APPRECIATES IT...
...I'M NOT GONNA LET IT DIE.
ALERT.
THE NEXT PAYROLL IS DUE IN 36 HOURS.
WHAT?!

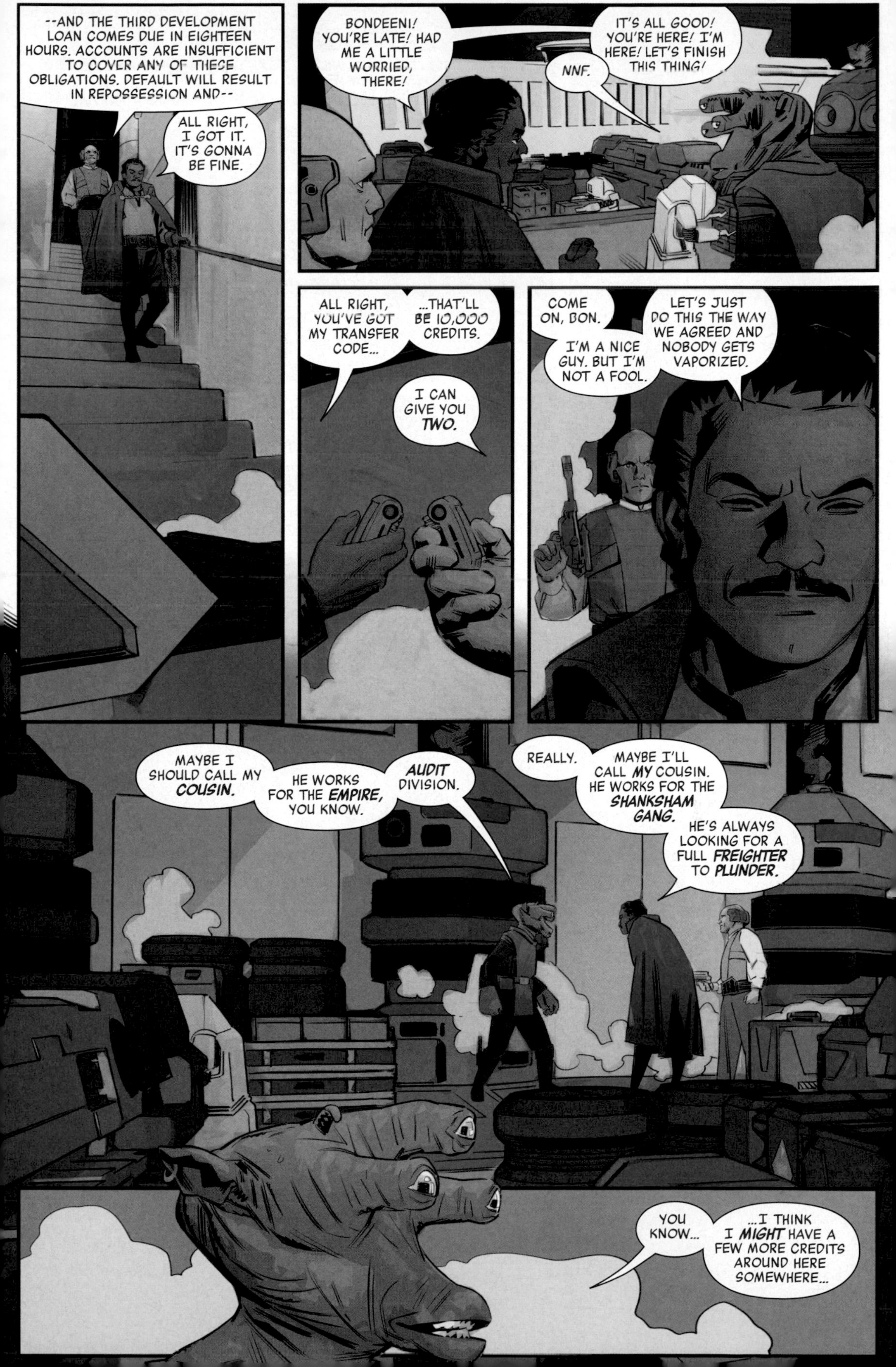
--AND THE THIRD DEVELOPMENT LOAN COMES DUE IN EIGHTEEN HOURS. ACCOUNTS ARE INSUFFICIENT TO COVER ANY OF THESE OBLIGATIONS. DEFAULT WILL RESULT IN REPOSSESSION AND--
ALL RIGHT, I GOT IT. IT'S GONNA BE FINE.
BONDEENI! YOU'RE LATE! HAD ME A LITTLE WORRIED, THERE!
IT'S ALL GOOD! YOU'RE HERE! I'M HERE! LET'S FINISH THIS THING!
NNF.
ALL RIGHT, YOU'VE GOT MY TRANSFER CODE...
...THAT'LL BE 10,000 CREDITS.
I CAN GIVE YOU TWO.
COME ON, BON.
I'M A NICE GUY. BUT I'M NOT A FOOL.
LET'S JUST DO THIS THE WAY WE AGREED AND NOBODY GETS VAPORIZED.
MAYBE I SHOULD CALL MY COUSIN.
HE WORKS FOR THE EMPIRE, YOU KNOW.
AUDIT DIVISION.
REALLY.
MAYBE I'LL CALL MY COUSIN. HE WORKS FOR THE SHANKSHAM GANG.
HE'S ALWAYS LOOKING FOR A FULL FREIGHTER TO PLUNDER.
YOU KNOW...
...I THINK I MIGHT HAVE A FEW MORE CREDITS AROUND HERE SOMEWHERE...

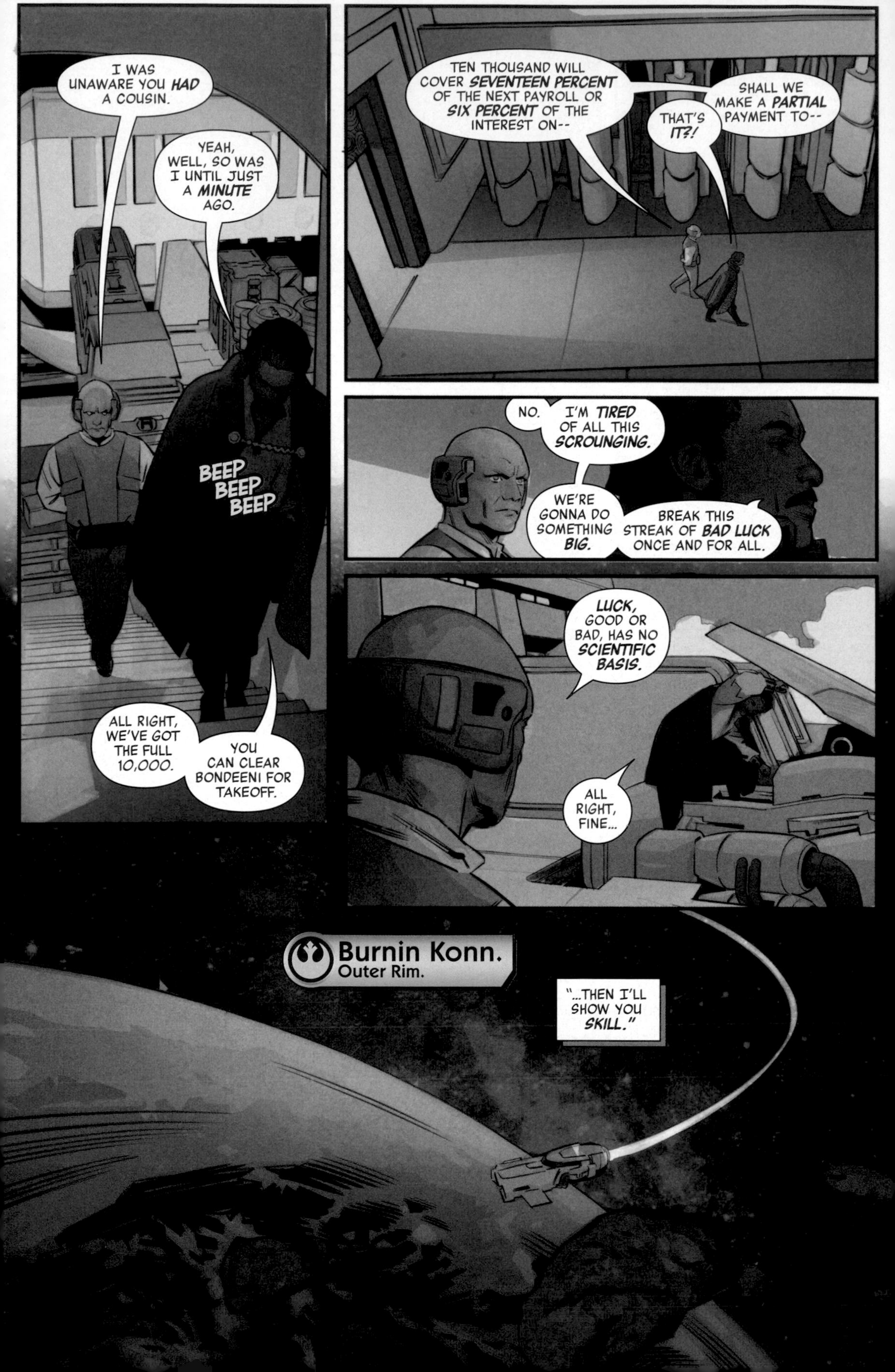
I WAS UNAWARE YOU HAD A COUSIN.
YEAH, WELL, SO WAS I UNTIL JUST A MINUTE AGO.
BEEP BEEP BEEP
ALL RIGHT, WE'VE GOT THE FULL 10,000.
YOU CAN CLEAR BONDEENI FOR TAKEOFF.
TEN THOUSAND WILL COVER SEVENTEEN PERCENT OF THE NEXT PAYROLL OR SIX PERCENT OF THE INTEREST ON--
THAT'S IT?!
SHALL WE MAKE A PARTIAL PAYMENT TO--
NO.
I'M TIRED OF ALL THIS SCROUNGING.
WE'RE GONNA DO SOMETHING BIG.
BREAK THIS STREAK OF BAD LUCK ONCE AND FOR ALL.
LUCK, GOOD OR BAD, HAS NO SCIENTIFIC BASIS.
ALL RIGHT, FINE...
Burnin Konn.
Outer Rim.
"...THEN I'LL SHOW YOU SKILL."

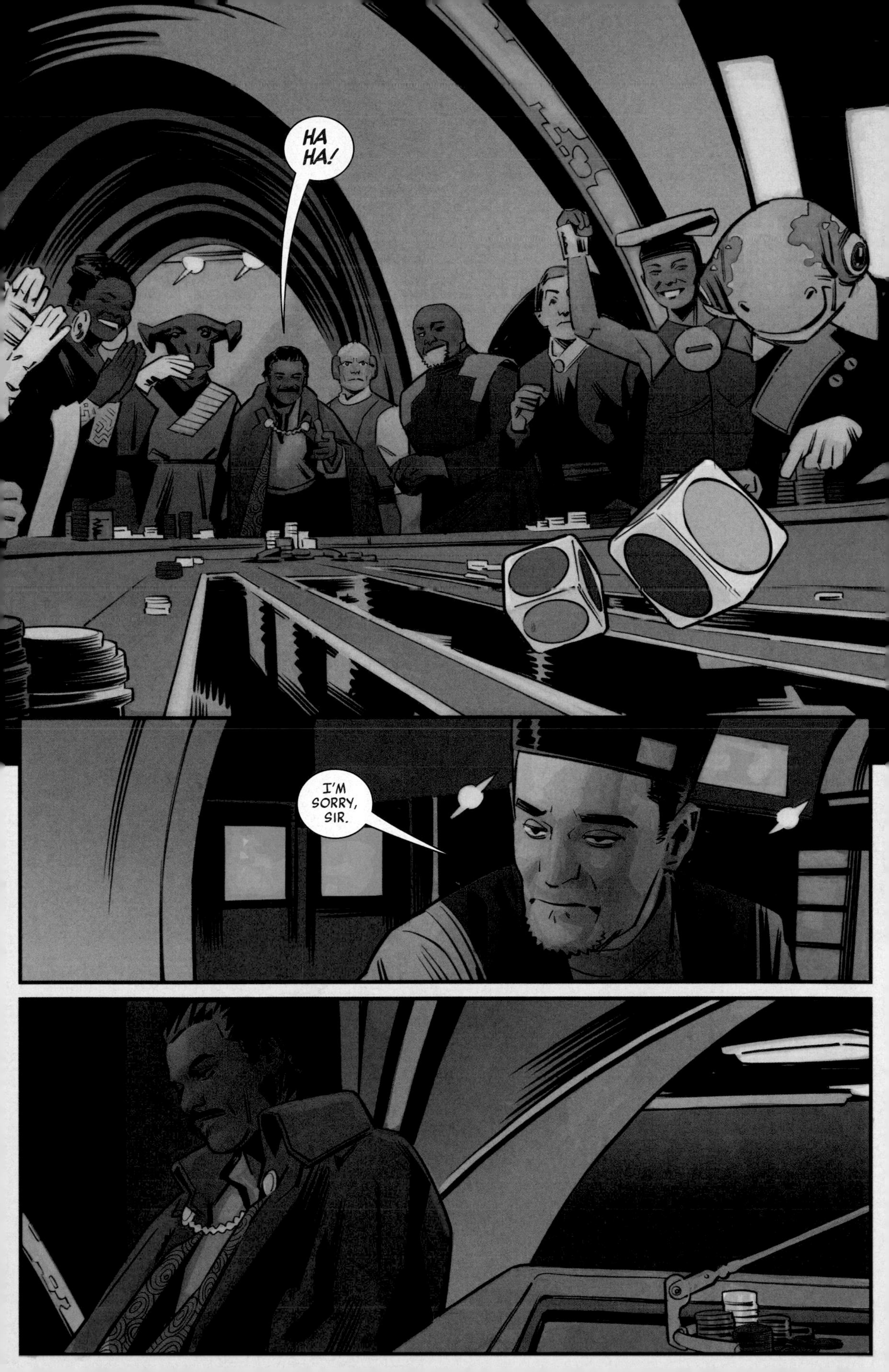
HA HA!
I'M SORRY, SIR.

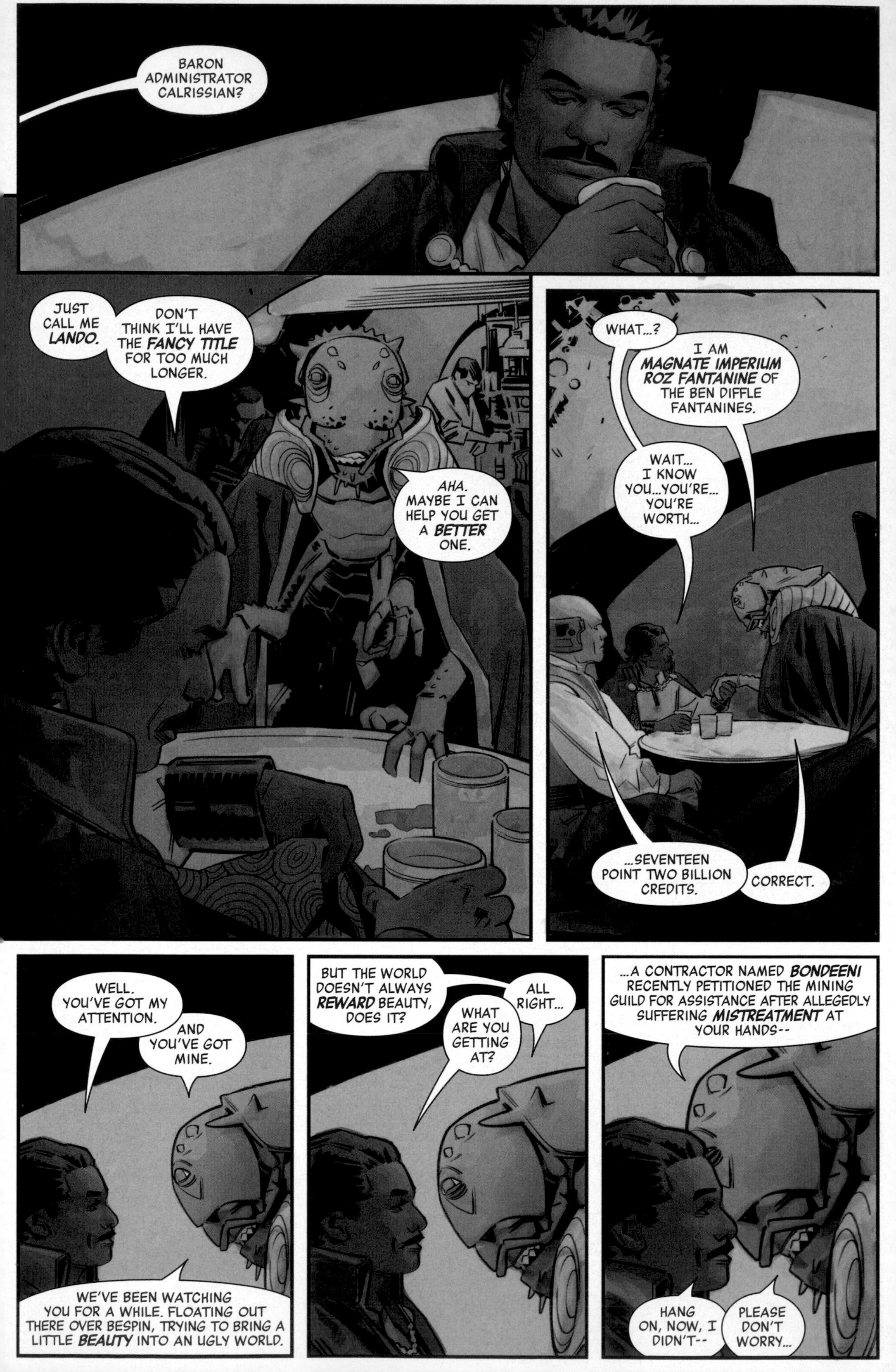
BARON ADMINISTRATOR CALRISSIAN?
JUST CALL ME LANDO.
DON'T THINK I'LL HAVE THE FANCY TITLE FOR TOO MUCH LONGER.
AHA. MAYBE I CAN HELP YOU GET A BETTER ONE.
WHAT...?
I AM MAGNATE IMPERIUM ROZ FANTANINE OF THE BEN DIFFLE FANTANINES.
WAIT... I KNOW YOU...YOU'RE... YOU'RE WORTH...
...SEVENTEEN POINT TWO BILLION CREDITS.
CORRECT.
WELL. YOU'VE GOT MY ATTENTION.
AND YOU'VE GOT MINE.
WE'VE BEEN WATCHING YOU FOR A WHILE. FLOATING OUT THERE OVER BESPIN, TRYING TO BRING A LITTLE BEAUTY INTO AN UGLY WORLD.
BUT THE WORLD DOESN'T ALWAYS REWARD BEAUTY, DOES IT?
ALL RIGHT...
WHAT ARE YOU GETTING AT?
...A CONTRACTOR NAMED BONDEENI RECENTLY PETITIONED THE MINING GUILD FOR ASSISTANCE AFTER ALLEGEDLY SUFFERING MISTREATMENT AT YOUR HANDS--
HANG ON, NOW, I DIDN'T--
PLEASE DON'T WORRY...

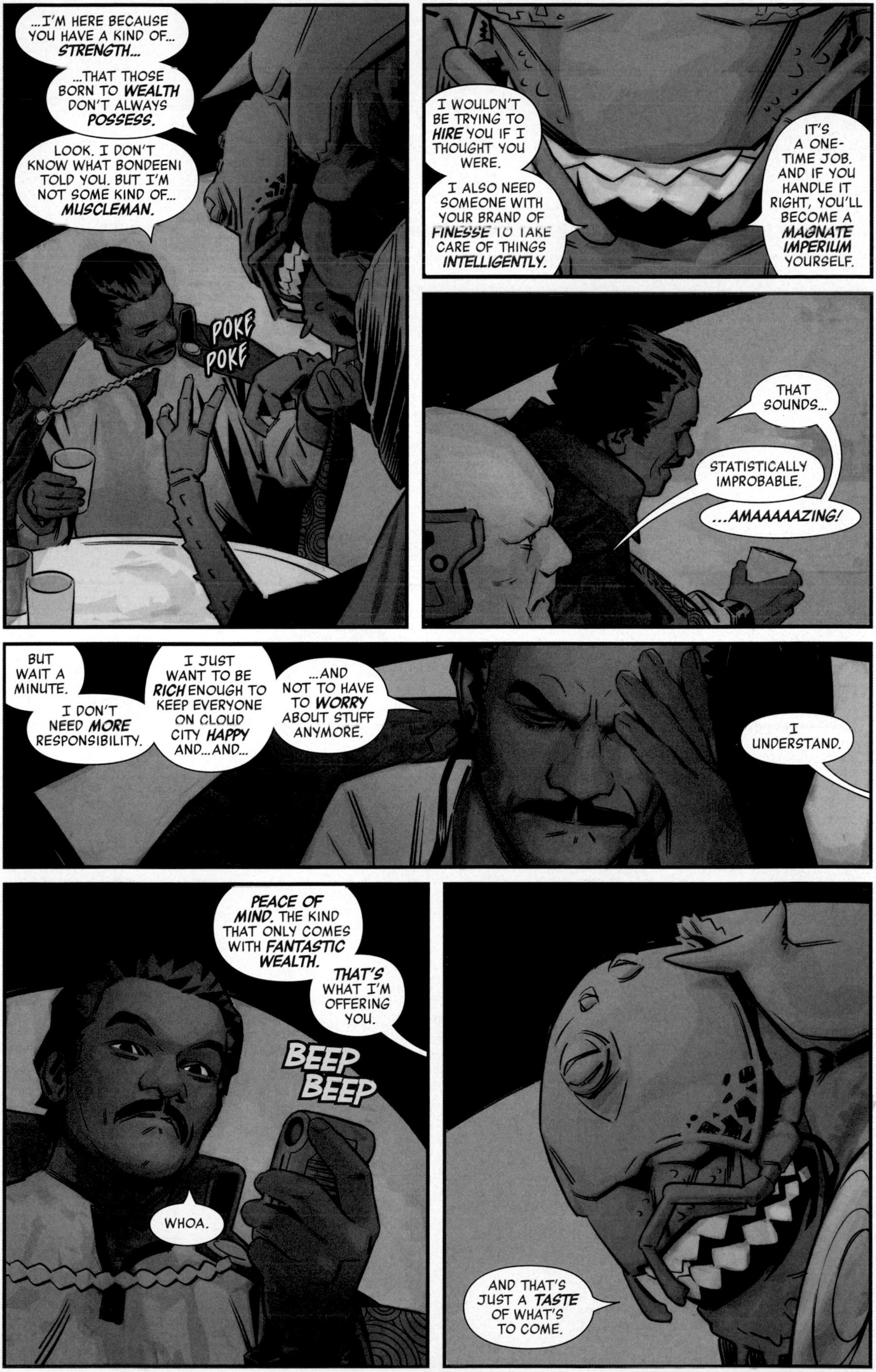
...I'M HERE BECAUSE YOU HAVE A KIND OF... STRENGTH...
...THAT THOSE BORN TO WEALTH DON'T ALWAYS POSSESS.
LOOK. I DON'T KNOW WHAT BONDEENI TOLD YOU. BUT I'M NOT SOME KIND OF... MUSCLEMAN.
POKE POKE
I WOULDN'T BE TRYING TO HIRE YOU IF I THOUGHT YOU WERE.
I ALSO NEED SOMEONE WITH YOUR BRAND OF FINESSE TO TAKE CARE OF THINGS INTELLIGENTLY.
IT'S A ONE-TIME JOB. AND IF YOU HANDLE IT RIGHT, YOU'LL BECOME A MAGNATE IMPERIUM YOURSELF.
THAT SOUNDS...
STATISTICALLY IMPROBABLE.
...AMAAAAAZING!
BUT WAIT A MINUTE.
I DON'T NEED MORE RESPONSIBILITY.
I JUST WANT TO BE RICH ENOUGH TO KEEP EVERYONE ON CLOUD CITY HAPPY AND...AND...
...AND NOT TO HAVE TO WORRY ABOUT STUFF ANYMORE.
I UNDERSTAND.
PEACE OF MIND. THE KIND THAT ONLY COMES WITH FANTASTIC WEALTH.
THAT'S WHAT I'M OFFERING YOU.
BEEP BEEP
WHOA.
AND THAT'S JUST A TASTE OF WHAT'S TO COME.

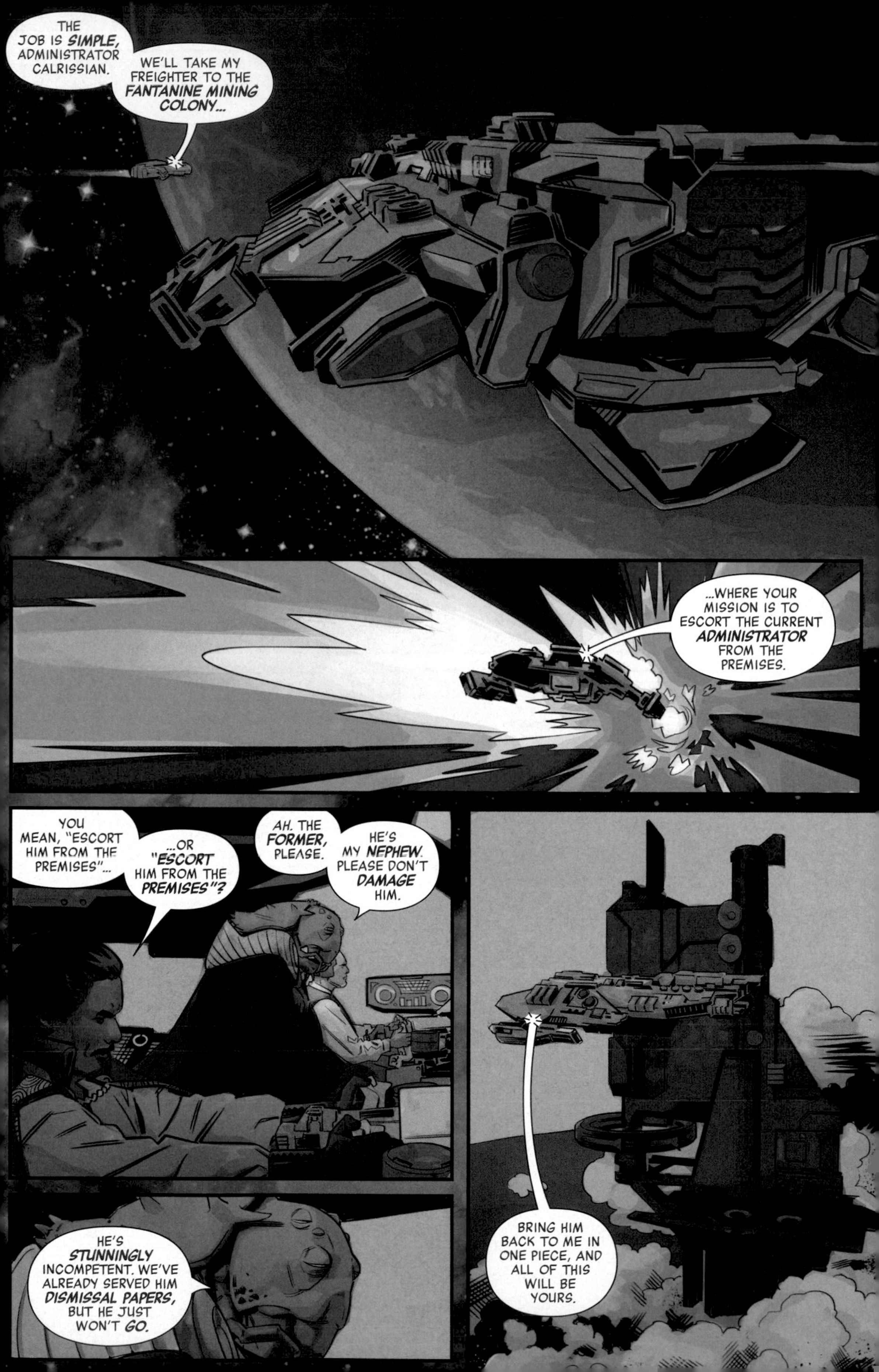

THE JOB IS SIMPLE, ADMINISTRATOR CALRISSIAN.
WE'LL TAKE MY FREIGHTER TO THE FANTANINE MINING COLONY...
...WHERE YOUR MISSION IS TO ESCORT THE CURRENT ADMINISTRATOR FROM THE PREMISES.
YOU MEAN, "ESCORT HIM FROM THE PREMISES"...
...OR "ESCORT HIM FROM THE PREMISES"?
AH. THE FORMER, PLEASE.
HE'S MY NEPHEW. PLEASE DON'T DAMAGE HIM.
HE'S STUNNINGLY INCOMPETENT. WE'VE ALREADY SERVED HIM DISMISSAL PAPERS, BUT HE JUST WON'T GO.
BRING HIM BACK TO ME IN ONE PIECE, AND ALL OF THIS WILL BE YOURS.

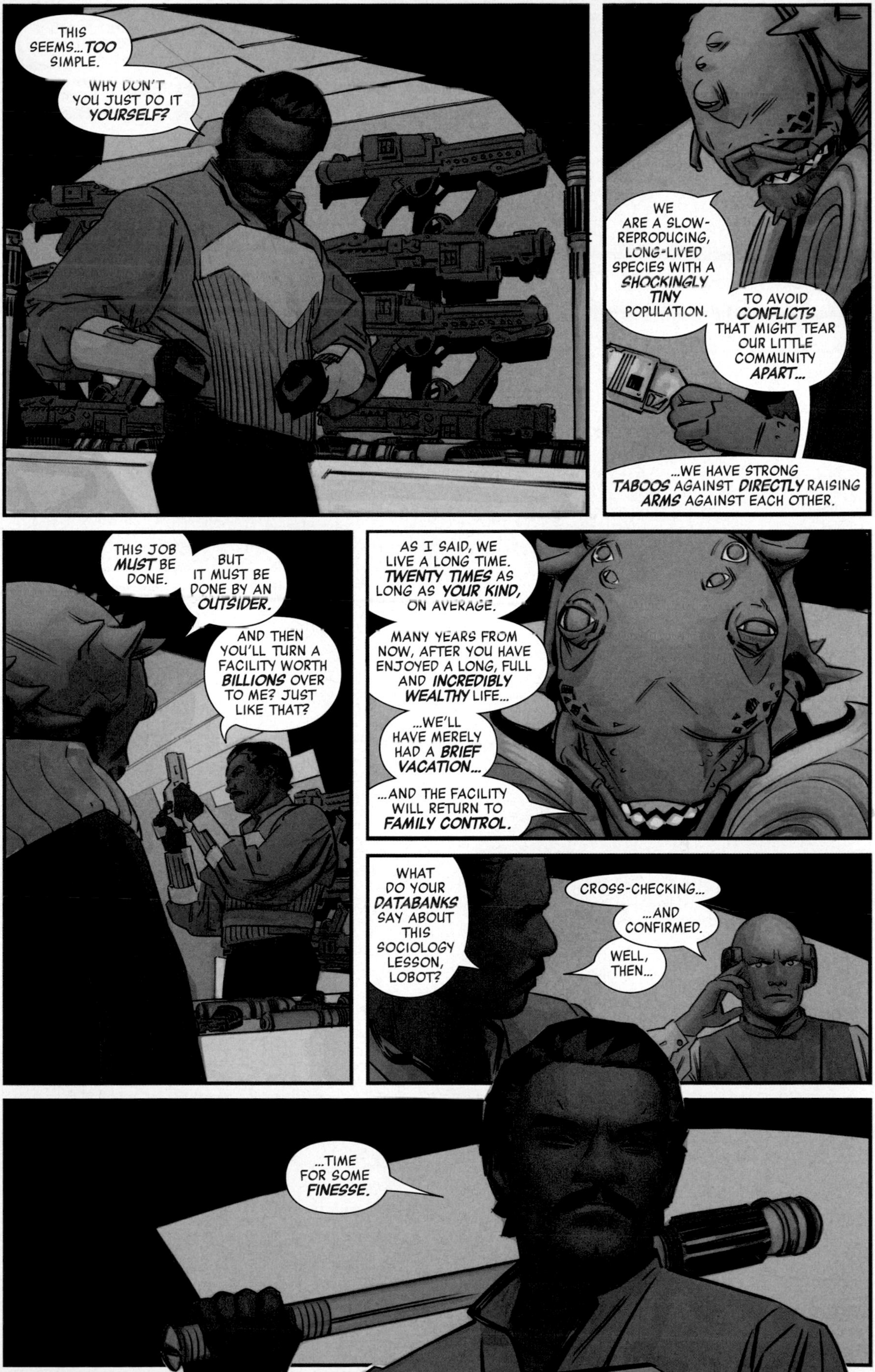
THIS SEEMS...TOO SIMPLE.
WHY DON'T YOU JUST DO IT YOURSELF?
WE ARE A SLOW-REPRODUCING, LONG-LIVED SPECIES WITH A SHOCKINGLY TINY POPULATION.
TO AVOID CONFLICTS THAT MIGHT TEAR OUR LITTLE COMMUNITY APART...
...WE HAVE STRONG TABOOS AGAINST DIRECTLY RAISING ARMS AGAINST EACH OTHER.
THIS JOB MUST BE DONE.
BUT IT MUST BE DONE BY AN OUTSIDER.
AND THEN YOU'LL TURN A FACILITY WORTH BILLIONS OVER TO ME? JUST LIKE THAT?
AS I SAID, WE LIVE A LONG TIME. TWENTY TIMES AS LONG AS YOUR KIND, ON AVERAGE.
MANY YEARS FROM NOW, AFTER YOU HAVE ENJOYED A LONG, FULL AND INCREDIBLY WEALTHY LIFE...
...WE'LL HAVE MERELY HAD A BRIEF VACATION...
...AND THE FACILITY WILL RETURN TO FAMILY CONTROL.
WHAT DO YOUR DATABANKS SAY ABOUT THIS SOCIOLOGY LESSON, LOBOT?
CROSS-CHECKING...
...AND CONFIRMED.
WELL, THEN...
...TIME FOR SOME FINESSE.

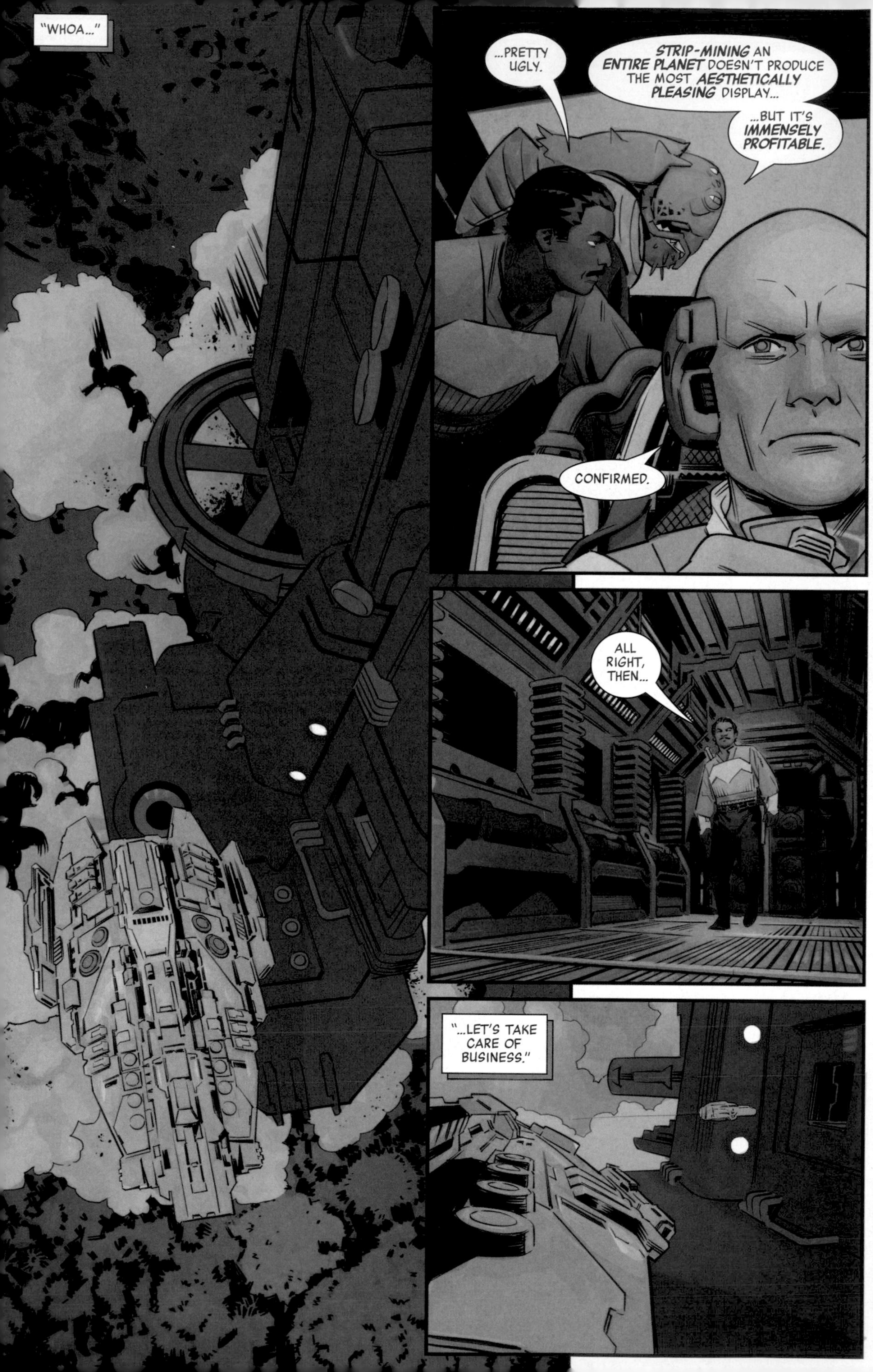
"WHOA..."
...PRETTY UGLY.
STRIP-MINING AN ENTIRE PLANET DOESN'T PRODUCE THE MOST AESTHETICALLY PLEASING DISPLAY...
...BUT IT'S IMMENSELY PROFITABLE.
CONFIRMED.
ALL RIGHT, THEN...
"...LET'S TAKE CARE OF BUSINESS."

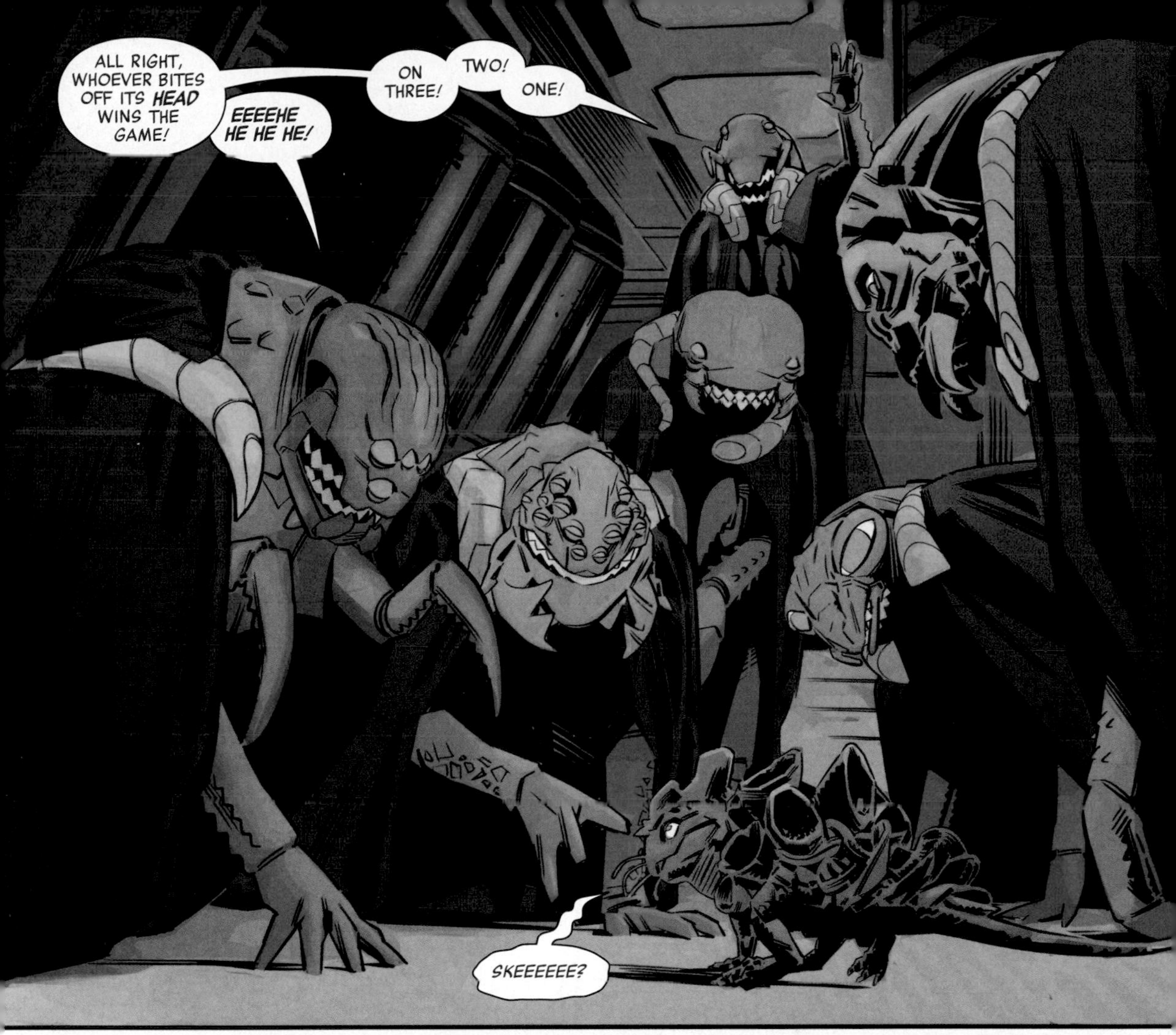
ALL RIGHT, WHOEVER BITES OFF ITS HEAD WINS THE GAME!
EEEEHE HE HE HE!
ON THREE!
TWO!
ONE!
SKEEEEEE?
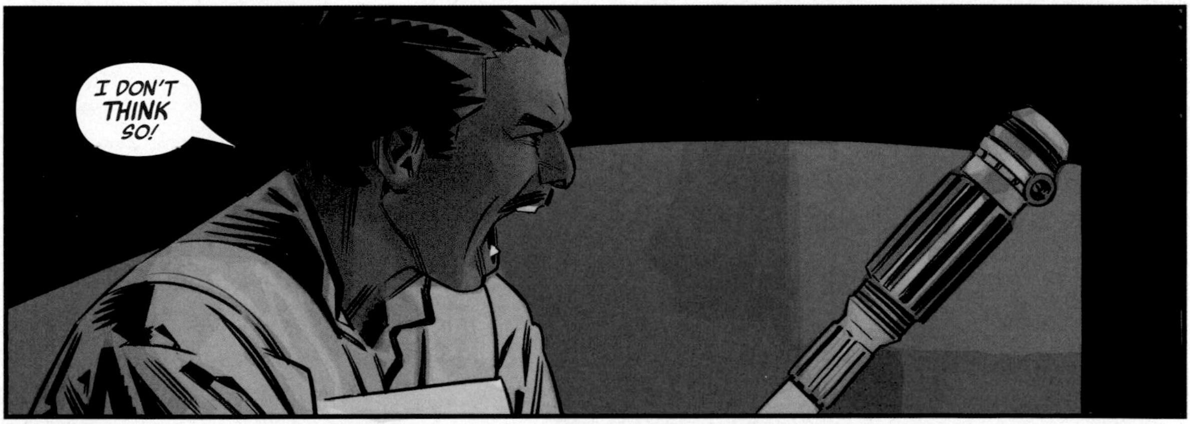
I DON'T THINK SO!
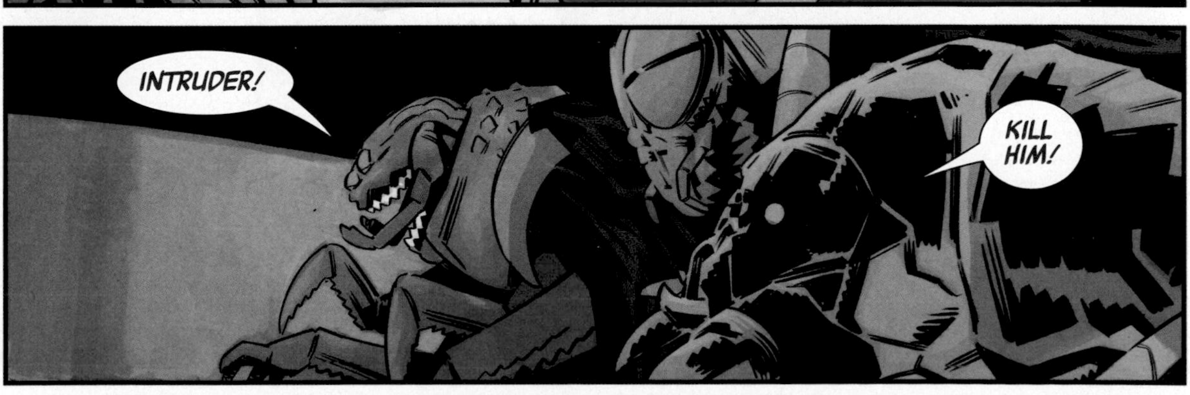
INTRUDER!
KILL HIM!

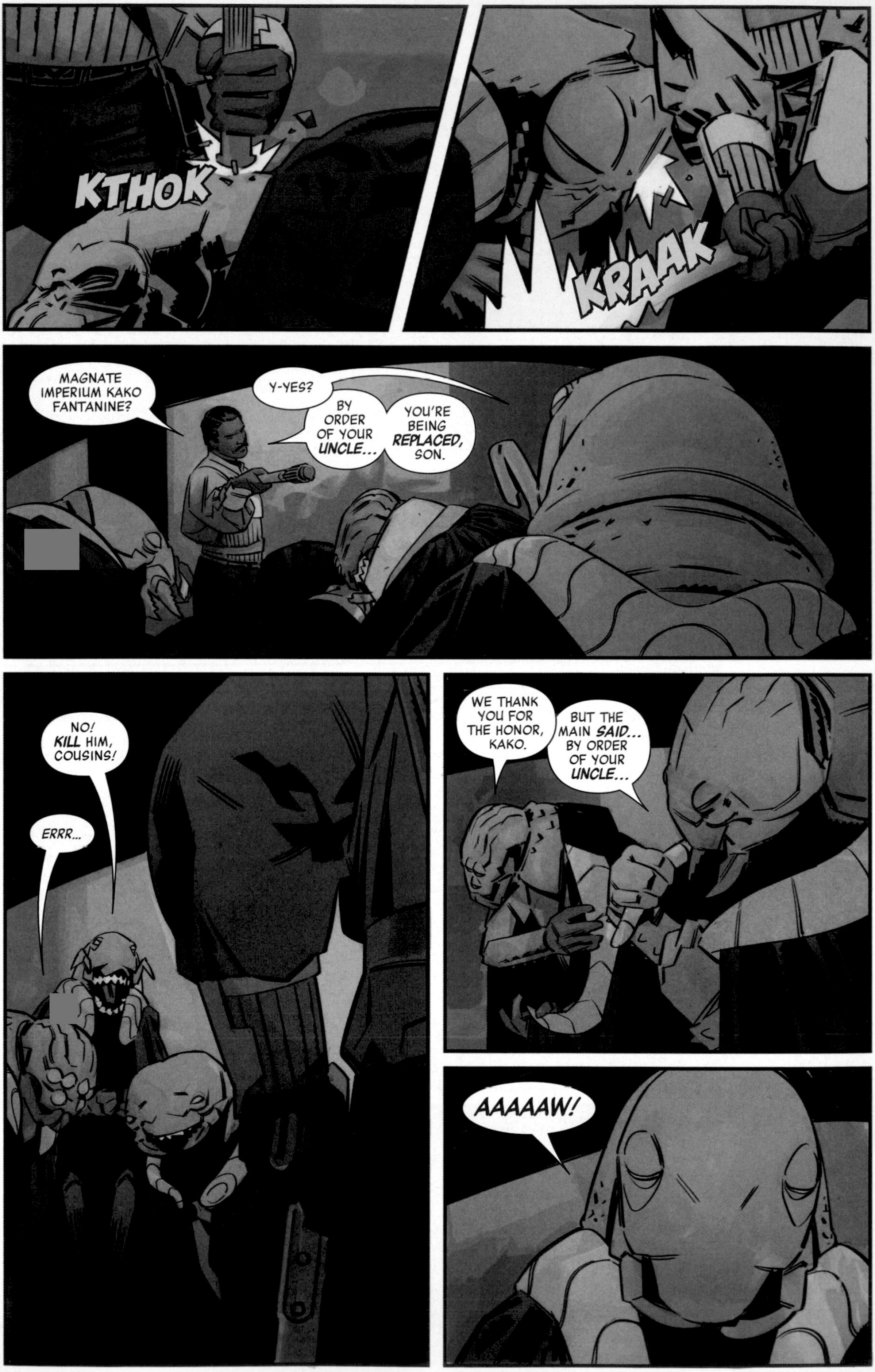
KTHOK
KRAAK
MAGNATE IMPERIUM KAKO FANTANINE?
Y-YES?
BY ORDER OF YOUR UNCLE...
YOU'RE BEING REPLACED, SON.
NO! KILL HIM, COUSINS!
ERRR...
WE THANK YOU FOR THE HONOR, KAKO.
BUT THE MAIN SAID... BY ORDER OF YOUR UNCLE...
AAAAAW!

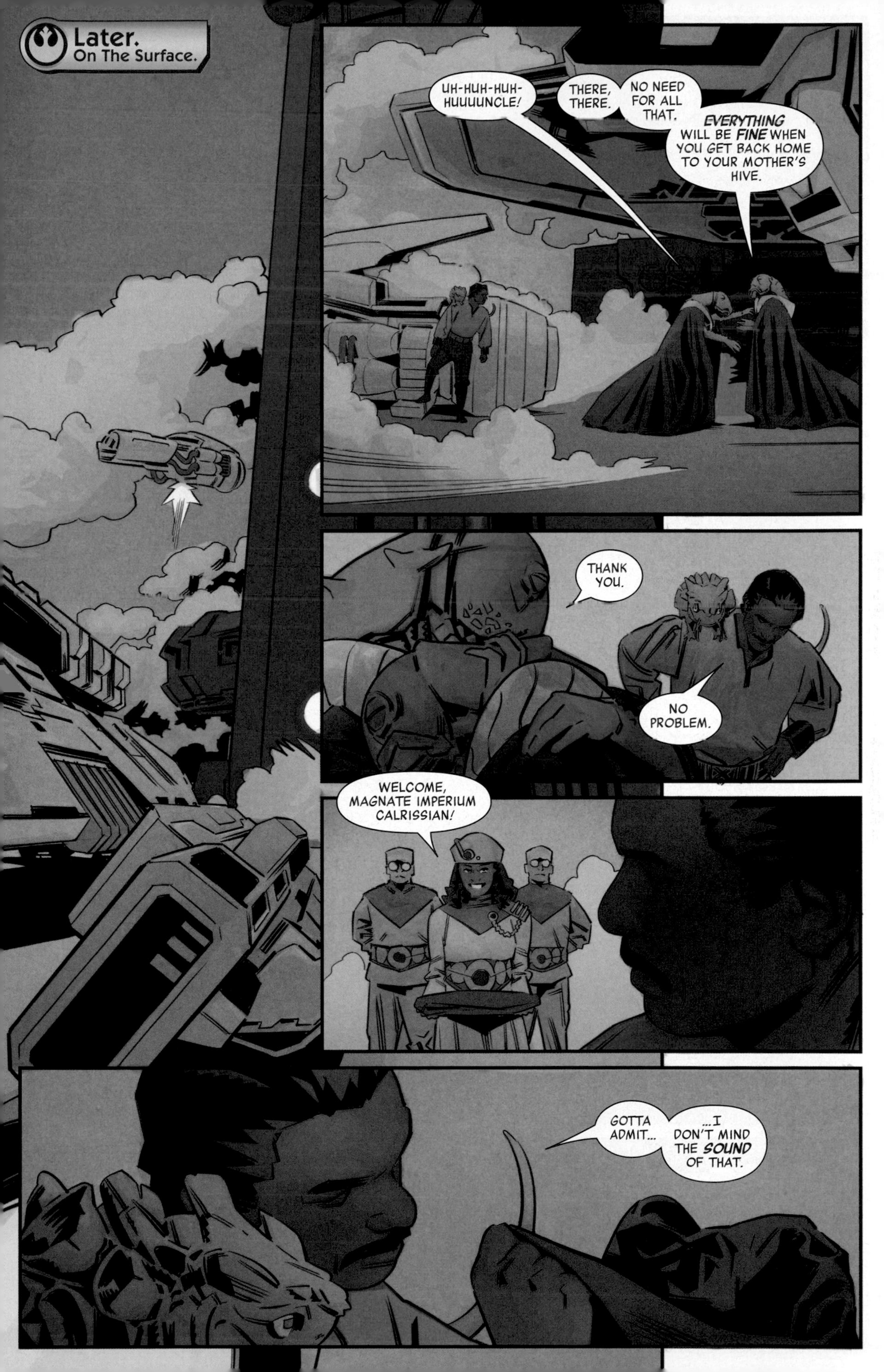
Later.
On The Surface.
UH-HUH-HUH-HUUUUNCLE!
THERE, THERE.
NO NEED FOR ALL THAT.
EVERYTHING WILL BE FINE WHEN YOU GET BACK HOME TO YOUR MOTHER'S HIVE.
THANK YOU.
NO PROBLEM.
WELCOME, MAGNATE IMPERIUM CALRISSIAN!
GOTTA ADMIT...
...I DON'T MIND THE SOUND OF THAT.

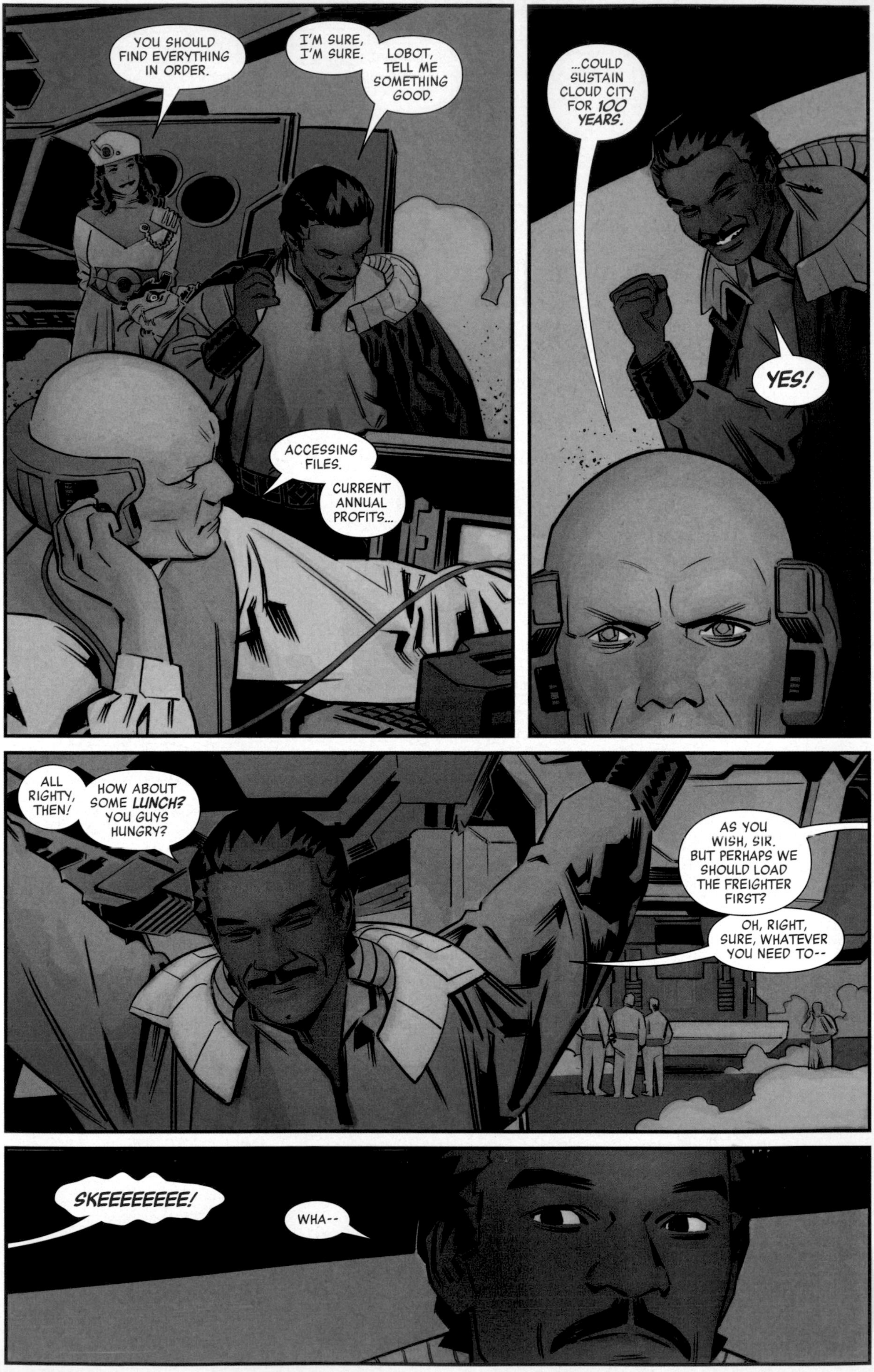
YOU SHOULD FIND EVERYTHING IN ORDER.
I'M SURE, I'M SURE.
LOBOT, TELL ME SOMETHING GOOD.
ACCESSING FILES.
CURRENT ANNUAL PROFITS...
...COULD SUSTAIN CLOUD CITY FOR 100 YEARS.
YES!
ALL RIGHTY, THEN!
HOW ABOUT SOME LUNCH? YOU GUYS HUNGRY?
AS YOU WISH, SIR. BUT PERHAPS WE SHOULD LOAD THE FREIGHTER FIRST?
OH, RIGHT, SURE, WHATEVER YOU NEED TO--
SKEEEEEEEE!
WHA--

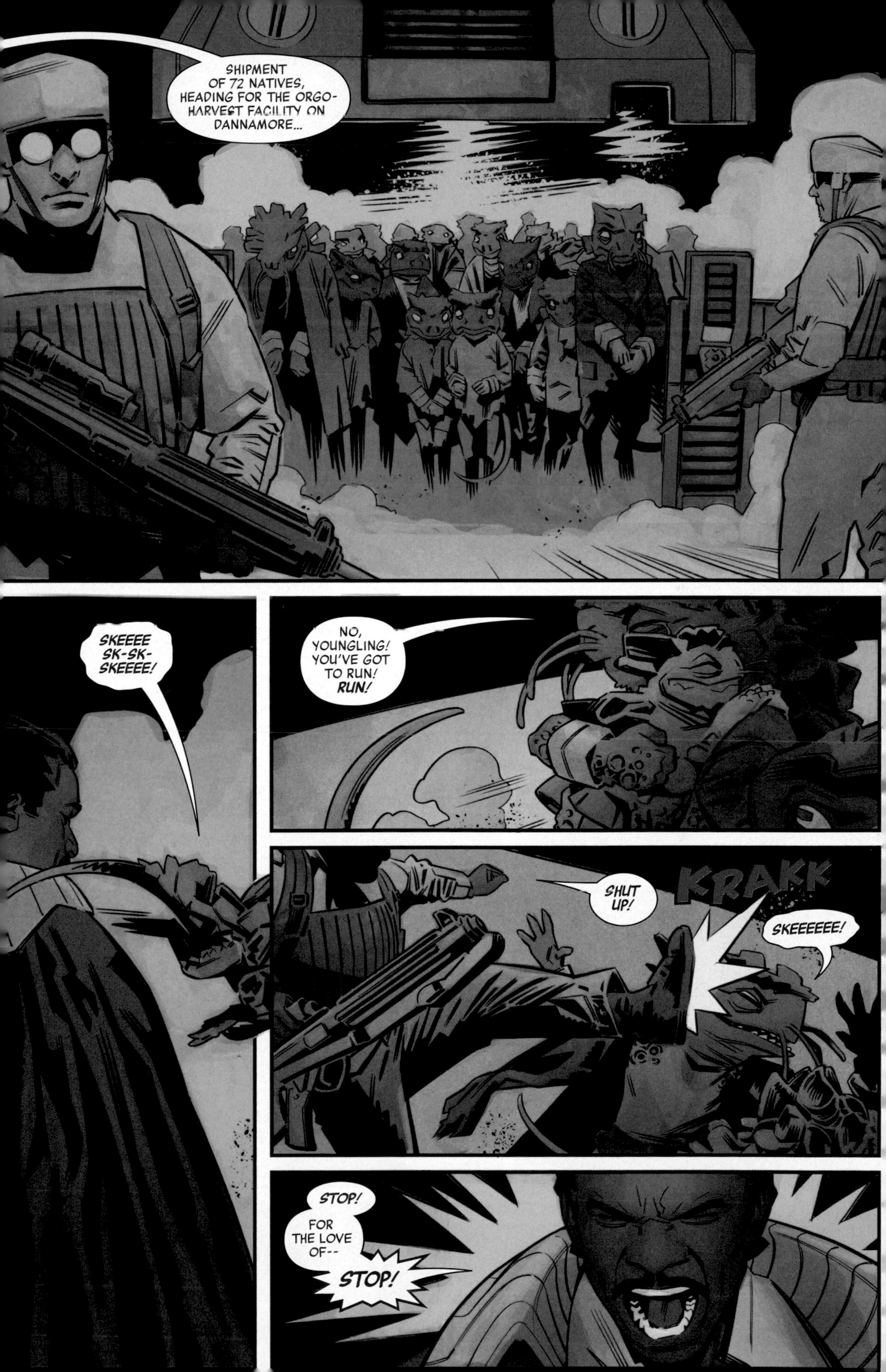
SHIPMENT OF 72 NATIVES, HEADING FOR THE ORGO-HARVEST FACILITY ON DANNAMORE...
SKEEEE SK-SK-SKEEEE!
NO, YOUNGLING! YOU'VE GOT TO RUN! RUN!
SHUT UP!
KRAKK
SKEEEEEE!
STOP!
FOR THE LOVE OF--
STOP!

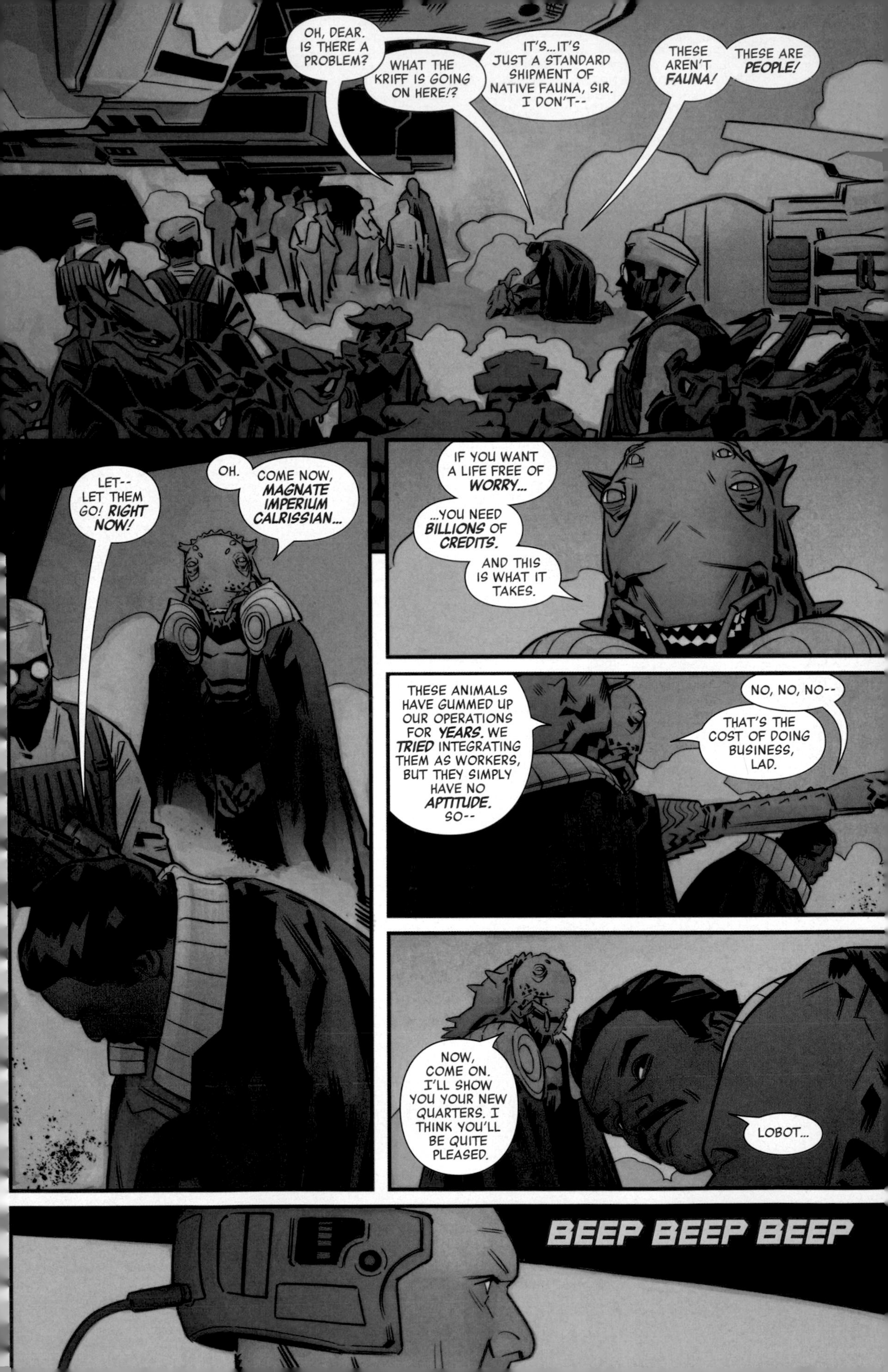
OH, DEAR. IS THERE A PROBLEM?
WHAT THE KRIFF IS GOING ON HERE!?
IT'S...IT'S JUST A STANDARD SHIPMENT OF NATIVE FAUNA, SIR. I DON'T--
THESE AREN'T FAUNA!
THESE ARE PEOPLE!
LET-- LET THEM GO! RIGHT NOW!
OH.
COME NOW, MAGNATE IMPERIUM CALRISSIAN...
IF YOU WANT A LIFE FREE OF WORRY...
...YOU NEED BILLIONS OF CREDITS.
AND THIS IS WHAT IT TAKES.
THESE ANIMALS HAVE GUMMED UP OUR OPERATIONS FOR YEARS. WE TRIED INTEGRATING THEM AS WORKERS, BUT THEY SIMPLY HAVE NO APTITUDE. SO--
NO, NO, NO--
THAT'S THE COST OF DOING BUSINESS, LAD.
NOW, COME ON. I'LL SHOW YOU YOUR NEW QUARTERS. I THINK YOU'LL BE QUITE PLEASED.
LOBOT...
BEEP BEEP BEEP

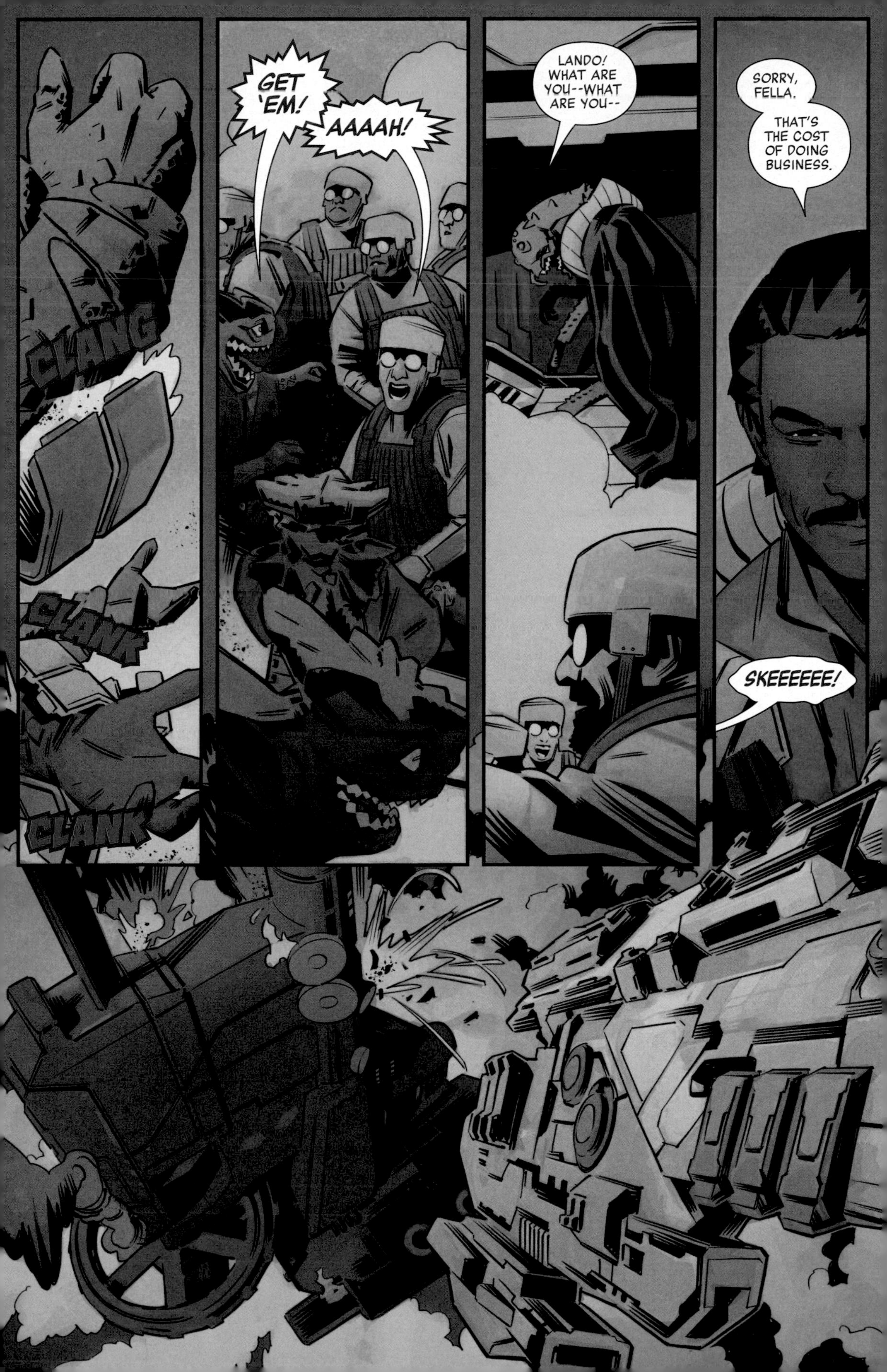

CLANG
CLANK
CLANK
GET 'EM!
AAAAH!
LANDO! WHAT ARE YOU--WHAT ARE YOU--
SORRY, FELLA.
THAT'S THE COST OF DOING BUSINESS.
SKEEEEEE!

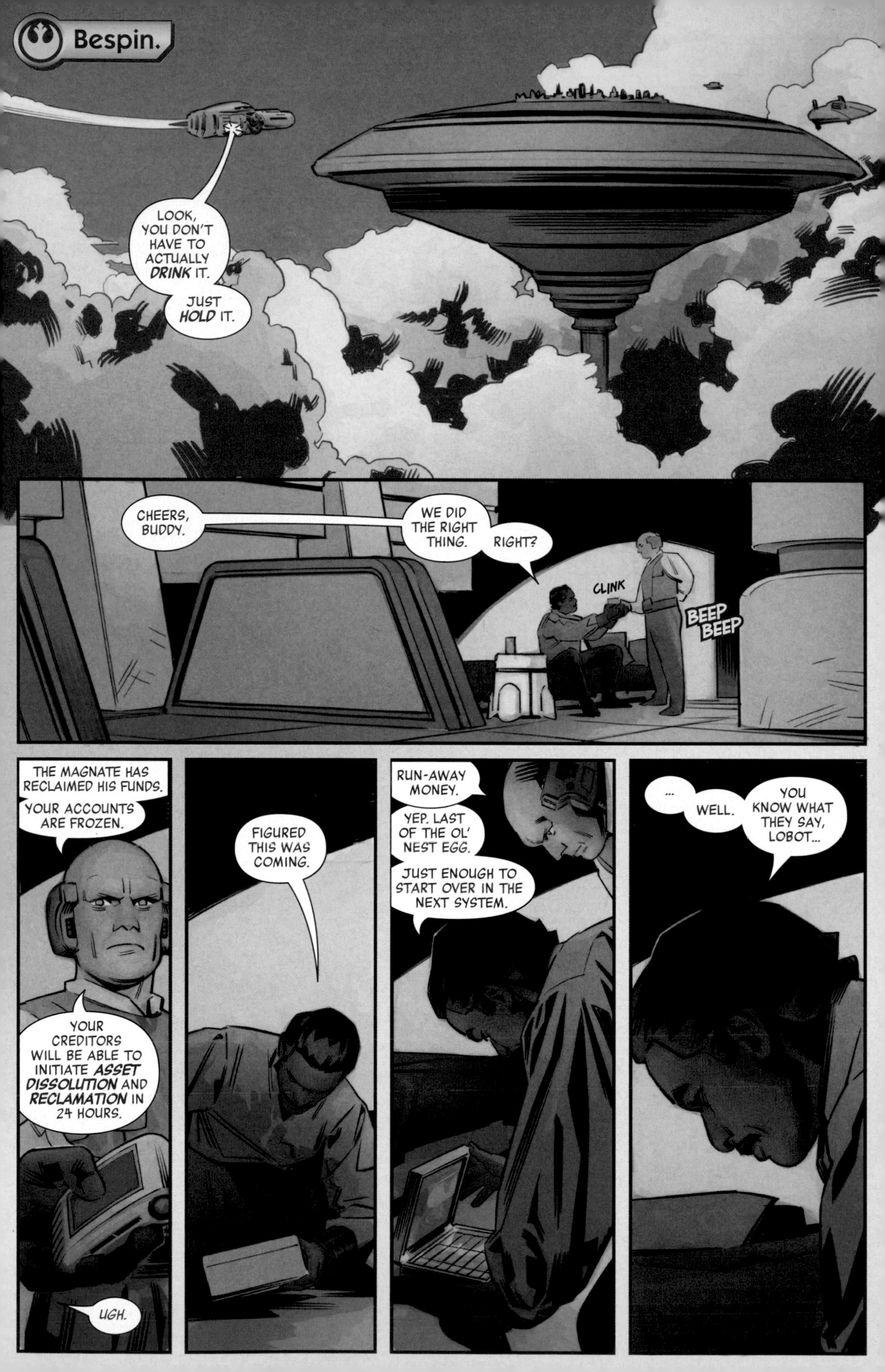

Bespin.
LOOK, YOU DON'T HAVE TO ACTUALLY DRINK IT.
JUST HOLD IT.
CHEERS, BUDDY.
WE DID THE RIGHT THING.
RIGHT?
CLINK
BEEP BEEP
THE MAGNATE HAS RECLAIMED HIS FUNDS.
YOUR ACCOUNTS ARE FROZEN.
YOUR CREDITORS WILL BE ABLE TO INITIATE ASSET DISSOLUTION AND RECLAMATION IN 24 HOURS.
UGH.
FIGURED THIS WAS COMING.
RUN-AWAY MONEY.
YEP. LAST OF THE OL' NEST EGG.
JUST ENOUGH TO START OVER IN THE NEXT SYSTEM.
...
WELL.
YOU KNOW WHAT THEY SAY, LOBOT...

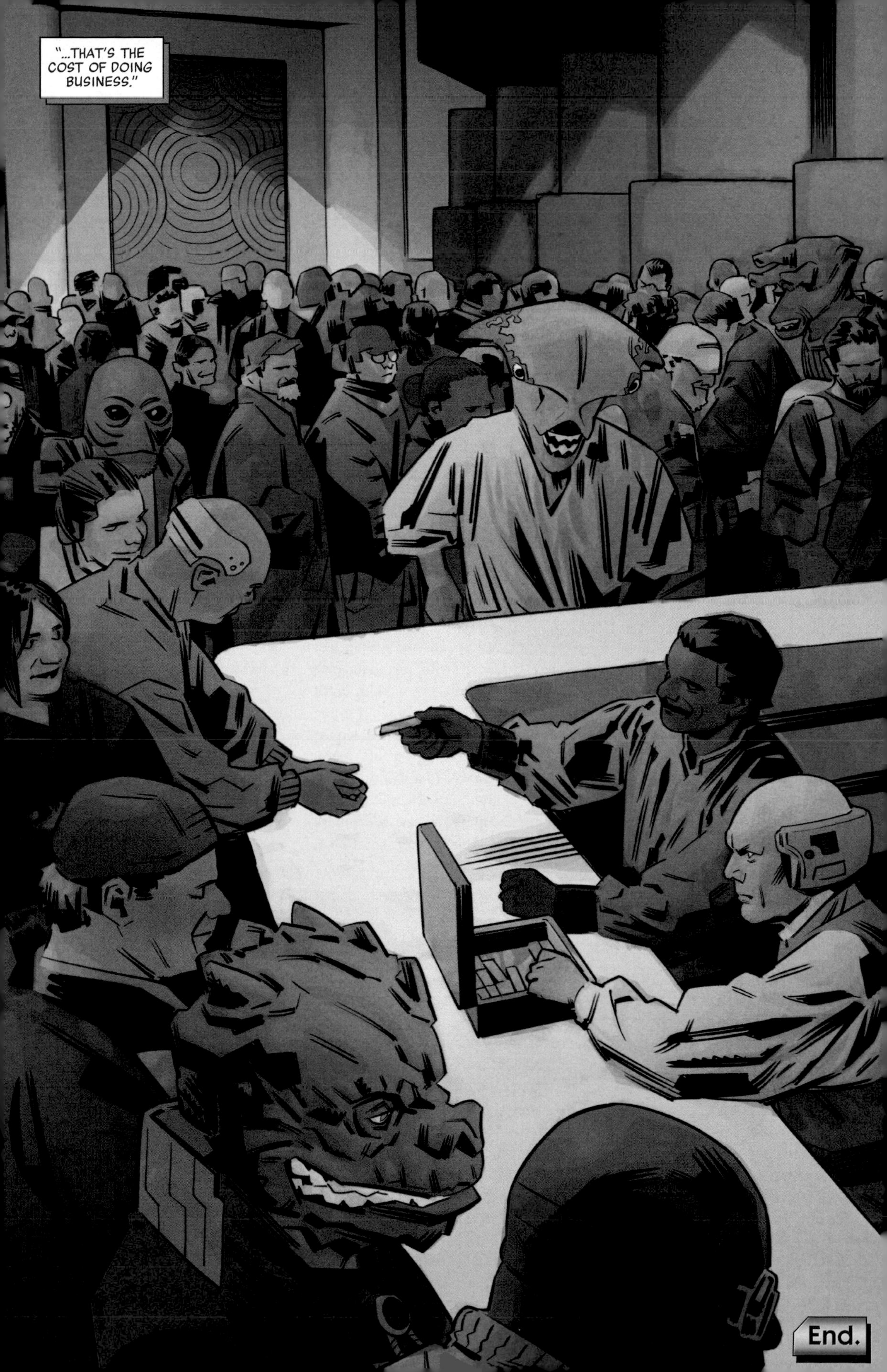
"...THAT'S THE COST OF DOING BUSINESS."
End.

LEAVE IT TO LANDO

From Con Games to Combat, Lando Calrissian is Coolness with a Cape

By Glenn Greenberg

"Why, you slimy, double-crossing, no-good swindler. You've got a lot of guts coming here, after what you pulled."

With that less-than-warm welcome to Han Solo on the landing pad of Cloud City in 1980's *The Empire Strikes Back*, Lando Calrissian made a particularly memorable entrance into the *Star Wars* saga. And when it was revealed that the disdainful greeting was actually just a playful fake-out—within a larger, far more serious deception, since Darth Vader was already there and pulling Lando's strings—audiences came to realize that with Calrissian, there's a lot more than meets the eye. You could never be sure what he would do next.

That came with the territory. Han had described Lando to Princess Leia as a "card player, gambler, scoundrel" who had "conned somebody" out of the tibanna gas mine he was now running. Lando himself told Han and Leia that he was now "responsible"—a byproduct of his business success. So had he really become a legitimate executive, or was he still a smooth-talking con artist? Either way, throughout the Imperial presence at Cloud City, Lando was forced to play every bad hand he was dealt, leading him to betray his old friend, adhere to the ever-worsening terms of his deal with Vader, and, ultimately, abandon the prosperous life he had built for himself.

THE IMPORTANCE OF BEING LANDO

In *Empire*, Lando was more than just a new character with an abundance of charisma dressed in a sleek outfit with a flowing cape. He brought to the *Star Wars* saga greater racial diversity. Author Adilifu Nama, in his 2008 book *Black Space: Imagining Race in Science Fiction Film*, even wrote that Lando had "offered a new benchmark in the status of black representation in science fiction cinema."

For actor Billy Dee Williams, who brought Lando to life on the big screen, the character's skin color was perhaps beside the point. "Lando Calrissian—I love the name; the name alone is fantastic," he told *Starlog* magazine in 1980. Williams also felt that Lando was "charming, adventurous, bumbling. And that's the best hero you can create. I love guys who bumble through life, who bump into walls, who trip over themselves. They're much more human."

Part of being human, of course, is to grow and mature. Audiences got to see Lando do just that in 1983's *Return of the Jedi*, in which he fully committed to—and risked his life for—causes bigger than himself, namely the rescue of Han from Jabba the Hutt and the Rebel attack on

the second Death Star. During the making of the film, Williams told an interviewer that playing Calrissian worked well for him because "I'm like Lando—he's always in transition. He has to be—that's where the fun is."

THE CANONICAL CALRISSIAN

The moment in *Empire* when it was revealed that Lando used to own the *Millennium Falcon* fired the imaginations of many fans, who began to wonder what kinds of adventures Calrissian had when he owned the ship. (Lando's mention of his "little maneuver at the Battle of Taanab," in *Return of the Jedi*, had a similar effect.) It took nearly 40 years, but audiences finally got an official glimpse of that earlier period of his life in 2018's *Solo: A Star Wars Story*, with Donald Glover playing the young Lando. Glover had pursued the role from the moment the film was first announced.

"[Lando] was my first toy--I just love that character," Glover told Jimmy Kimmel during a TV interview. He even consulted with Williams on how to play the part with authenticity. According to Glover, the original Lando offered only this bit of sage advice: "Just be charming."

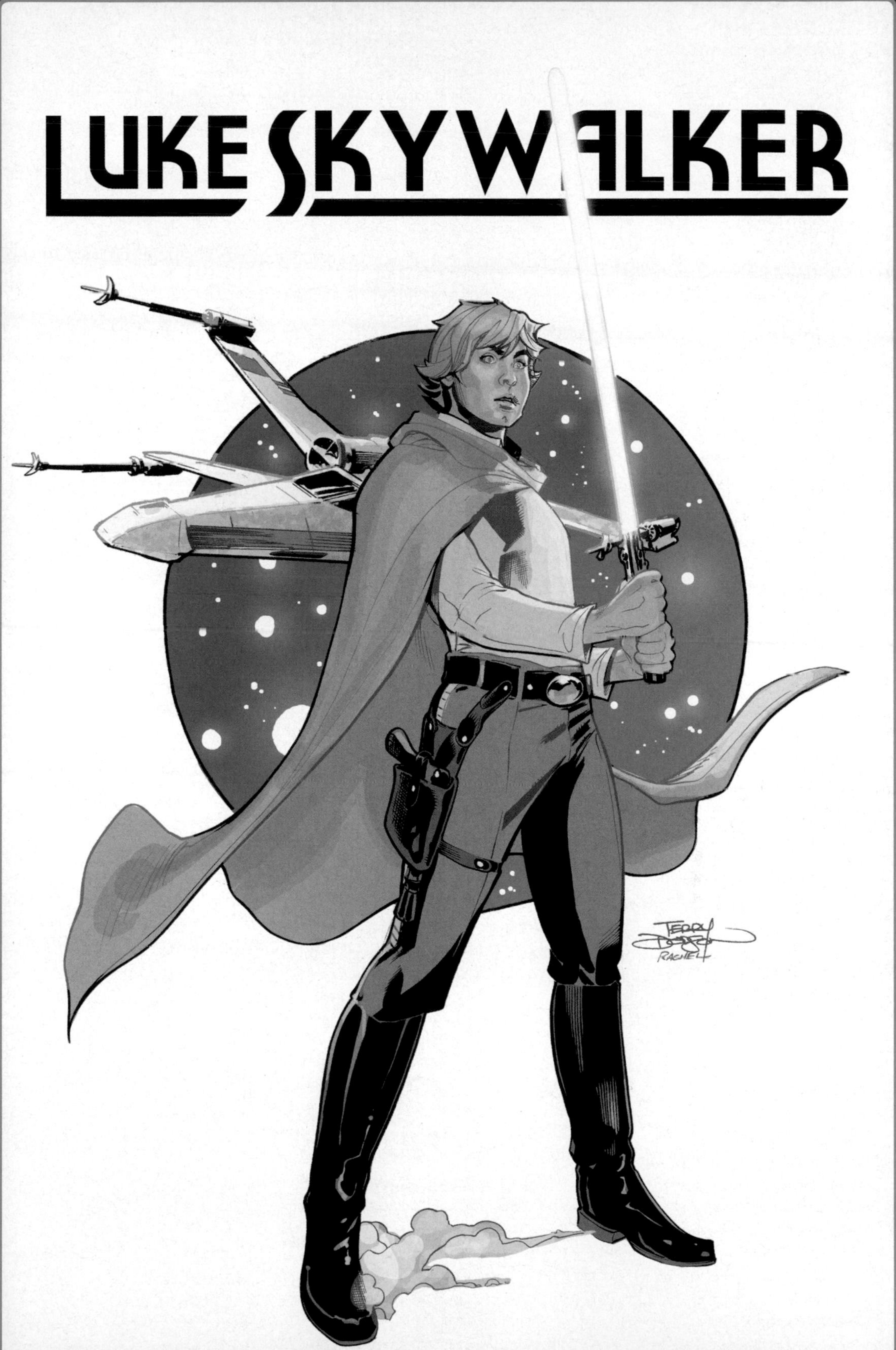
LUKE SKYWALKER
TERRY DODSON
RACHEL

"FIGHT OR FLIGHT"

For years, the heroic Rebel Alliance has fought to free the galaxy from the evil Galactic Empire. But the Emperor and his powerful apprentice Darth Vader are close to crushing the freedom fighters once and for all — and turning the young Rebel hero and Jedi-in-training, Luke Skywalker, to the dark side might all but ensure their victory. As Luke grows stronger in the ways of the Force, so do the challenges — and temptations — he faces. . . .

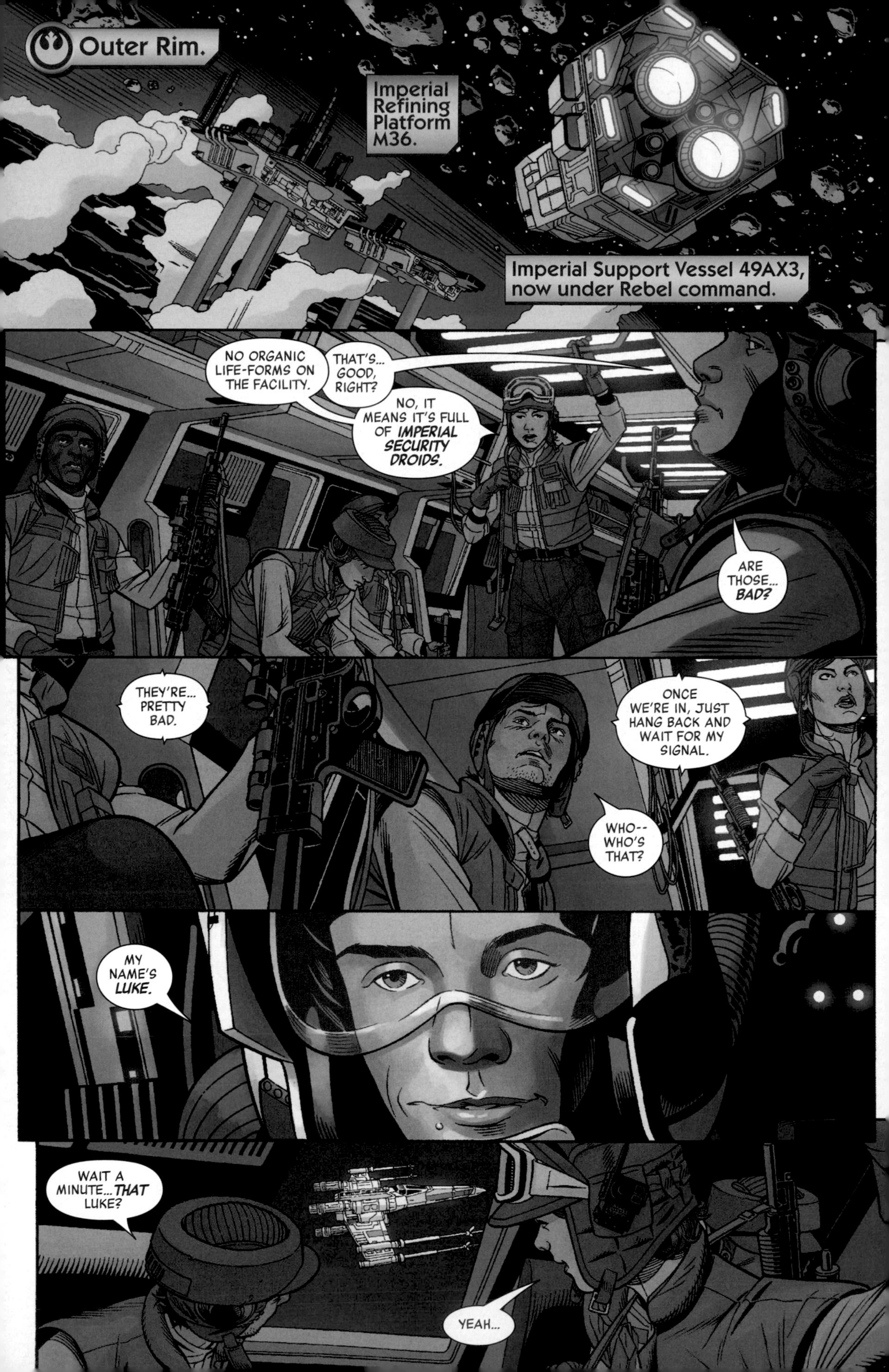

Outer Rim.
Imperial Refining Platform M36.
Imperial Support Vessel 49AX3, now under Rebel command.
NO ORGANIC LIFE-FORMS ON THE FACILITY.
THAT'S... GOOD, RIGHT?
NO, IT MEANS IT'S FULL OF IMPERIAL SECURITY DROIDS.
ARE THOSE... BAD?
THEY'RE... PRETTY BAD.
ONCE WE'RE IN, JUST HANG BACK AND WAIT FOR MY SIGNAL.
WHO-- WHO'S THAT?
MY NAME'S LUKE.
WAIT A MINUTE... THAT LUKE?
YEAH...

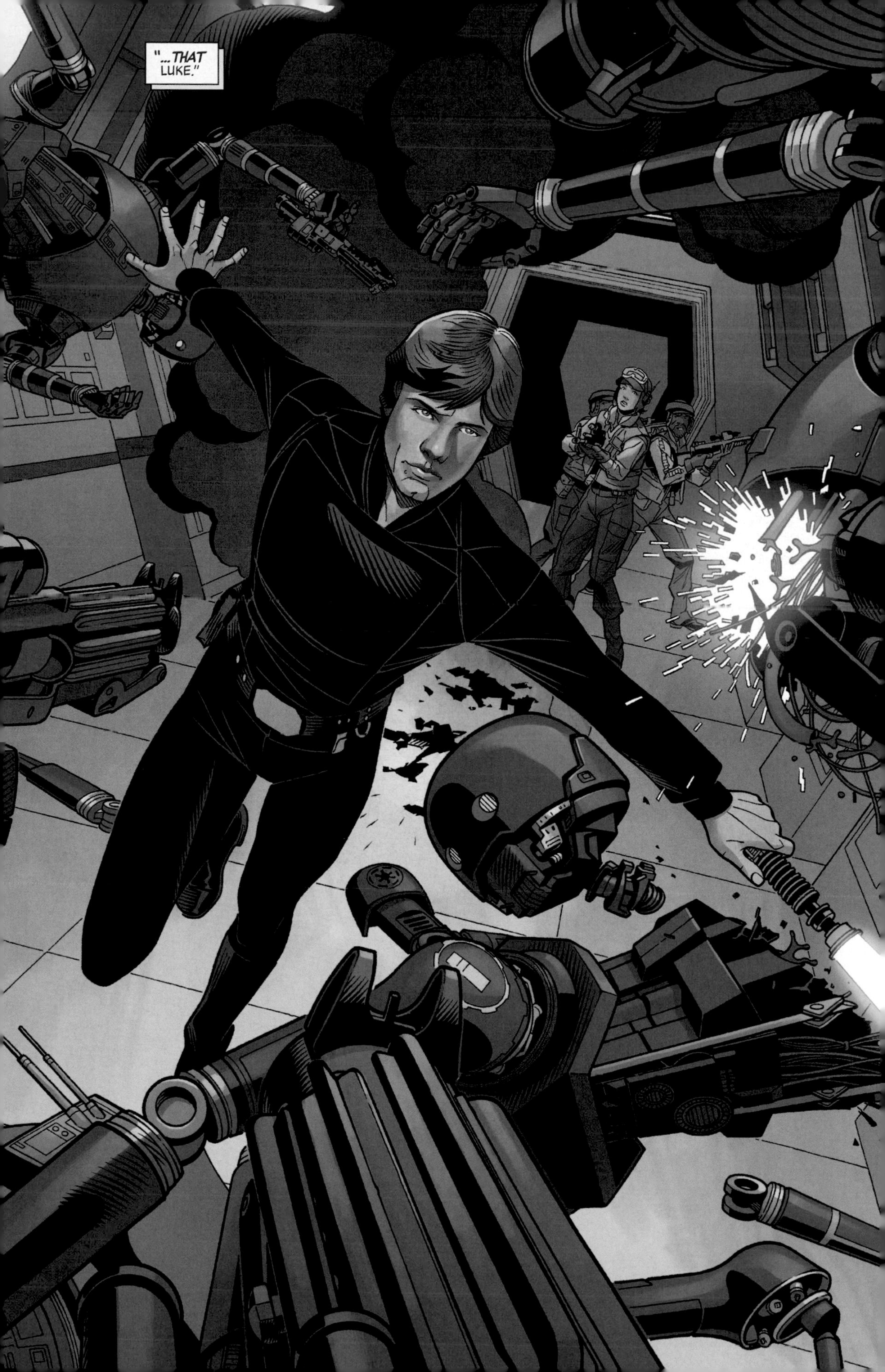
"...THAT LUKE."

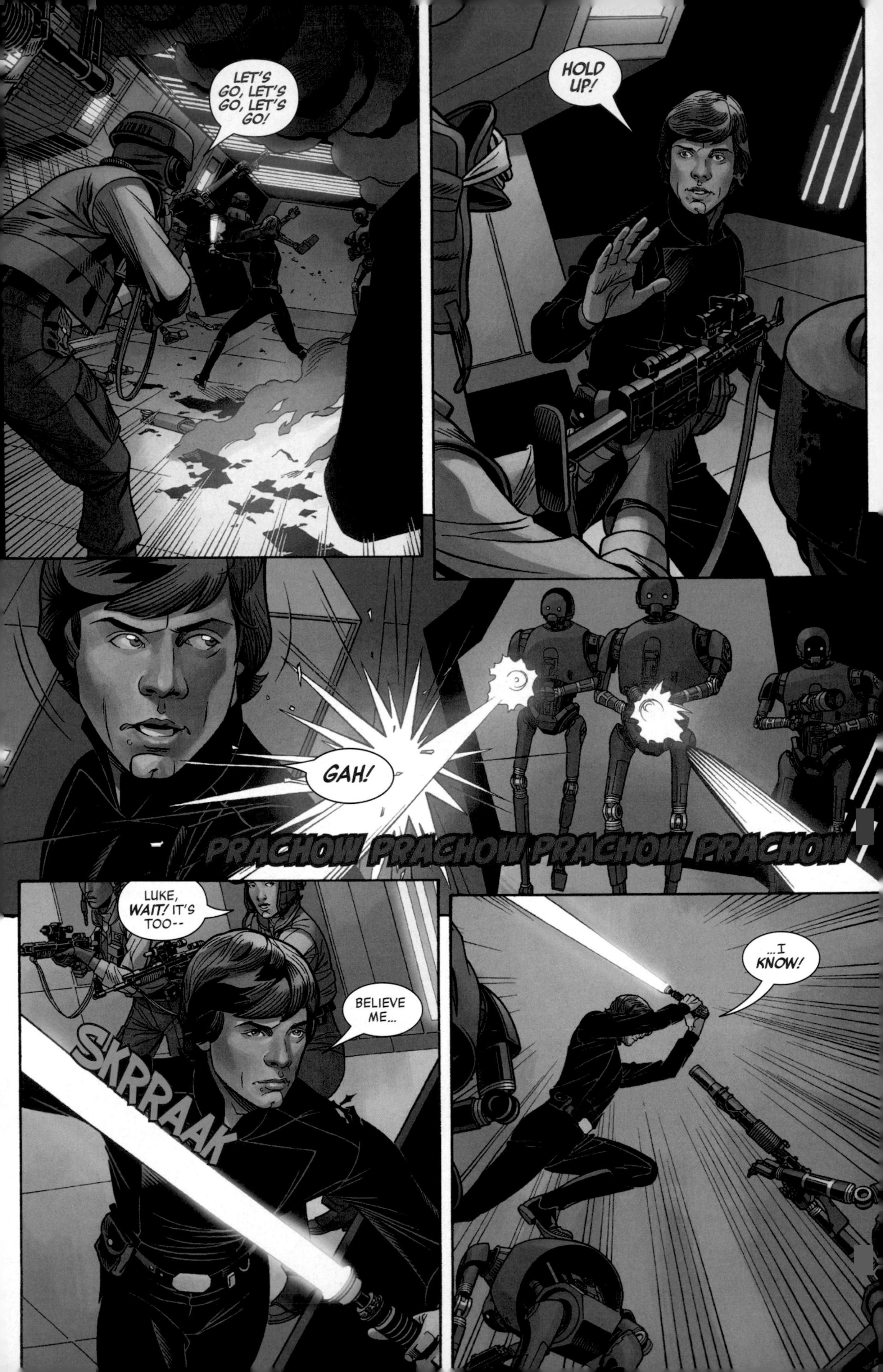
LET'S GO, LET'S GO, LET'S GO!
HOLD UP!
GAH!
PRACHOW PRACHOW PRACHOW PRACHOW
LUKE, WAIT! IT'S TOO--
BELIEVE ME...
SKRRAAK
...I KNOW!

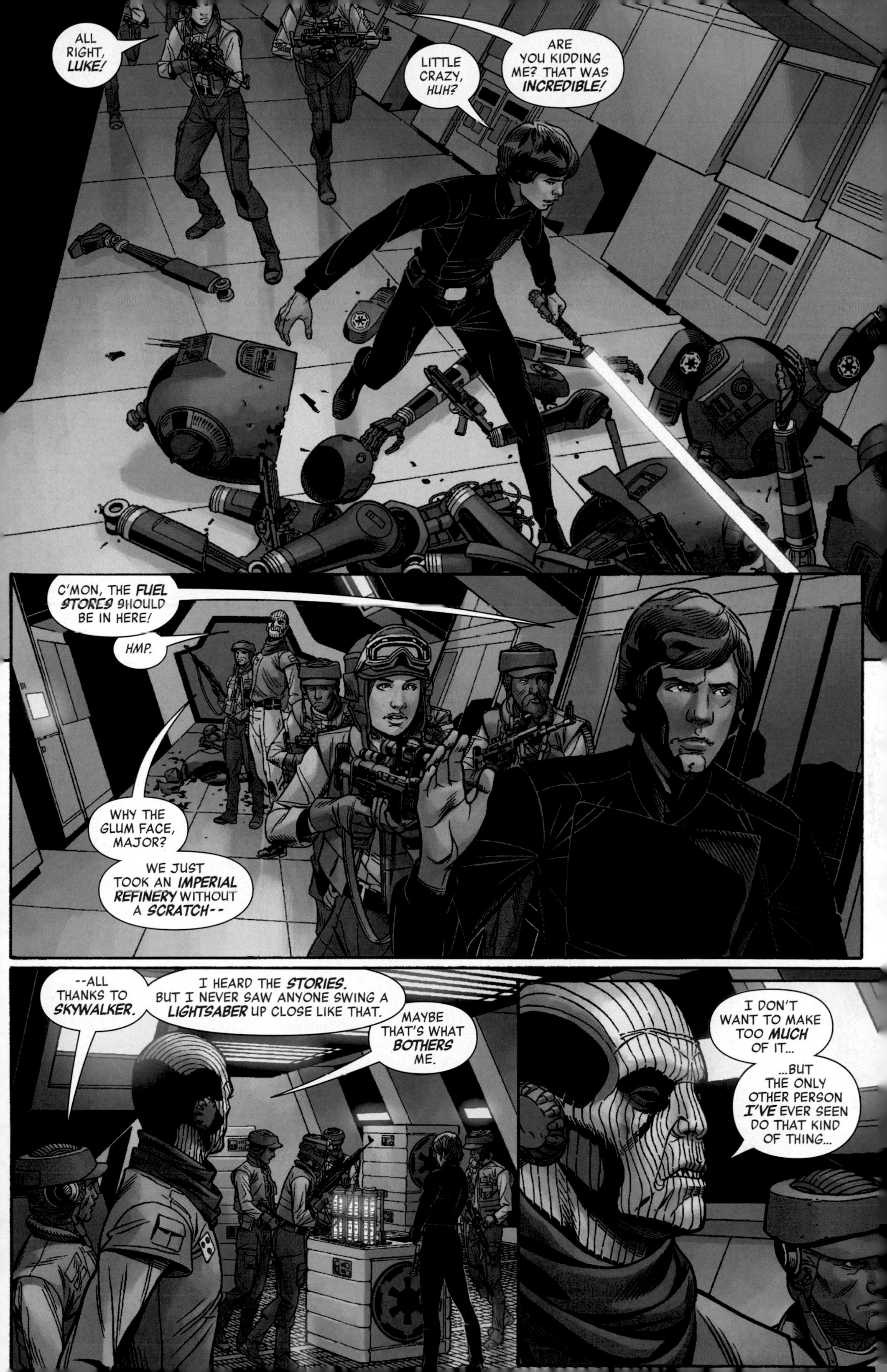
ALL RIGHT, LUKE!
ARE YOU KIDDING ME? THAT WAS INCREDIBLE!
LITTLE CRAZY, HUH?
C'MON, THE FUEL STORES SHOULD BE IN HERE!
HMP.
WHY THE GLUM FACE, MAJOR?
WE JUST TOOK AN IMPERIAL REFINERY WITHOUT A SCRATCH--
--ALL THANKS TO SKYWALKER.
I HEARD THE STORIES. BUT I NEVER SAW ANYONE SWING A LIGHTSABER UP CLOSE LIKE THAT.
MAYBE THAT'S WHAT BOTHERS ME.
I DON'T WANT TO MAKE TOO MUCH OF IT...
...BUT THE ONLY OTHER PERSON I'VE EVER SEEN DO THAT KIND OF THING...

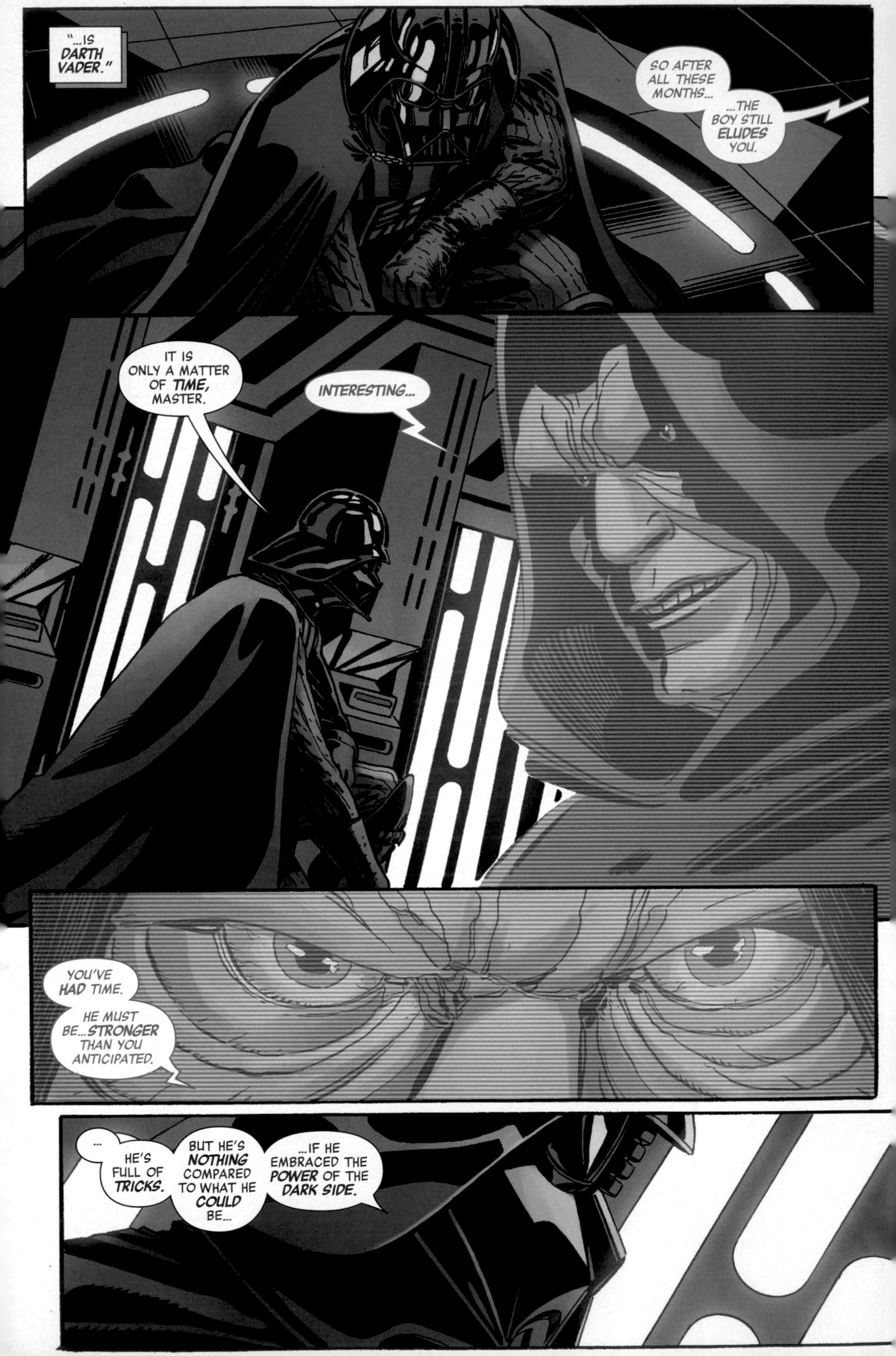
"...IS DARTH VADER."
SO AFTER ALL THESE MONTHS...
...THE BOY STILL ELUDES YOU.
IT IS ONLY A MATTER OF TIME, MASTER.
INTERESTING...
YOU'VE HAD TIME.
HE MUST BE...STRONGER THAN YOU ANTICIPATED.
...
HE'S FULL OF TRICKS.
BUT HE'S NOTHING COMPARED TO WHAT HE COULD BE...
...IF HE EMBRACED THE POWER OF THE DARK SIDE.

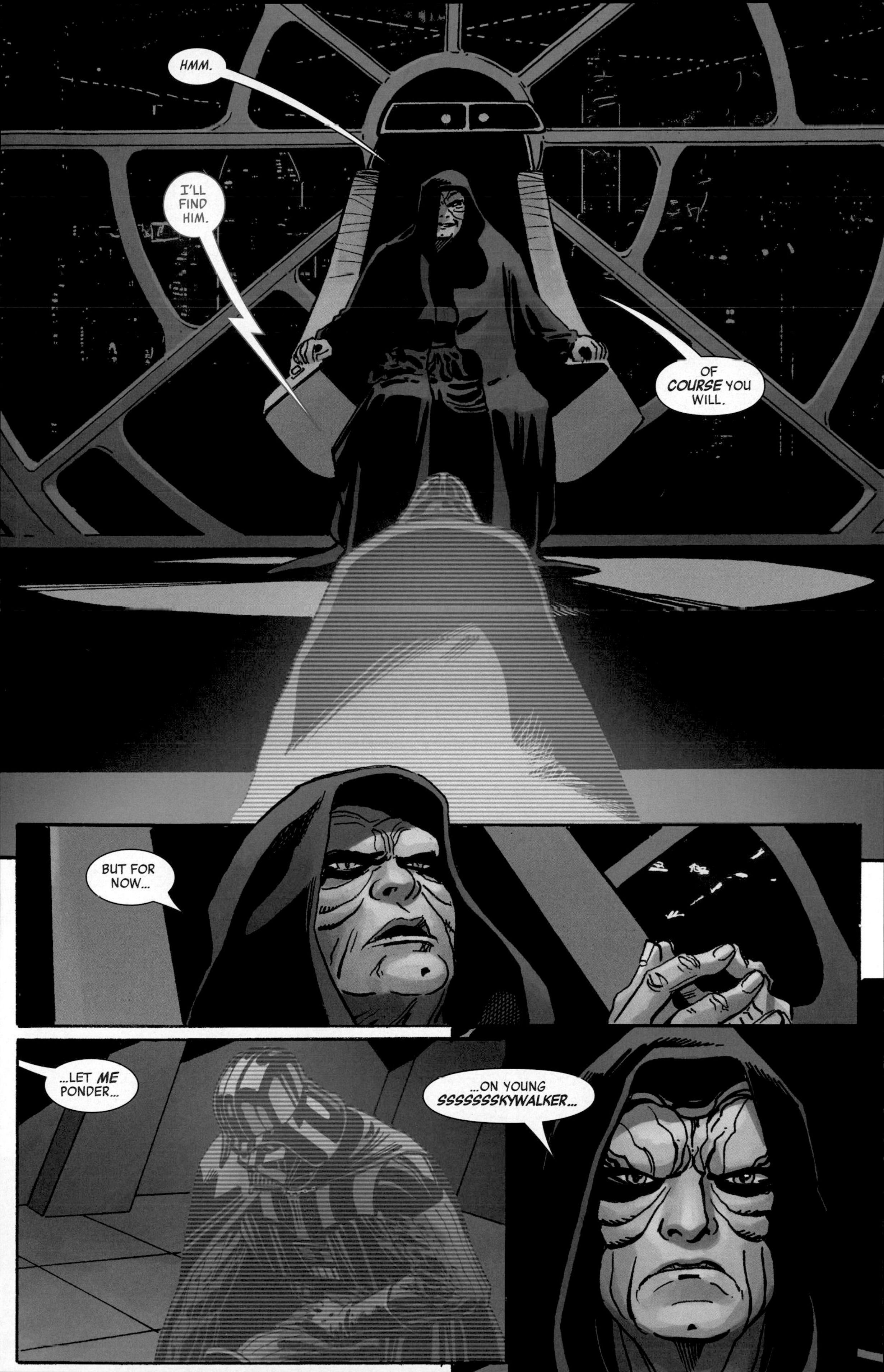
HMM.
I'LL FIND HIM.
OF COURSE YOU WILL.
BUT FOR NOW...
...LET ME PONDER...
...ON YOUNG SSSSSSSKYWALKER...

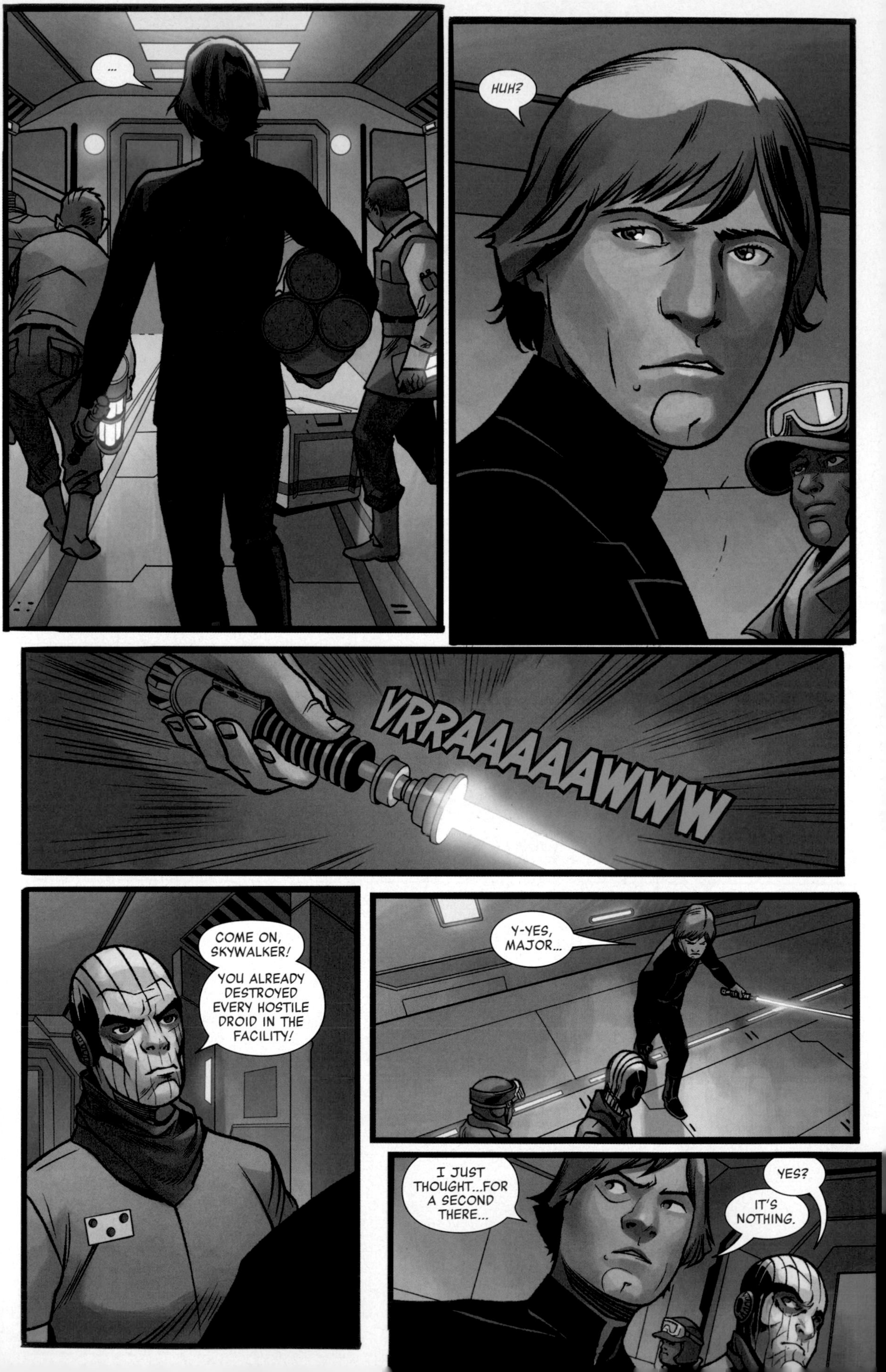

...
HUH?
VRRAAAAAAWWW
COME ON, SKYWALKER!
YOU ALREADY DESTROYED EVERY HOSTILE DROID IN THE FACILITY!
Y-YES, MAJOR...
I JUST THOUGHT...FOR A SECOND THERE...
YES?
IT'S NOTHING.

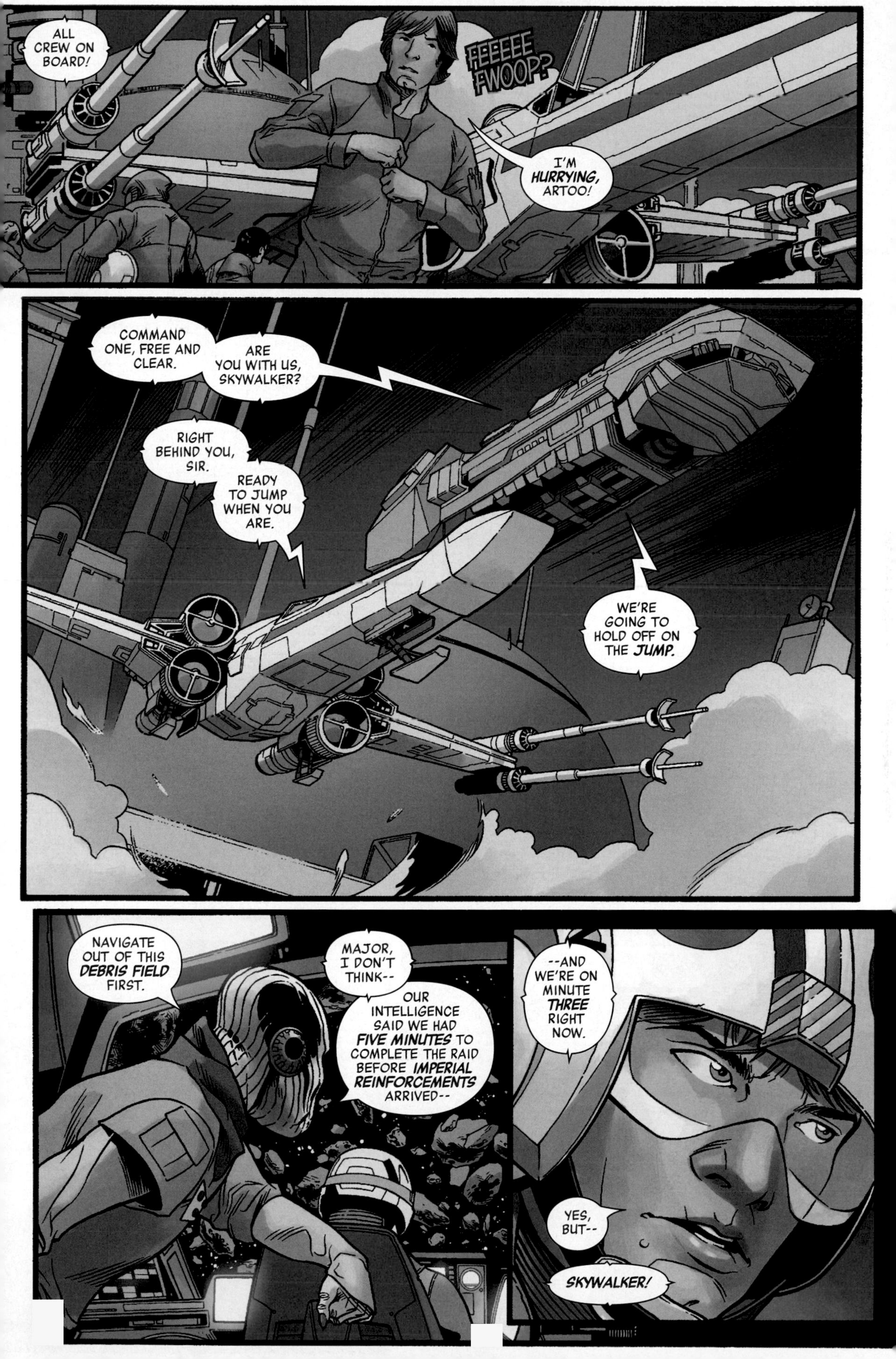
ALL CREW ON BOARD!
FEEEEE FWOOP?
I'M HURRYING, ARTOO!
COMMAND ONE, FREE AND CLEAR.
ARE YOU WITH US, SKYWALKER?
RIGHT BEHIND YOU, SIR.
READY TO JUMP WHEN YOU ARE.
WE'RE GOING TO HOLD OFF ON THE JUMP.
NAVIGATE OUT OF THIS DEBRIS FIELD FIRST.
MAJOR, I DON'T THINK--
OUR INTELLIGENCE SAID WE HAD FIVE MINUTES TO COMPLETE THE RAID BEFORE IMPERIAL REINFORCEMENTS ARRIVED--
--AND WE'RE ON MINUTE THREE RIGHT NOW.
YES, BUT--
SKYWALKER!

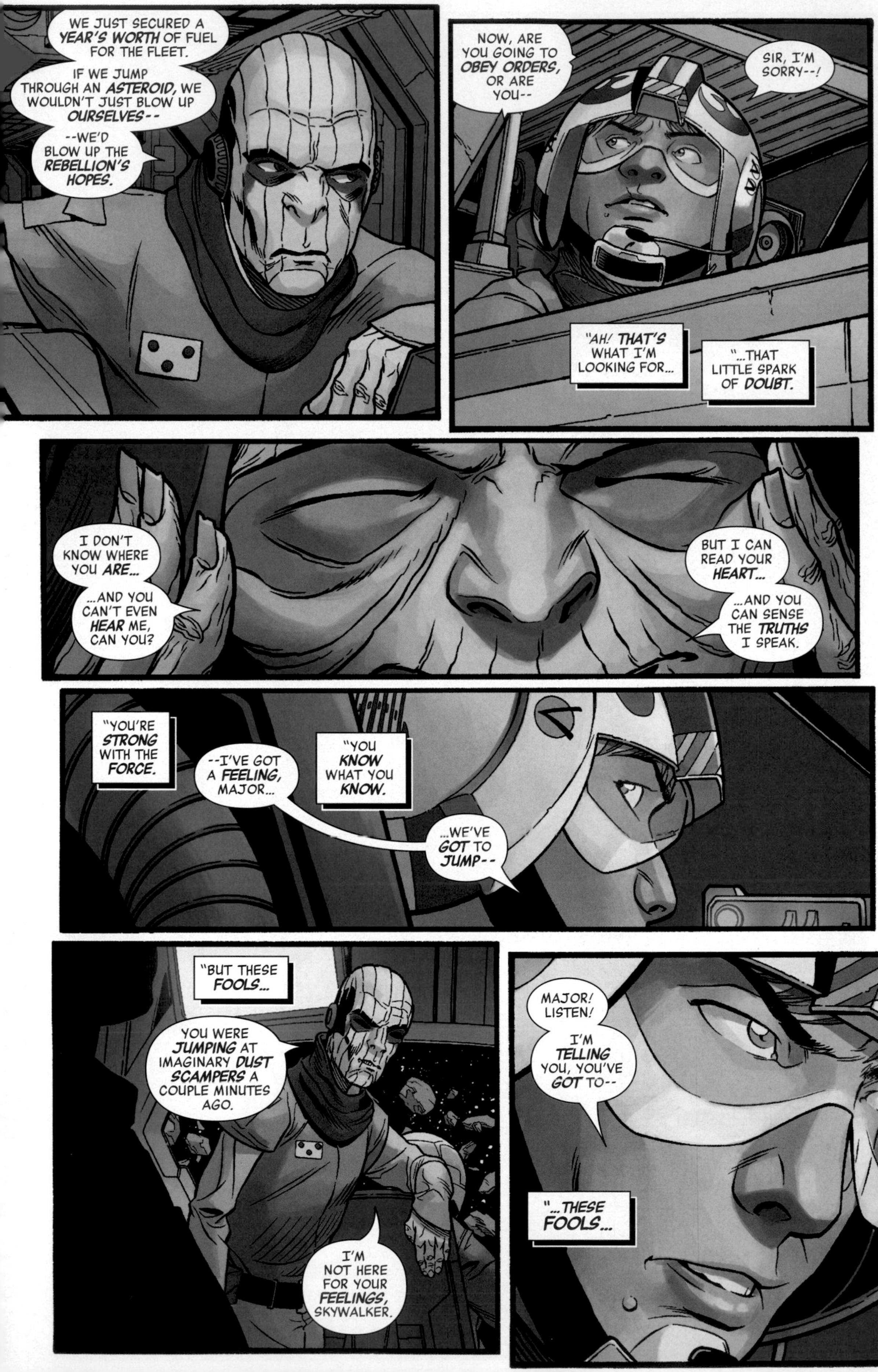
WE JUST SECURED A YEAR'S WORTH OF FUEL FOR THE FLEET.
IF WE JUMP THROUGH AN ASTEROID, WE WOULDN'T JUST BLOW UP OURSELVES--
--WE'D BLOW UP THE REBELLION'S HOPES.
NOW, ARE YOU GOING TO OBEY ORDERS, OR ARE YOU--
SIR, I'M SORRY--!
"AH! THAT'S WHAT I'M LOOKING FOR...
"...THAT LITTLE SPARK OF DOUBT.
I DON'T KNOW WHERE YOU ARE...
...AND YOU CAN'T EVEN HEAR ME, CAN YOU?
BUT I CAN READ YOUR HEART...
...AND YOU CAN SENSE THE TRUTHS I SPEAK.
"YOU'RE STRONG WITH THE FORCE.
--I'VE GOT A FEELING, MAJOR...
"YOU KNOW WHAT YOU KNOW.
...WE'VE GOT TO JUMP--
"BUT THESE FOOLS...
YOU WERE JUMPING AT IMAGINARY DUST SCAMPERS A COUPLE MINUTES AGO.
I'M NOT HERE FOR YOUR FEELINGS, SKYWALKER.
MAJOR! LISTEN!
I'M TELLING YOU, YOU'VE GOT TO--
"...THESE FOOLS...

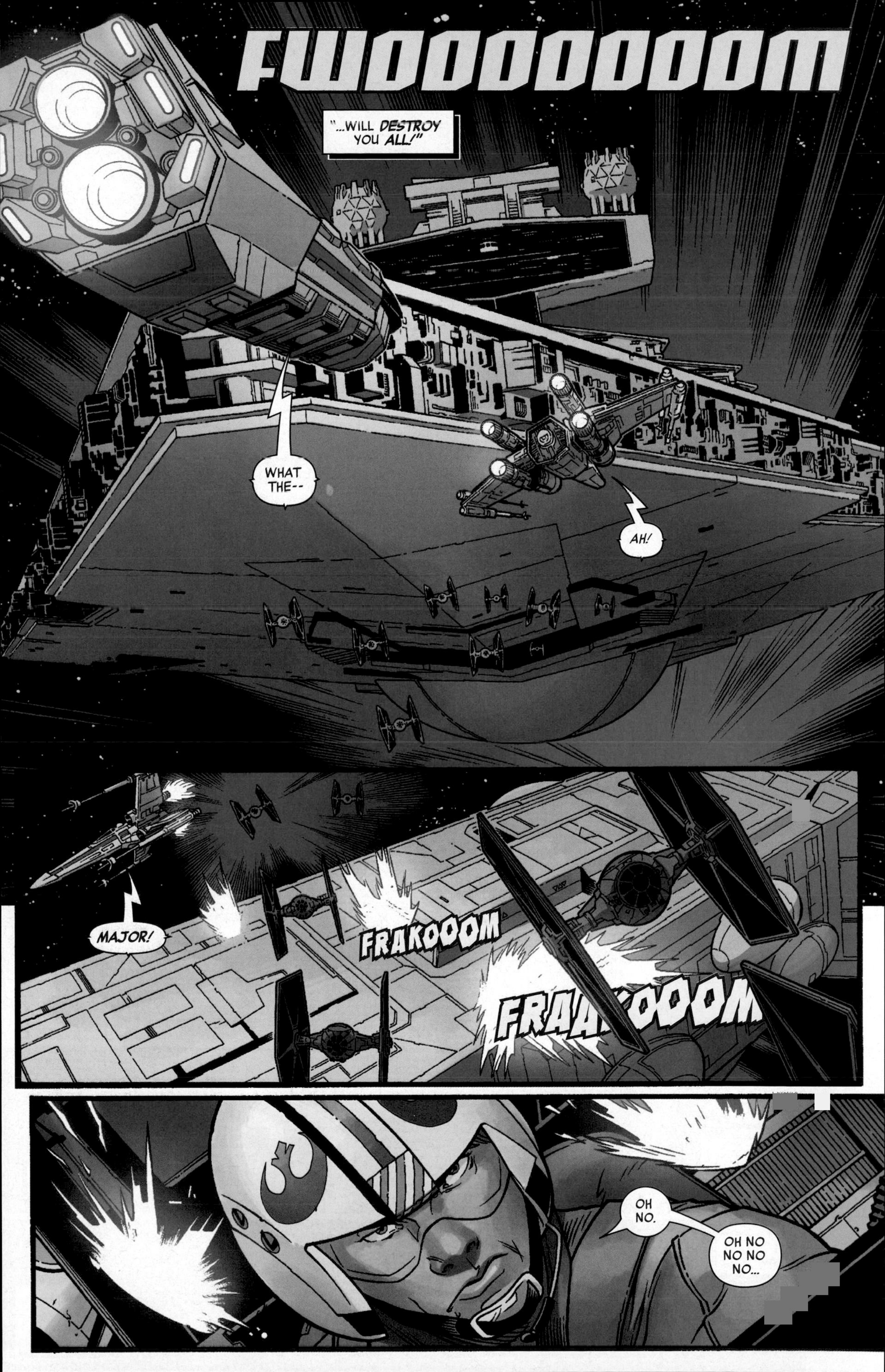
FWOOOOOOOOM
"...WILL DESTROY YOU ALL!"
WHAT THE--
AH!
MAJOR!
FRAKOOOM
FRAAKOOOM
OH NO.
OH NO NO NO NO...

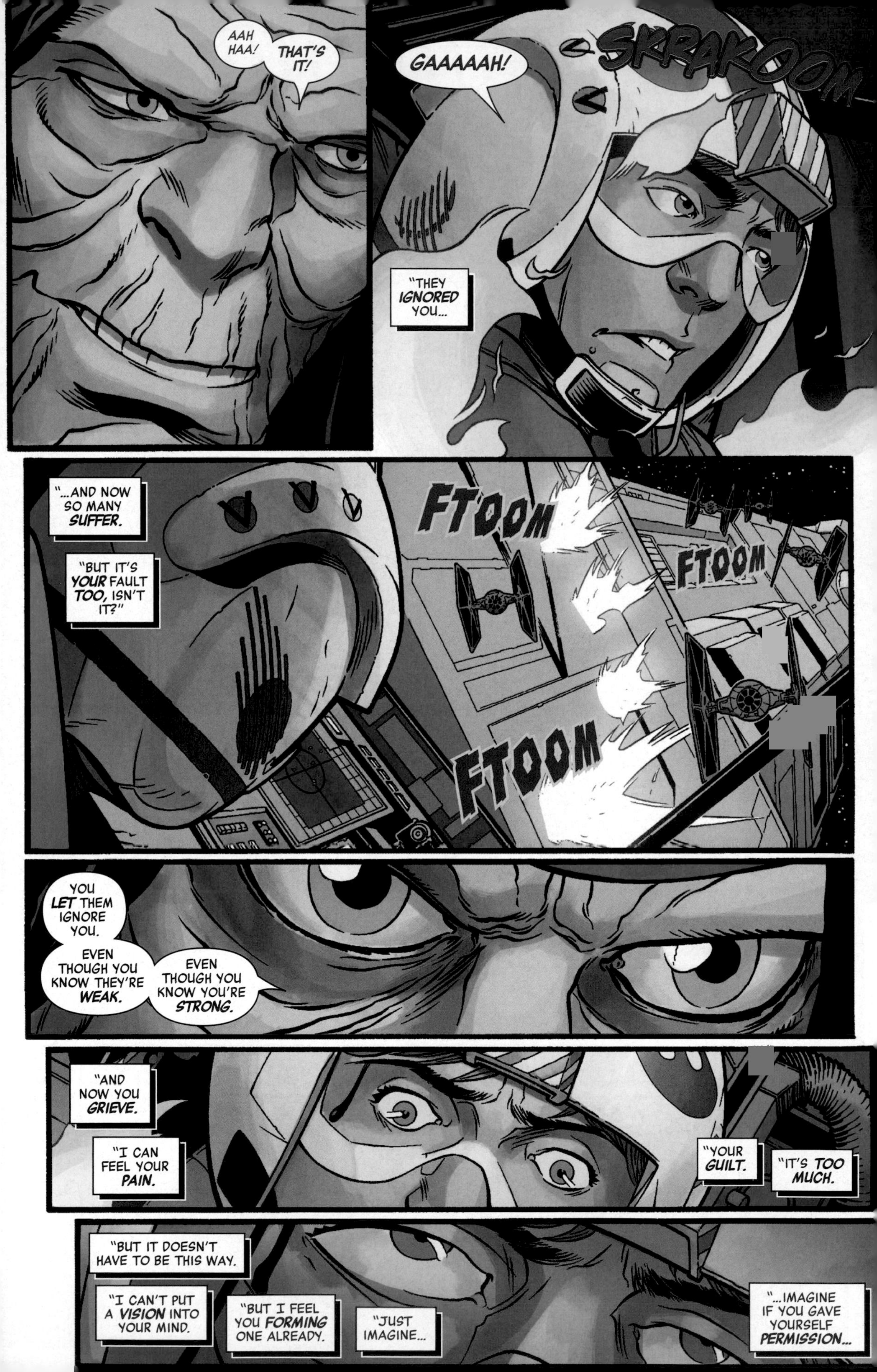
AAH HAA!
THAT'S IT!
GAAAAAH!
SKRAKOOM
"THEY IGNORED YOU...
"...AND NOW SO MANY SUFFER.
"BUT IT'S YOUR FAULT TOO, ISN'T IT?"
FTOOM
FTOOM
FTOOM
YOU LET THEM IGNORE YOU.
EVEN THOUGH YOU KNOW THEY'RE WEAK.
EVEN THOUGH YOU KNOW YOU'RE STRONG.
"AND NOW YOU GRIEVE.
"I CAN FEEL YOUR PAIN.
"YOUR GUILT.
"IT'S TOO MUCH.
"BUT IT DOESN'T HAVE TO BE THIS WAY.
"I CAN'T PUT A VISION INTO YOUR MIND.
"BUT I FEEL YOU FORMING ONE ALREADY.
"JUST IMAGINE...
"...IMAGINE IF YOU GAVE YOURSELF PERMISSION...

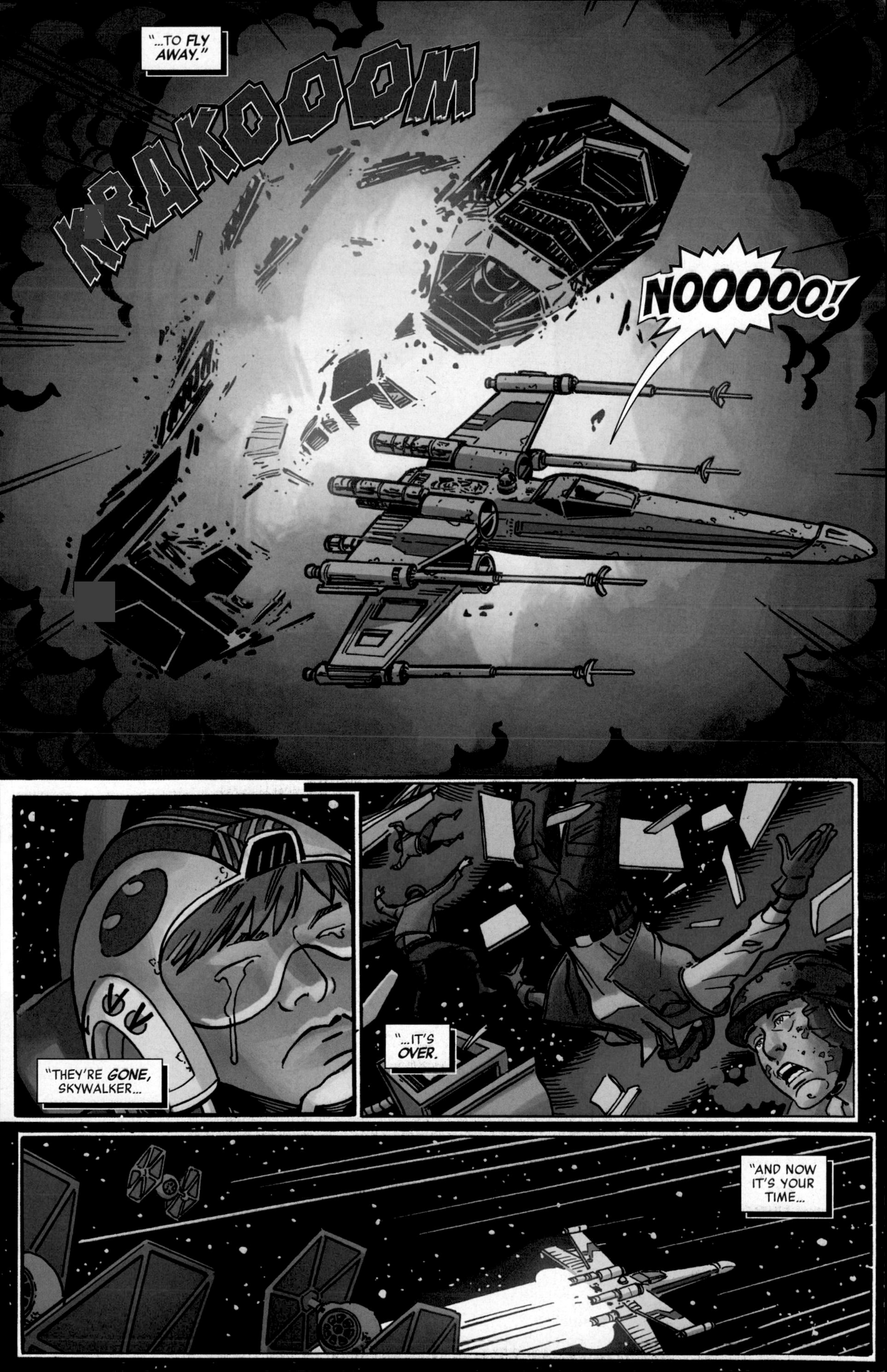
"...TO *FLY* *AWAY.*"
KRAKOOOM
NOOOOO!
"THEY'RE *GONE,* SKYWALKER...
"...IT'S *OVER.*
"AND NOW IT'S YOUR TIME...

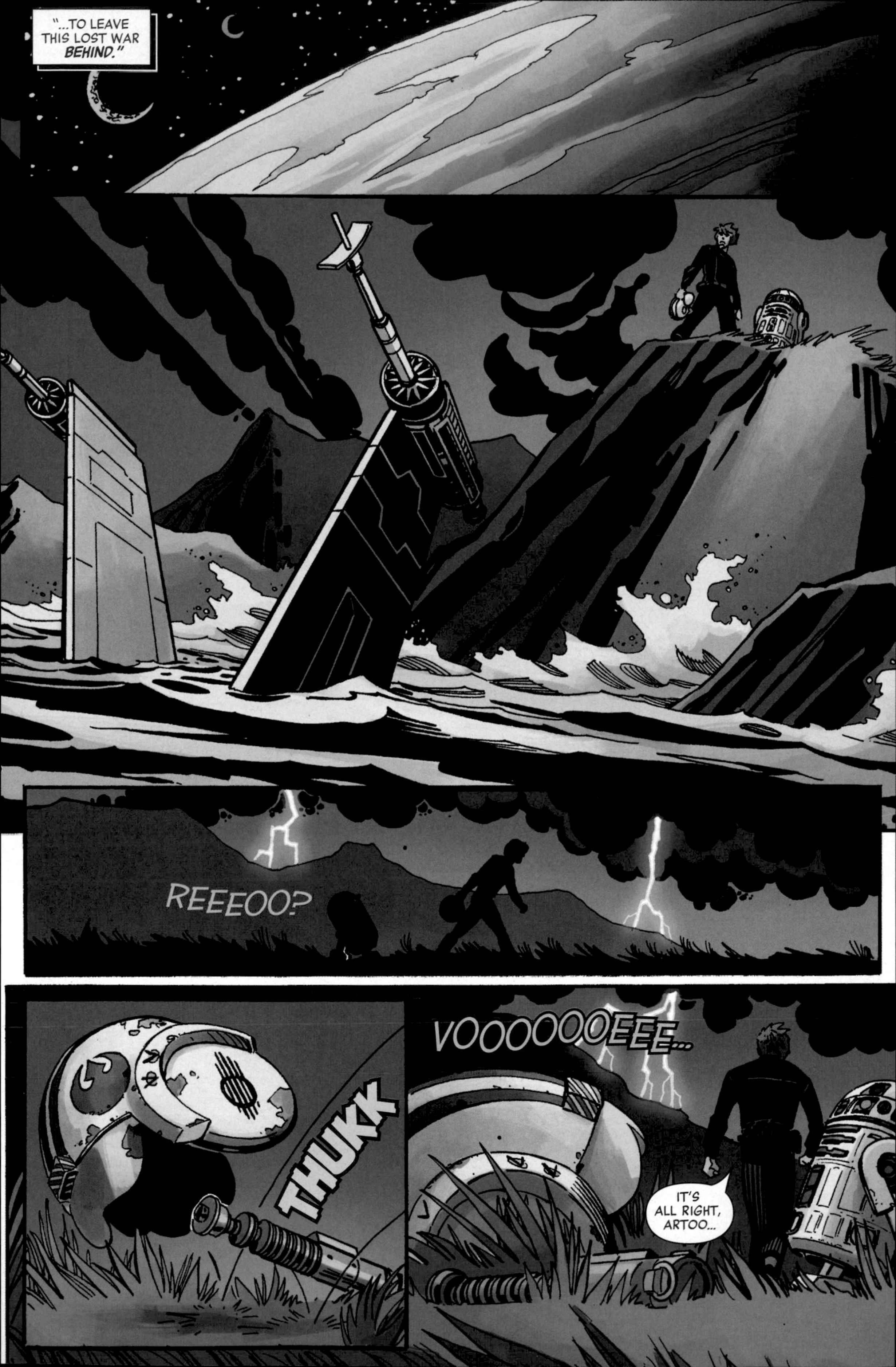
"...TO LEAVE THIS LOST WAR BEHIND."
REEEOO?
THUKK
VOOOOOOEEE...
IT'S ALL RIGHT, ARTOO...

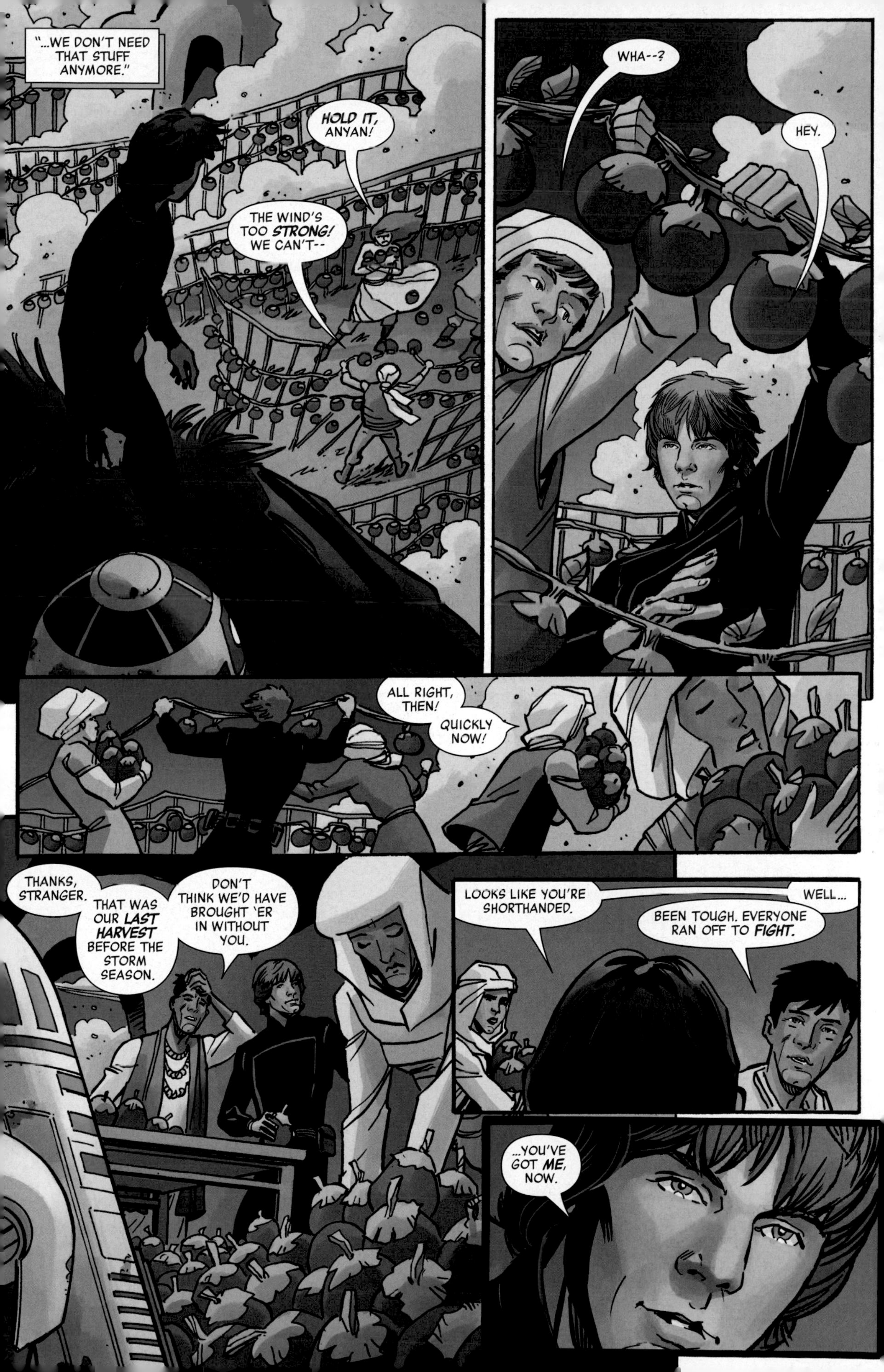
"...WE DON'T NEED THAT STUFF ANYMORE."
HOLD IT, ANYAN!
THE WIND'S TOO STRONG! WE CAN'T--
WHA--?
HEY.
ALL RIGHT, THEN!
QUICKLY NOW!
THANKS, STRANGER.
THAT WAS OUR LAST HARVEST BEFORE THE STORM SEASON.
DON'T THINK WE'D HAVE BROUGHT 'ER IN WITHOUT YOU.
LOOKS LIKE YOU'RE SHORTHANDED.
WELL...
BEEN TOUGH. EVERYONE RAN OFF TO FIGHT.
...YOU'VE GOT ME, NOW.

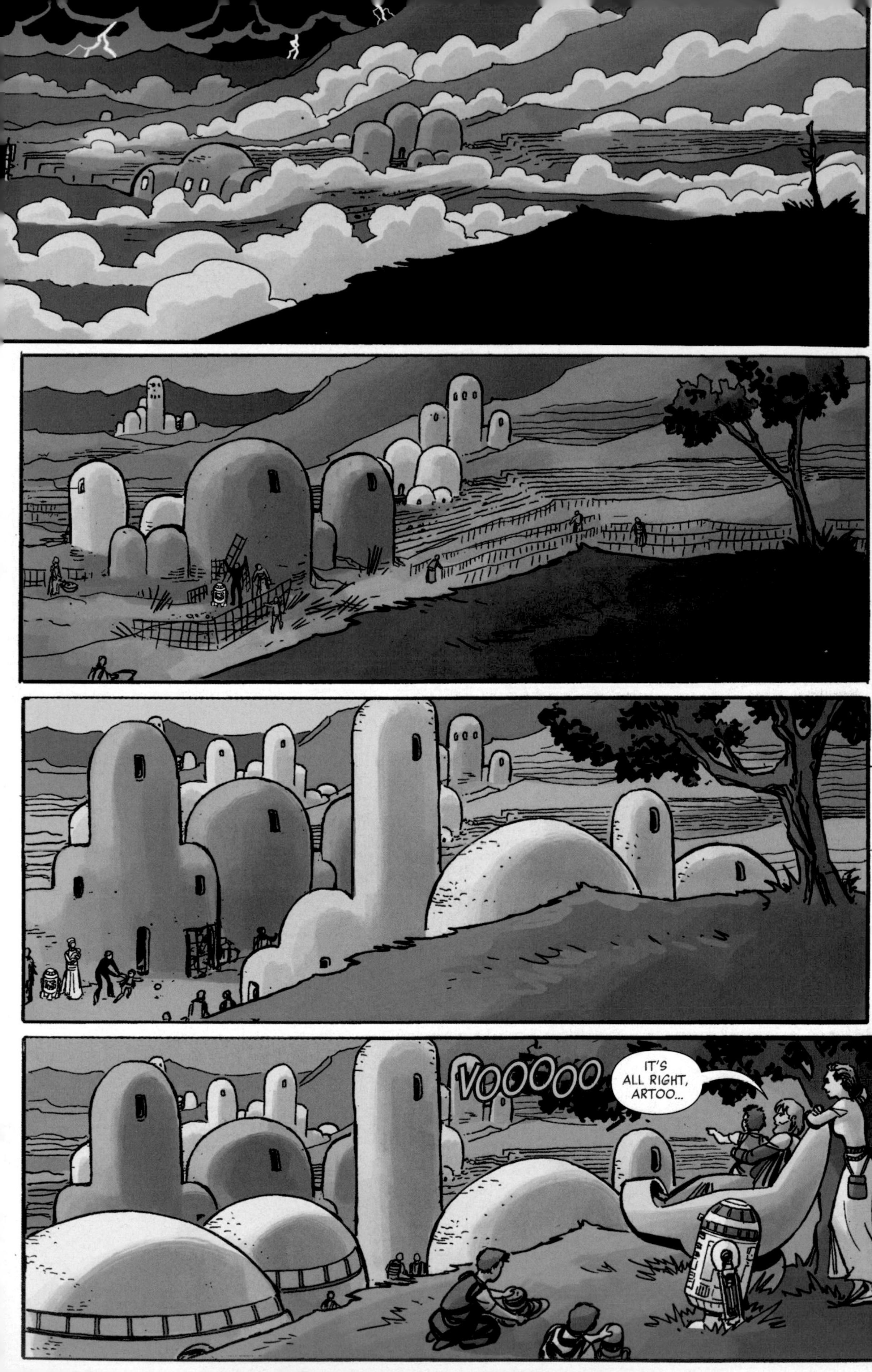
VOOOOO
IT'S ALL RIGHT, ARTOO...

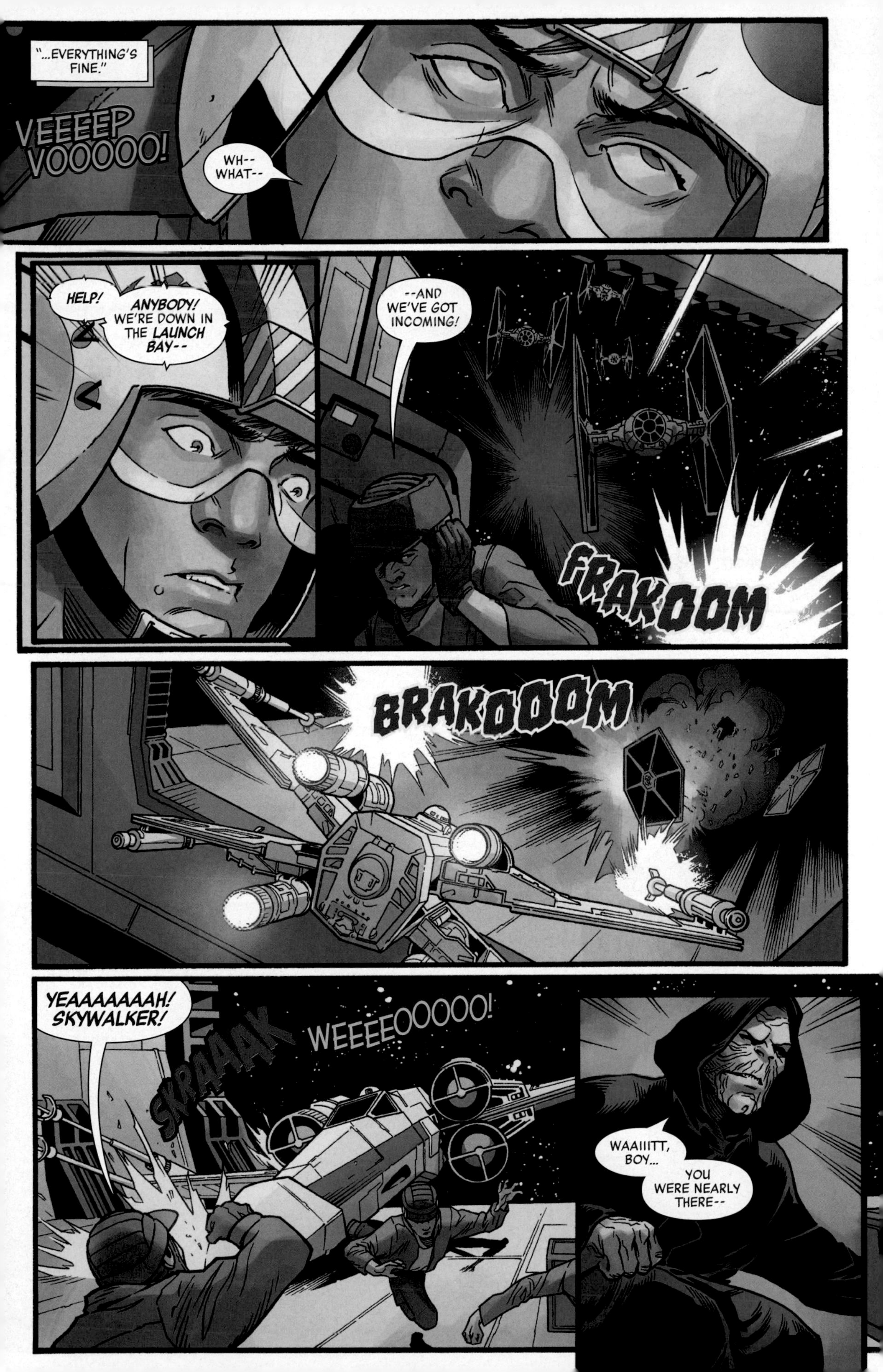
"...EVERYTHING'S FINE."
VEEEEP VOOOOO!
WH-- WHAT--
HELP!
ANYBODY! WE'RE DOWN IN THE LAUNCH BAY--
--AND WE'VE GOT INCOMING!
FRAKOOM
BRAKOOOM
YEAAAAAAAH! SKYWALKER!
SKRAAAK
WEEEEOOOOO!
WAAIIITT, BOY...
YOU WERE NEARLY THERE--

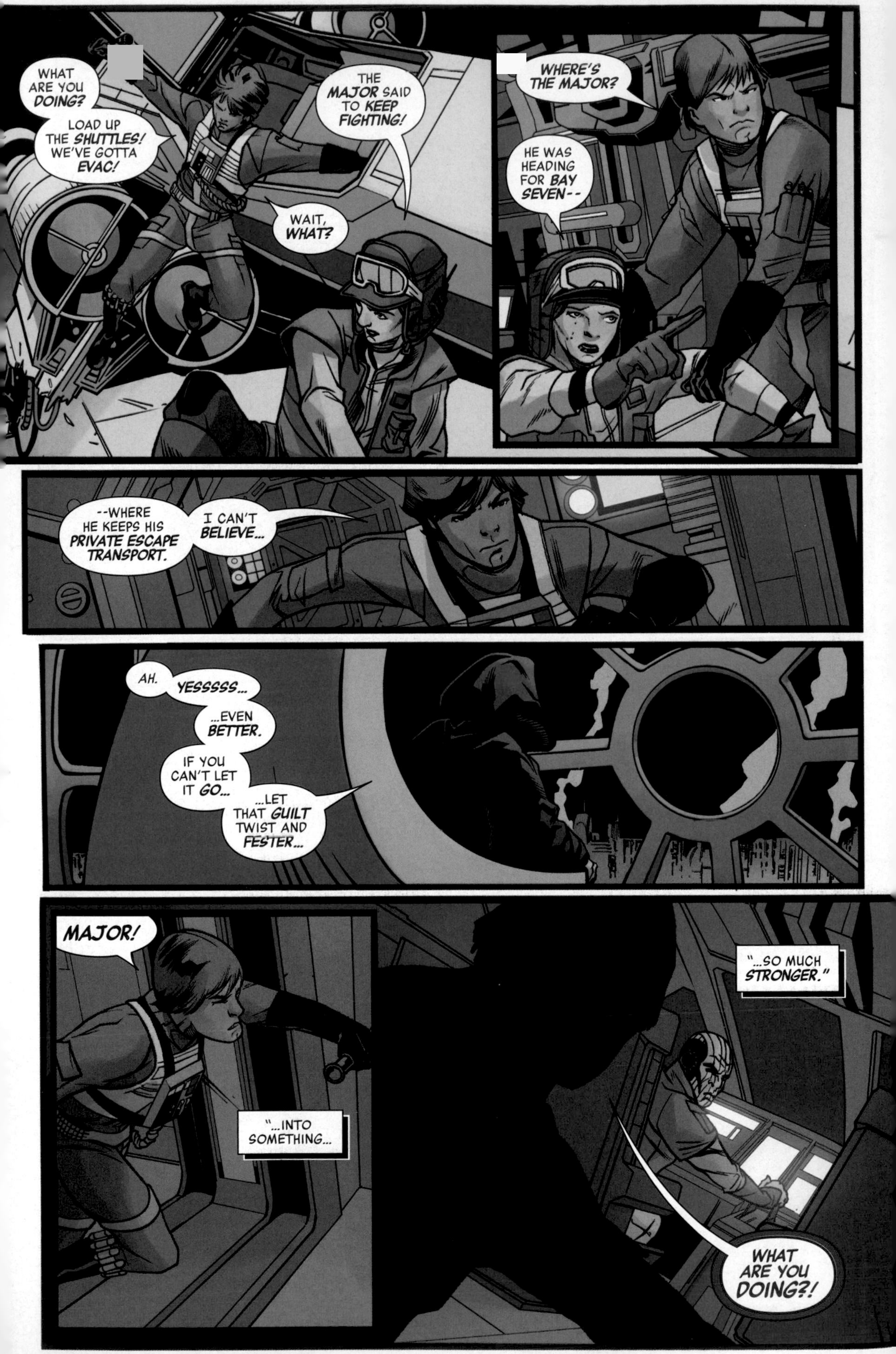

WHAT ARE YOU DOING?
LOAD UP THE SHUTTLES! WE'VE GOTTA EVAC!
THE MAJOR SAID TO KEEP FIGHTING!
WAIT, WHAT?
WHERE'S THE MAJOR?
HE WAS HEADING FOR BAY SEVEN--
--WHERE HE KEEPS HIS PRIVATE ESCAPE TRANSPORT.
I CAN'T BELIEVE...
AH.
YESSSSS...
...EVEN BETTER.
IF YOU CAN'T LET IT GO...
...LET THAT GUILT TWIST AND FESTER...
MAJOR!
"...INTO SOMETHING...
"...SO MUCH STRONGER."
WHAT ARE YOU DOING?!

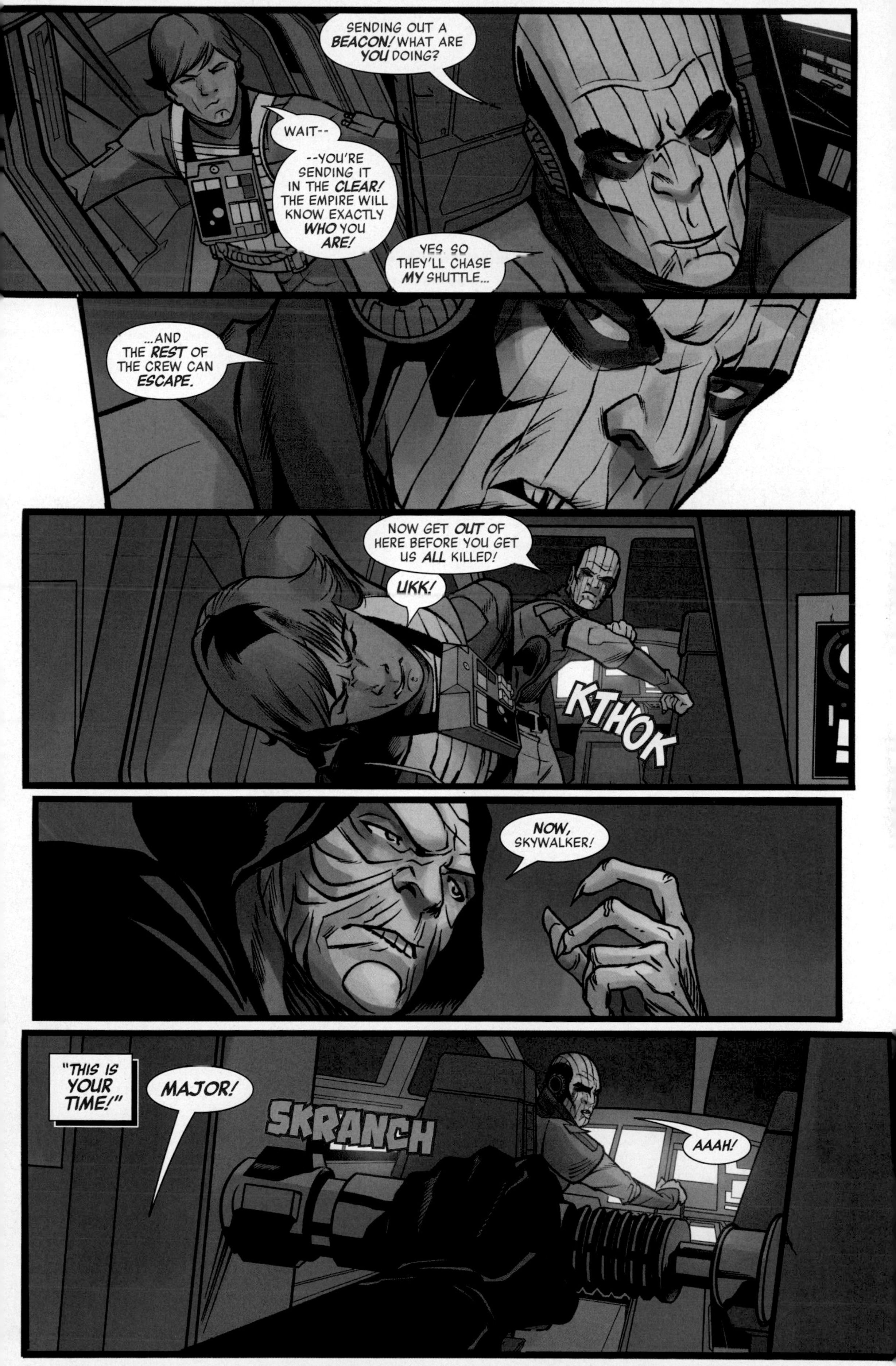
SENDING OUT A BEACON! WHAT ARE YOU DOING?
WAIT--
--YOU'RE SENDING IT IN THE CLEAR! THE EMPIRE WILL KNOW EXACTLY WHO YOU ARE!
YES. SO THEY'LL CHASE MY SHUTTLE...
...AND THE REST OF THE CREW CAN ESCAPE.
NOW GET OUT OF HERE BEFORE YOU GET US ALL KILLED!
UKK!
KTHOK
NOW, SKYWALKER!
"THIS IS YOUR TIME!"
MAJOR!
SKRANCH
AAAH!

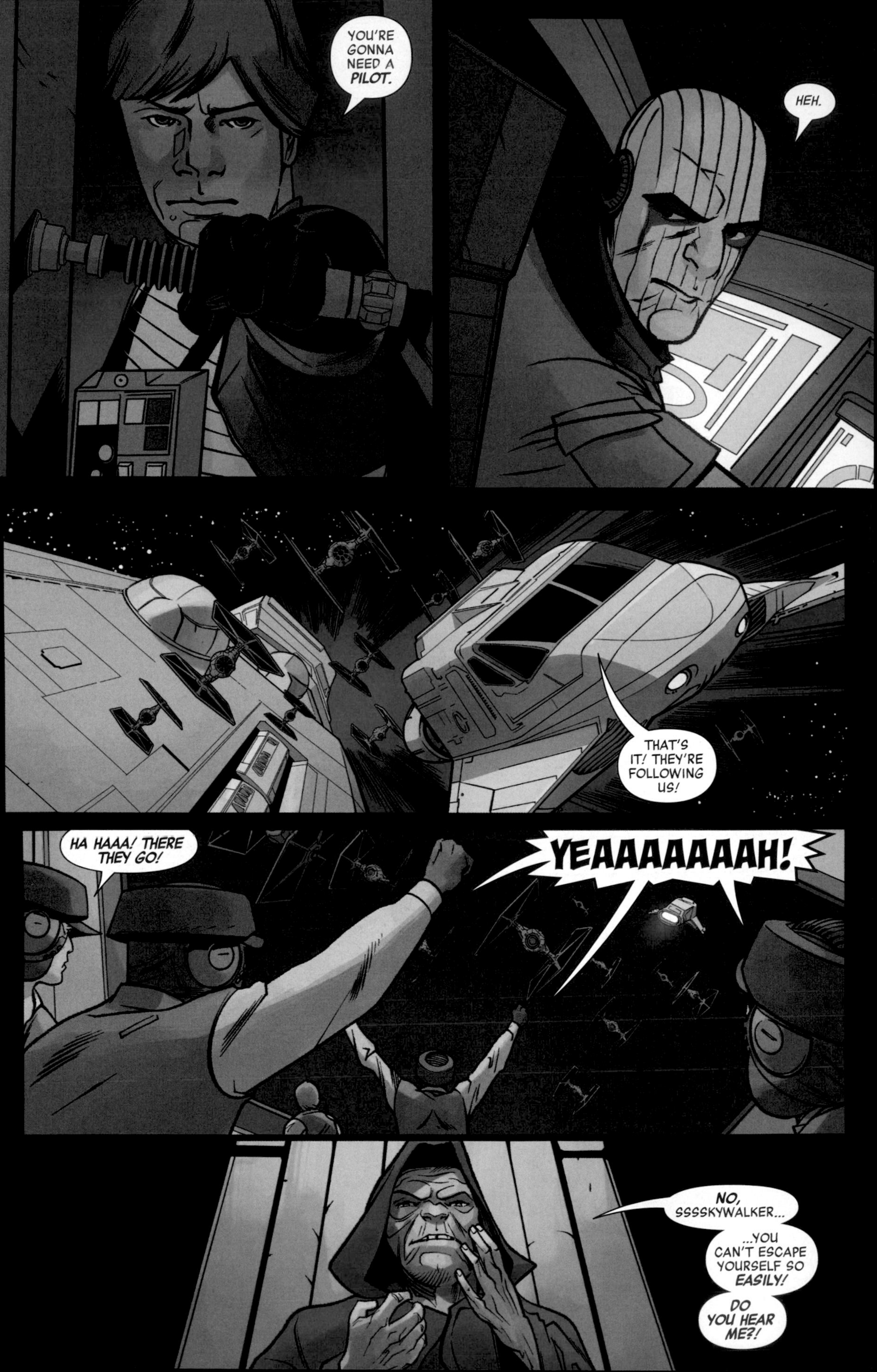
YOU'RE GONNA NEED A PILOT.
HEH.
THAT'S IT! THEY'RE FOLLOWING US!
HA HAAA! THERE THEY GO!
YEAAAAAAAH!
NO, SSSSKYWALKER...
...YOU CAN'T ESCAPE YOURSELF SO EASILY!
DO YOU HEAR ME?!

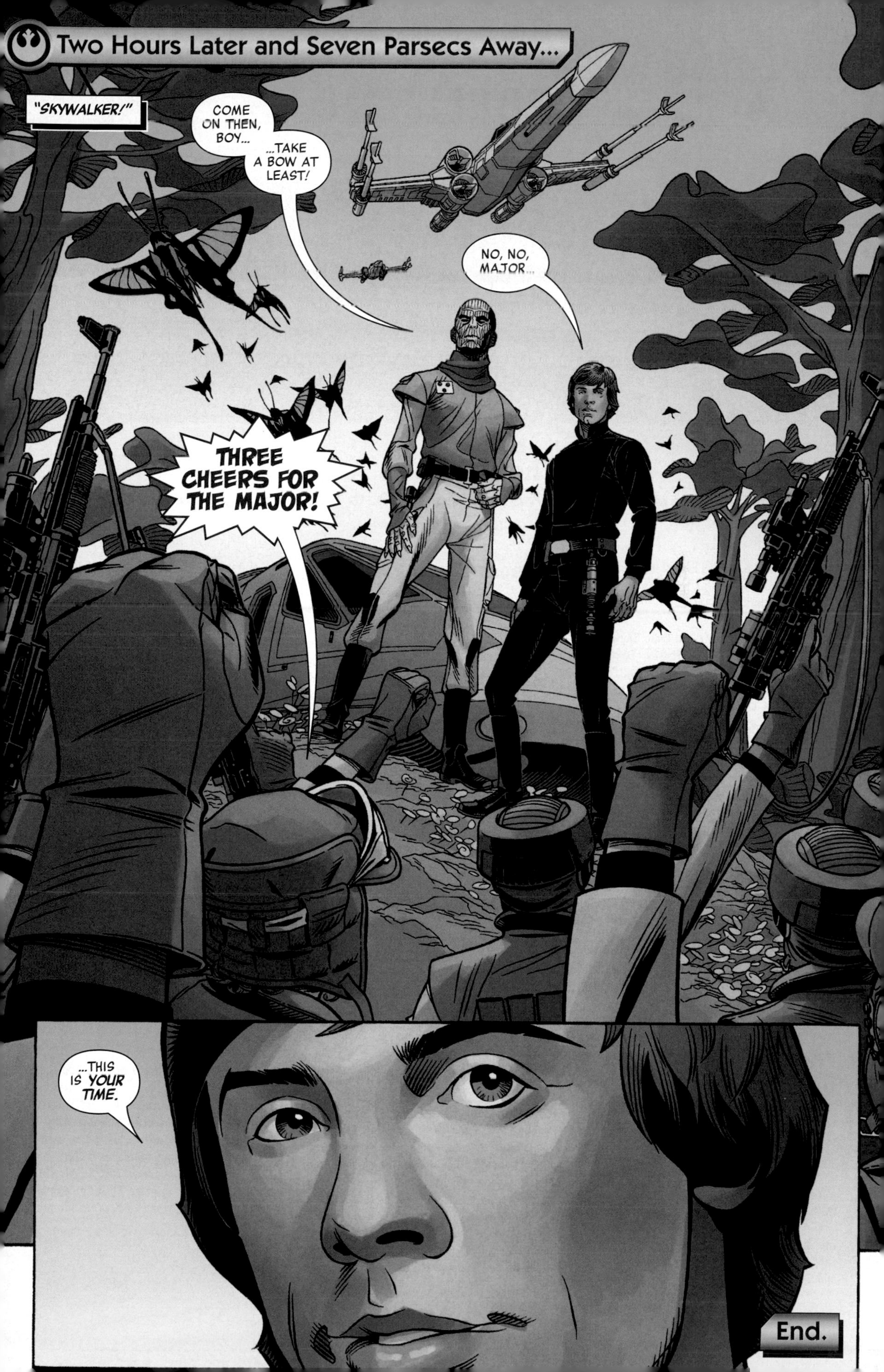
Two Hours Later and Seven Parsecs Away...
"SKYWALKER!"
COME ON THEN, BOY...
...TAKE A BOW AT LEAST!
NO, NO, MAJOR...
THREE CHEERS FOR THE MAJOR!
...THIS IS YOUR TIME.
End.

The Path of a Jedi

Luke Skywalker's journey from farmboy to Jedi Knight to legend has captivated a generation

By Glenn Greenberg

"All his life has he looked away—to the future, to the horizon. Never his mind on where he was, *hmm*? What he was doing."

That was how Yoda described Luke Skywalker in 1980's *The Empire Strikes Back*, in explanation for why he felt the young, Force-sensitive Rebel pilot was unfit for Jedi training. Luke had not yet won over the 900-year-old Jedi Master, but that description undoubtedly helped to solidify Skywalker's position as one of the most relatable characters in the *Star Wars* saga.

If the clever, confident Han Solo or the smart, bold Princess Leia are the characters we wish we were, Luke, despite his great powers and abilities, is the one who's probably most like us. As Yoda noted, and as we saw in the original *Star Wars*, Luke is the restless kid who dreams of leaving home and going on to bigger and better things. Once he's in the larger world, as he is in *Empire*, he screws up—and pays for it dearly. But Luke learns from his mistakes and emerges stronger and wiser. Who can't relate to that?

Mark Hamill, who plays Luke, says he recognized how important this aspect of the character would be to the overall narrative the first time he read the script for *Star Wars*.

"You need a Luke as the character in the piece that the youngest members of the audience can look at and relate to," he told this writer during an interview that will be published in *RetroFan* #5 (Summer 2019 issue). "Of all those characters in *Star Wars*, I think the kids would be most comfortable hanging around *me*, because I'm most like them. . . . You can get intimidated being around royalty or a space pirate."

THE ROOTS OF SKYWALKER

In Luke, writer/director George Lucas created a character very much in the classic heroic tradition, inspired heavily by the various myths and fairy tales that fueled his research as he developed the saga. Luke especially had much in common with King Arthur, another hero and leader who came forth from humble beginnings, was raised by surrogate parents, grew up unaware of his unique lineage and was eventually called to action to save the world around him, with a wizard for a mentor and a special sword as his signature weapon.

Lucas himself related to Luke, perhaps more than any of the other characters he created for that galaxy far, far away. As he told film critic Leonard Maltin on *Entertainment Tonight* in 1999, his favorite moment in *Star Wars* was when Luke stood on the desert of Tatooine and watched the twin suns set on the horizon. "It's the moment that's the most like me in terms of my view of what I do," Lucas said. "I'm sort of always standing out there looking at the sunset, thinking about where I'm going to go from here."

ADVENTURES UNTOLD

At the end of the original trilogy, we see Luke's "graduation" to the rank of full-fledged Jedi Knight. But despite numerous legends told in highly imaginative and exciting novels and comics, Luke's activities following *Return of the Jedi* remain, for the most part, shrouded in mystery. Hamill is amused that audiences never got to see Luke at his peak—he gets his Jedi license, so to speak, and then we don't see him again until he's an old man.

"I thought that was funny," Hamill says. "It would be like telling the trilogy of how James Bond got his license to kill, and once he becomes a spy, that's the end of the series."

THE POWER OF HOPE

Still, it can be argued that, aside from Darth Vader, Luke goes through the most fascinating character arc in the entire saga. Throughout the original trilogy, Luke is the youthful eternal optimist and man of action—he decides without hesitation to rescue Leia from her cell aboard the Death Star and to join the battle to destroy the space station. He rushes off, with his Jedi training unfinished, to save his friends and confront Vader, convinced he can defeat the Sith Lord. And, after he learns that Vader is his father, Luke chooses to try to reach the goodness that he believes still lurks within the man who used to be Anakin Skywalker.

That's why it's so heartbreaking to see what's become of Luke in *The Last Jedi*—to see that, as a result of his failure with his nephew, he has become embittered, cynical, disconnected from the galaxy, from the Force, from his family, from *himself*.

But a key element of storytelling is that for a character to truly rise, he or she must first fall. What makes Luke's "comeback" confrontation with Kylo Ren so powerful and touching is that he had been at such a low point earlier in the film. Emerging from his failure and disillusionment, Luke Skywalker, in his final moments, is once again the hero, the symbol of hope, that he was when we first encountered him in 1977.

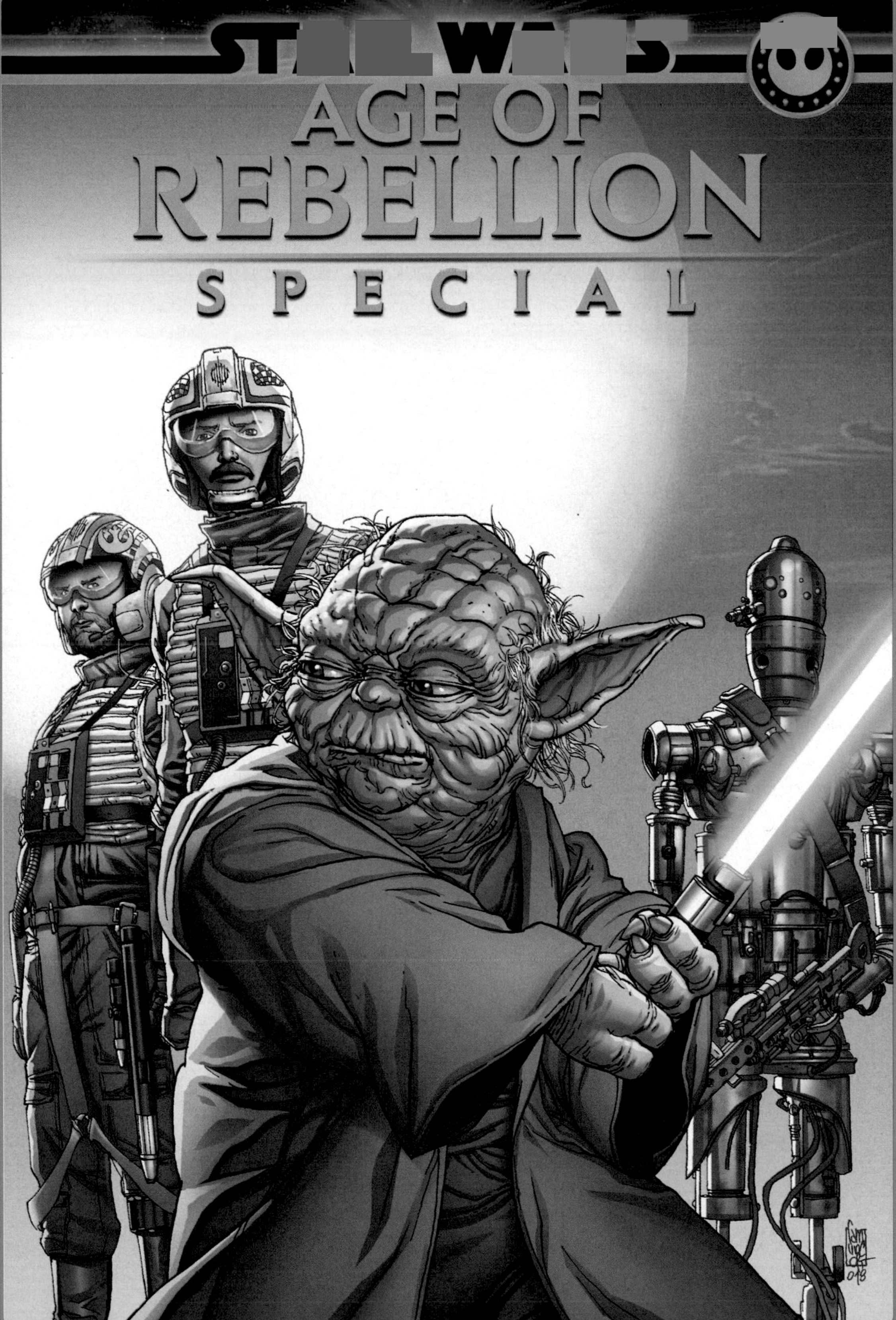
AGE OF
REBELLION
SPECIAL

"THE TRIAL OF DAGOBAH"

The downfall of the Republic has forced Yoda into exile. But the long years on the remote world of Dagobah haven't exactly been peaceful for the old Jedi Master. . . .

"STOLEN VALOR"

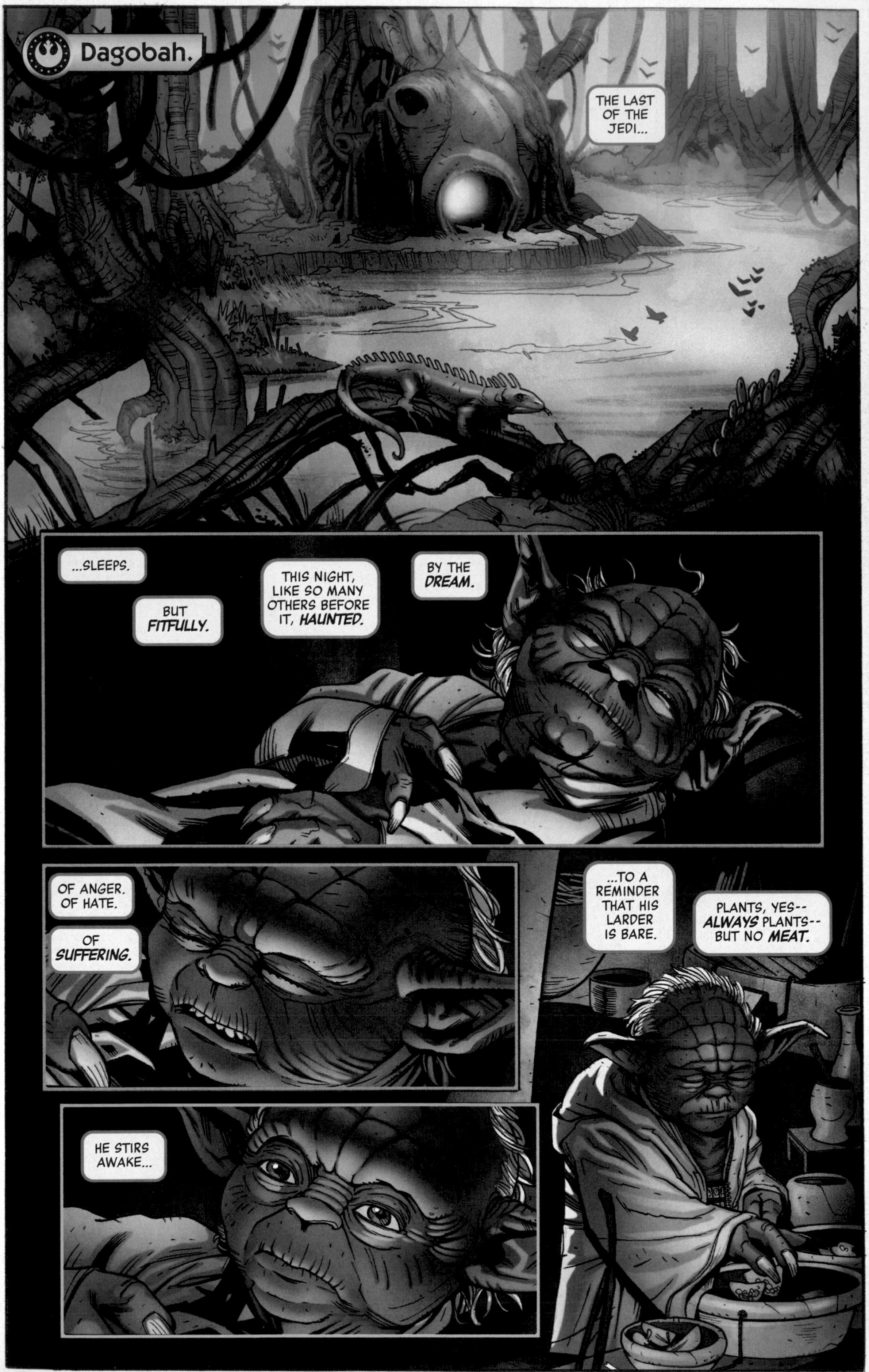
Dagobah.
THE LAST OF THE JEDI...
...SLEEPS.
BUT FITFULLY.
THIS NIGHT, LIKE SO MANY OTHERS BEFORE IT, HAUNTED.
BY THE DREAM.
OF ANGER. OF HATE.
OF SUFFERING.
HE STIRS AWAKE...
...TO A REMINDER THAT HIS LARDER IS BARE.
PLANTS, YES-- ALWAYS PLANTS-- BUT NO MEAT.

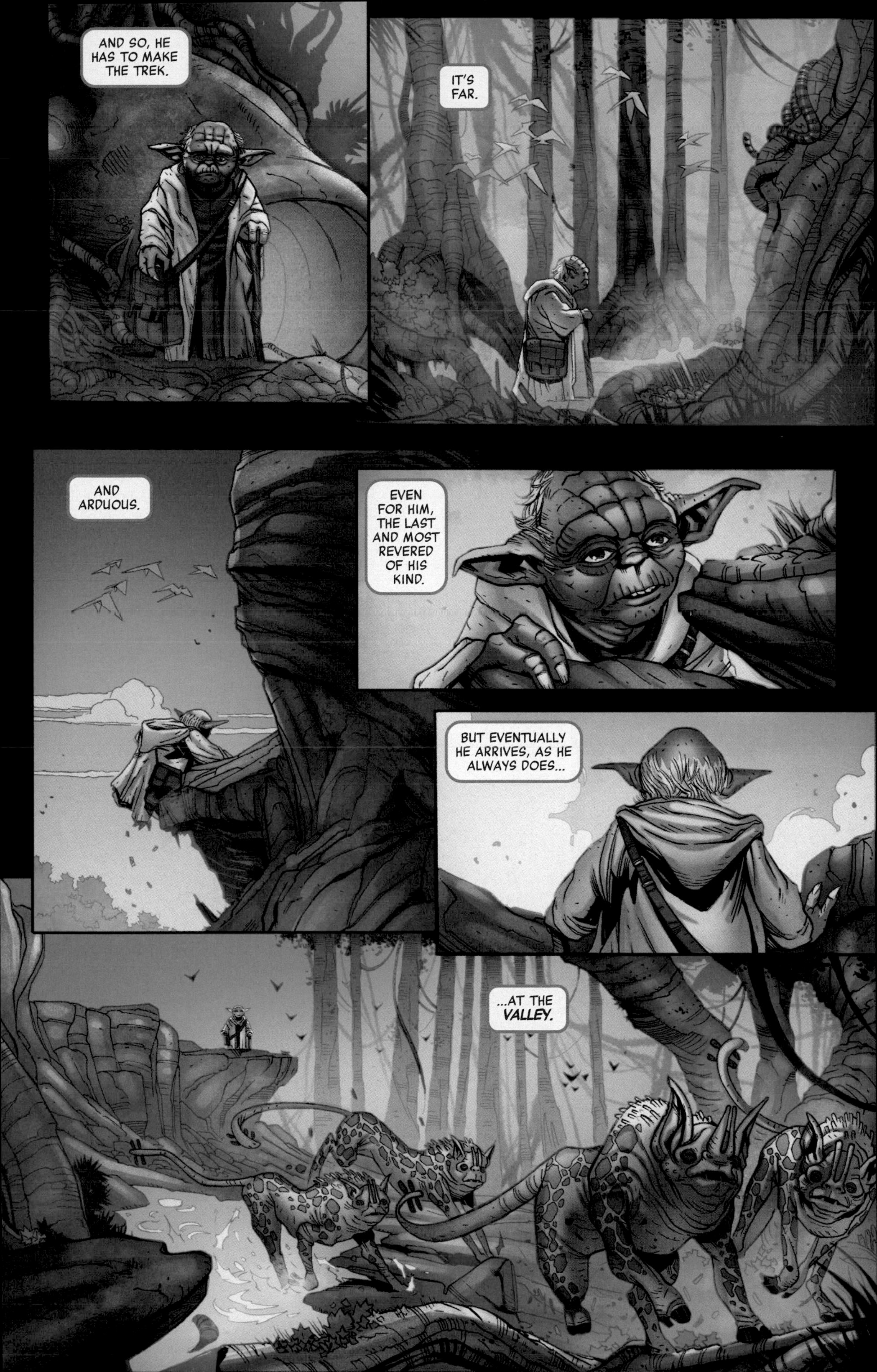
AND SO, HE HAS TO MAKE THE TREK.
IT'S FAR.
AND ARDUOUS.
EVEN FOR HIM, THE LAST AND MOST REVERED OF HIS KIND.
BUT EVENTUALLY HE ARRIVES, AS HE ALWAYS DOES...
...AT THE VALLEY.

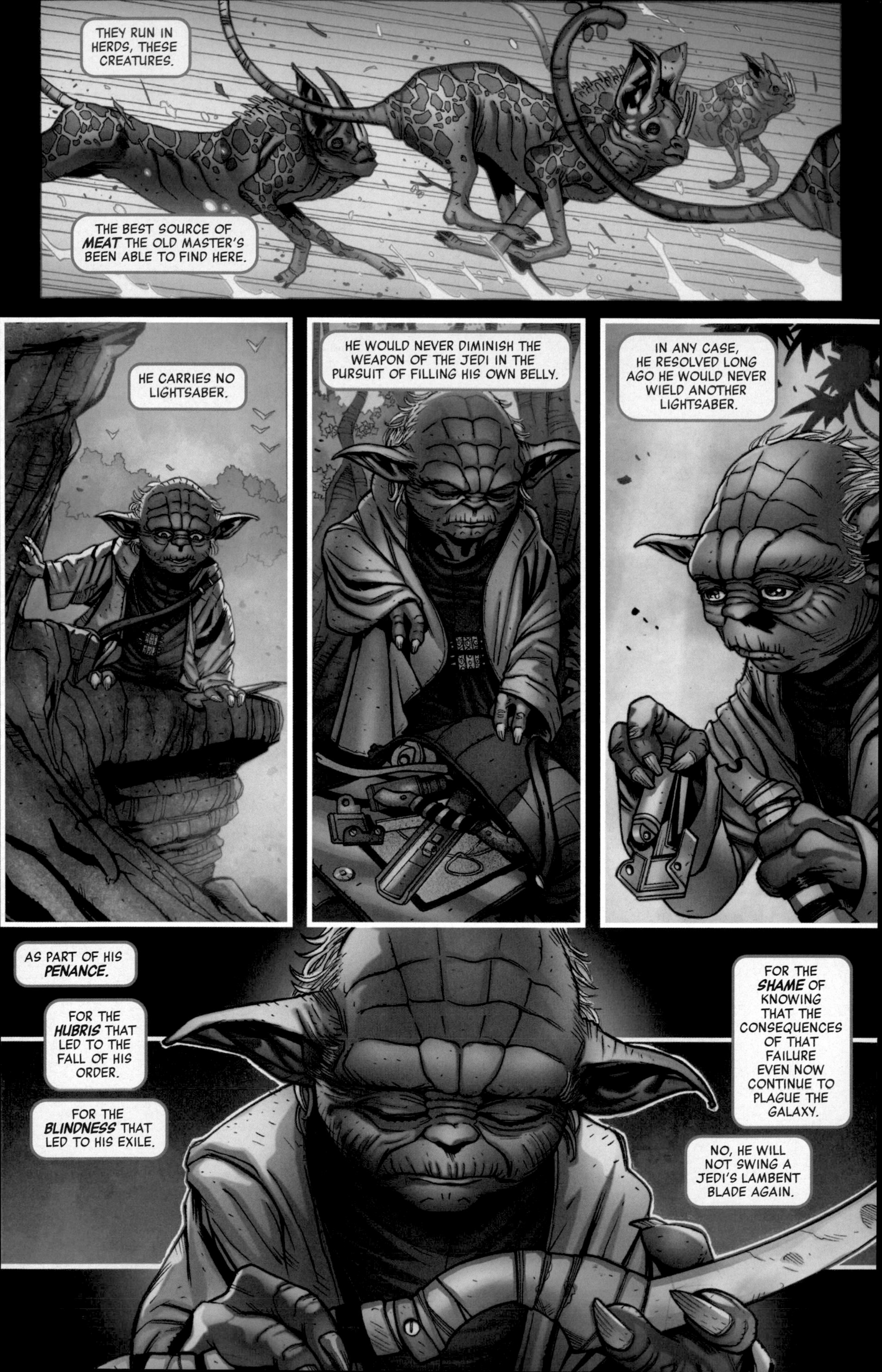
THEY RUN IN HERDS, THESE CREATURES.
THE BEST SOURCE OF MEAT THE OLD MASTER'S BEEN ABLE TO FIND HERE.
HE CARRIES NO LIGHTSABER.
HE WOULD NEVER DIMINISH THE WEAPON OF THE JEDI IN THE PURSUIT OF FILLING HIS OWN BELLY.
IN ANY CASE, HE RESOLVED LONG AGO HE WOULD NEVER WIELD ANOTHER LIGHTSABER.
AS PART OF HIS PENANCE.
FOR THE HUBRIS THAT LED TO THE FALL OF HIS ORDER.
FOR THE BLINDNESS THAT LED TO HIS EXILE.
FOR THE SHAME OF KNOWING THAT THE CONSEQUENCES OF THAT FAILURE EVEN NOW CONTINUE TO PLAGUE THE GALAXY.
NO, HE WILL NOT SWING A JEDI'S LAMBENT BLADE AGAIN.

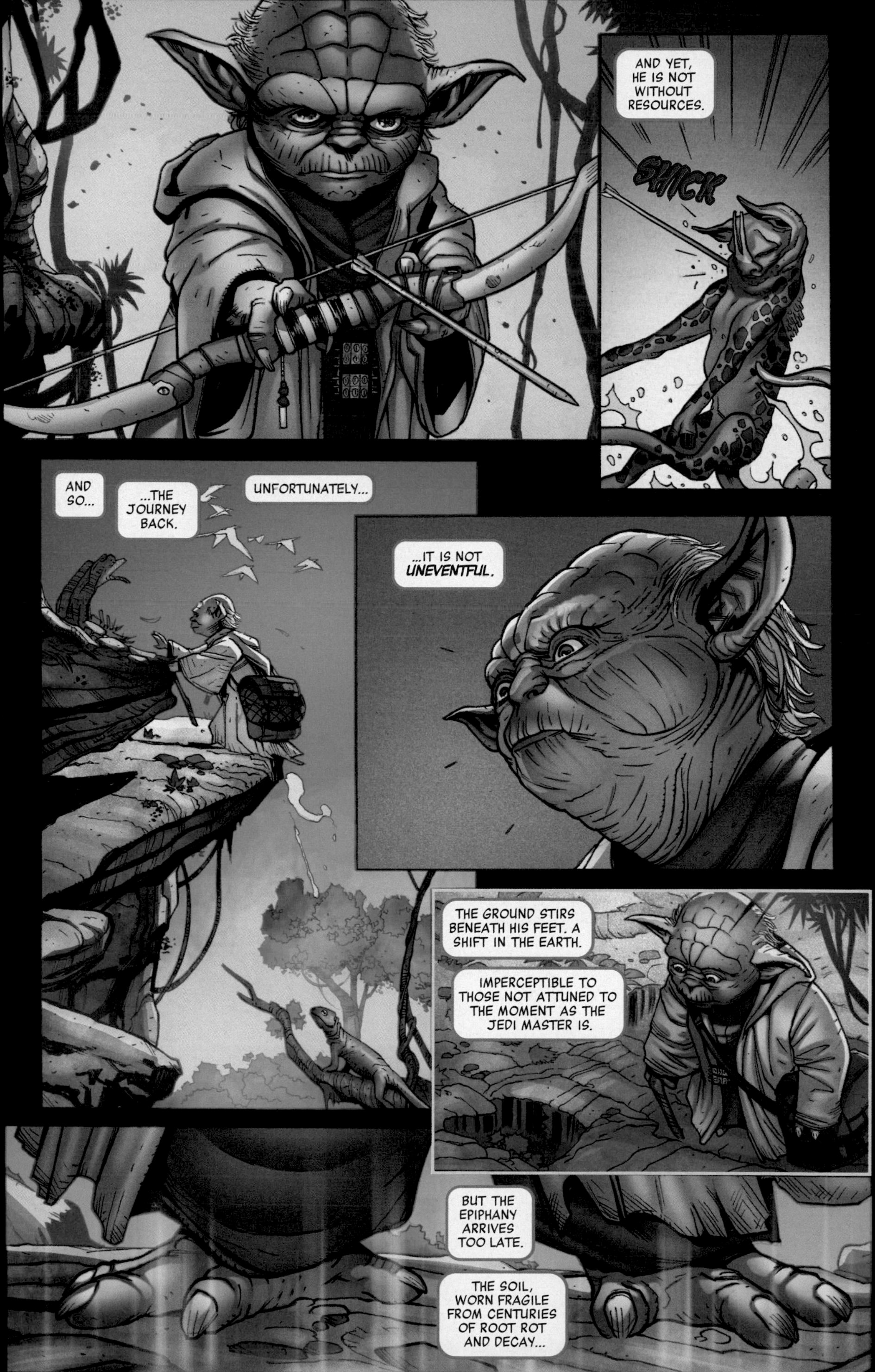
AND YET, HE IS NOT WITHOUT RESOURCES.
SHICK
AND SO...
...THE JOURNEY BACK.
UNFORTUNATELY...
...IT IS NOT UNEVENTFUL.
THE GROUND STIRS BENEATH HIS FEET. A SHIFT IN THE EARTH.
IMPERCEPTIBLE TO THOSE NOT ATTUNED TO THE MOMENT AS THE JEDI MASTER IS.
BUT THE EPIPHANY ARRIVES TOO LATE.
THE SOIL, WORN FRAGILE FROM CENTURIES OF ROOT ROT AND DECAY...

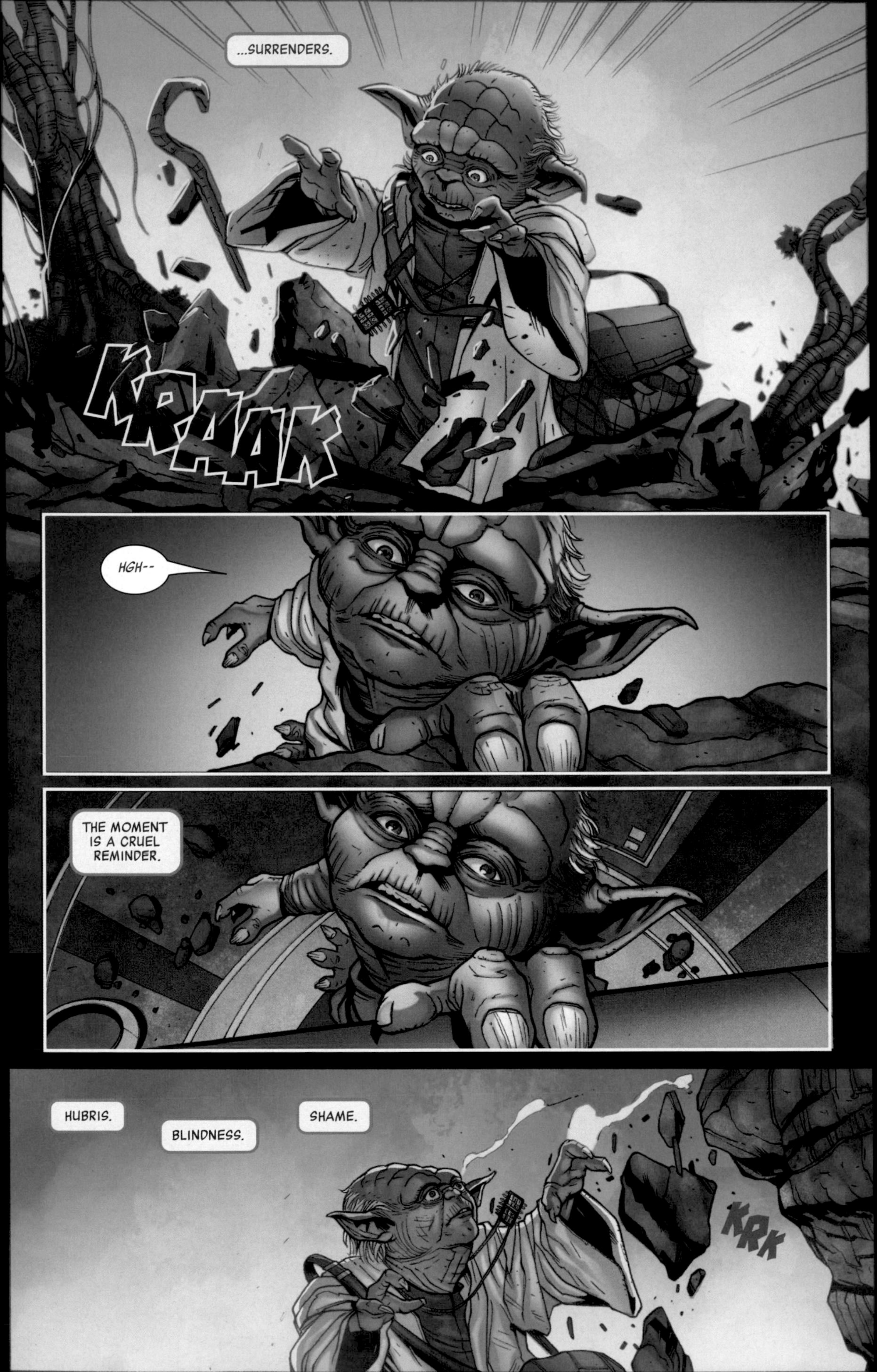
...SURRENDERS.
KRAAK
HGH--
THE MOMENT IS A CRUEL REMINDER.
HUBRIS.
BLINDNESS.
SHAME.
KRK

GGGN--

RRRUMM

THE PLANET RAINS ITS MASS DOWN ON HIM.

MBLLE

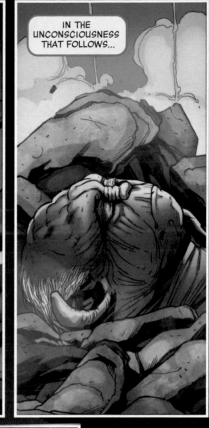

IN THE UNCONSCIOUSNESS THAT FOLLOWS...

...THE DREAM AGAIN.

HE SHOOTS AWAKE.

TO FIND HIMSELF TRAPPED.

BURIED ALIVE.

HIS REACTION IS UNEXPECTED.

HEEHEEHEEHEE...

THE MASTER LAUGHS.

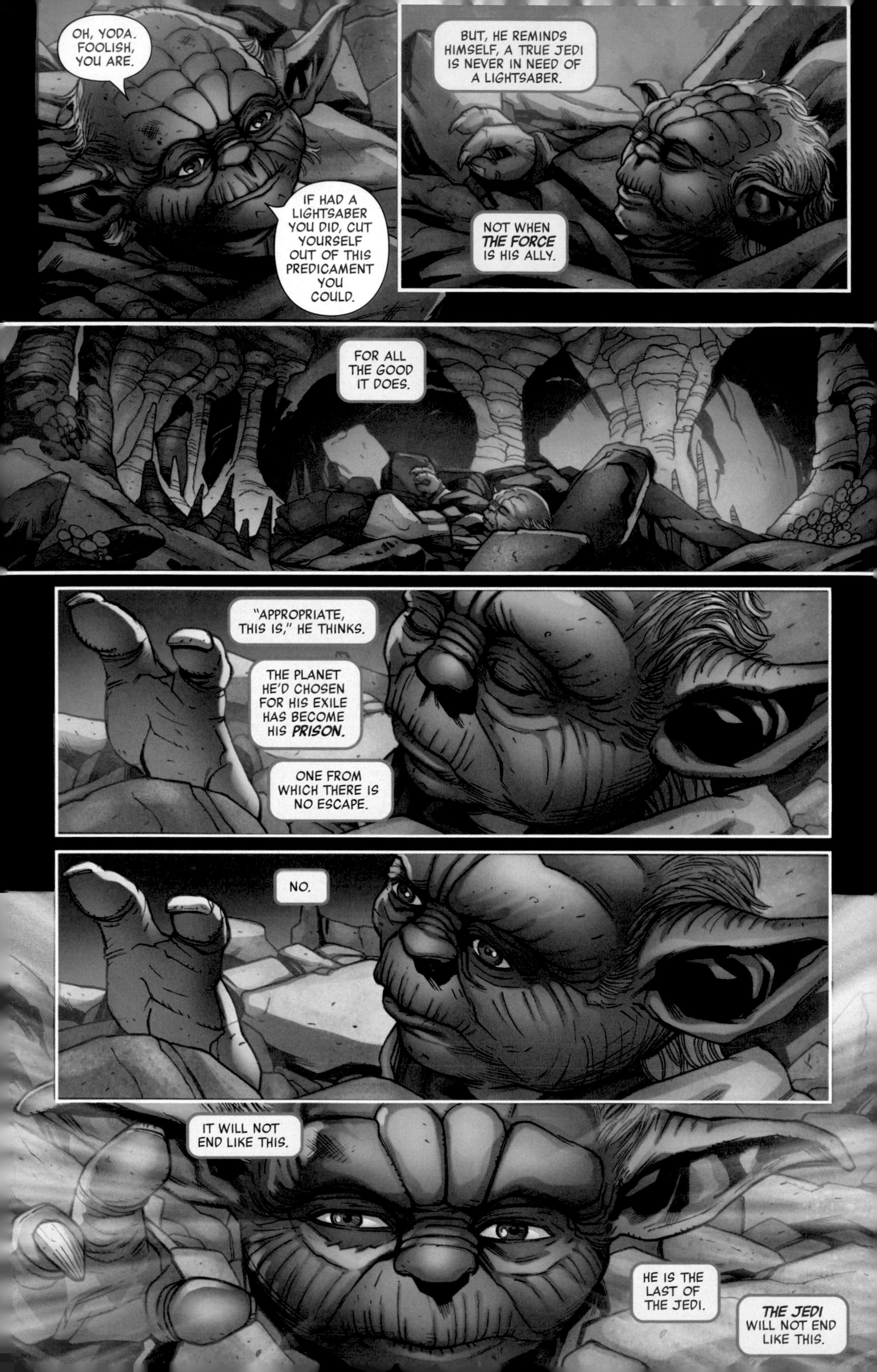
OH, YODA. FOOLISH, YOU ARE.
IF HAD A LIGHTSABER YOU DID, CUT YOURSELF OUT OF THIS PREDICAMENT YOU COULD.
BUT, HE REMINDS HIMSELF, A TRUE JEDI IS NEVER IN NEED OF A LIGHTSABER.
NOT WHEN *THE FORCE* IS HIS ALLY.
FOR ALL THE GOOD IT DOES.
"APPROPRIATE, THIS IS," HE THINKS.
THE PLANET HE'D CHOSEN FOR HIS EXILE HAS BECOME HIS *PRISON.*
ONE FROM WHICH THERE IS NO ESCAPE.
NO.
IT WILL NOT END LIKE THIS.
HE IS THE LAST OF THE JEDI.
THE JEDI WILL NOT END LIKE THIS.

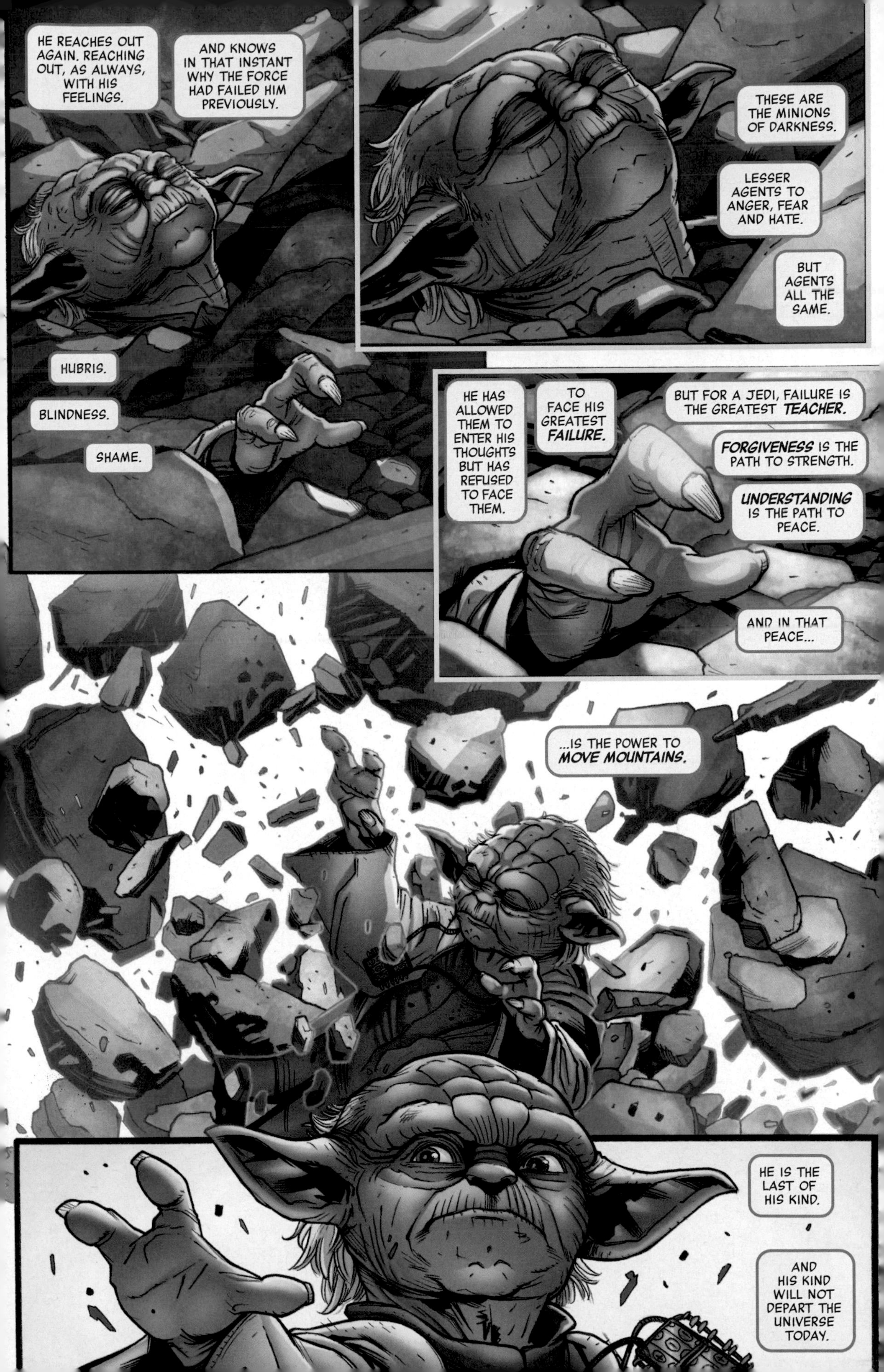
HE REACHES OUT AGAIN. REACHING OUT, AS ALWAYS, WITH HIS FEELINGS.
AND KNOWS IN THAT INSTANT WHY THE FORCE HAD FAILED HIM PREVIOUSLY.
HUBRIS.
BLINDNESS.
SHAME.
THESE ARE THE MINIONS OF DARKNESS.
LESSER AGENTS TO ANGER, FEAR AND HATE.
BUT AGENTS ALL THE SAME.
HE HAS ALLOWED THEM TO ENTER HIS THOUGHTS BUT HAS REFUSED TO FACE THEM.
TO FACE HIS GREATEST FAILURE.
BUT FOR A JEDI, FAILURE IS THE GREATEST TEACHER.
FORGIVENESS IS THE PATH TO STRENGTH.
UNDERSTANDING IS THE PATH TO PEACE.
AND IN THAT PEACE...
...IS THE POWER TO MOVE MOUNTAINS.
HE IS THE LAST OF HIS KIND.
AND HIS KIND WILL NOT DEPART THE UNIVERSE TODAY.

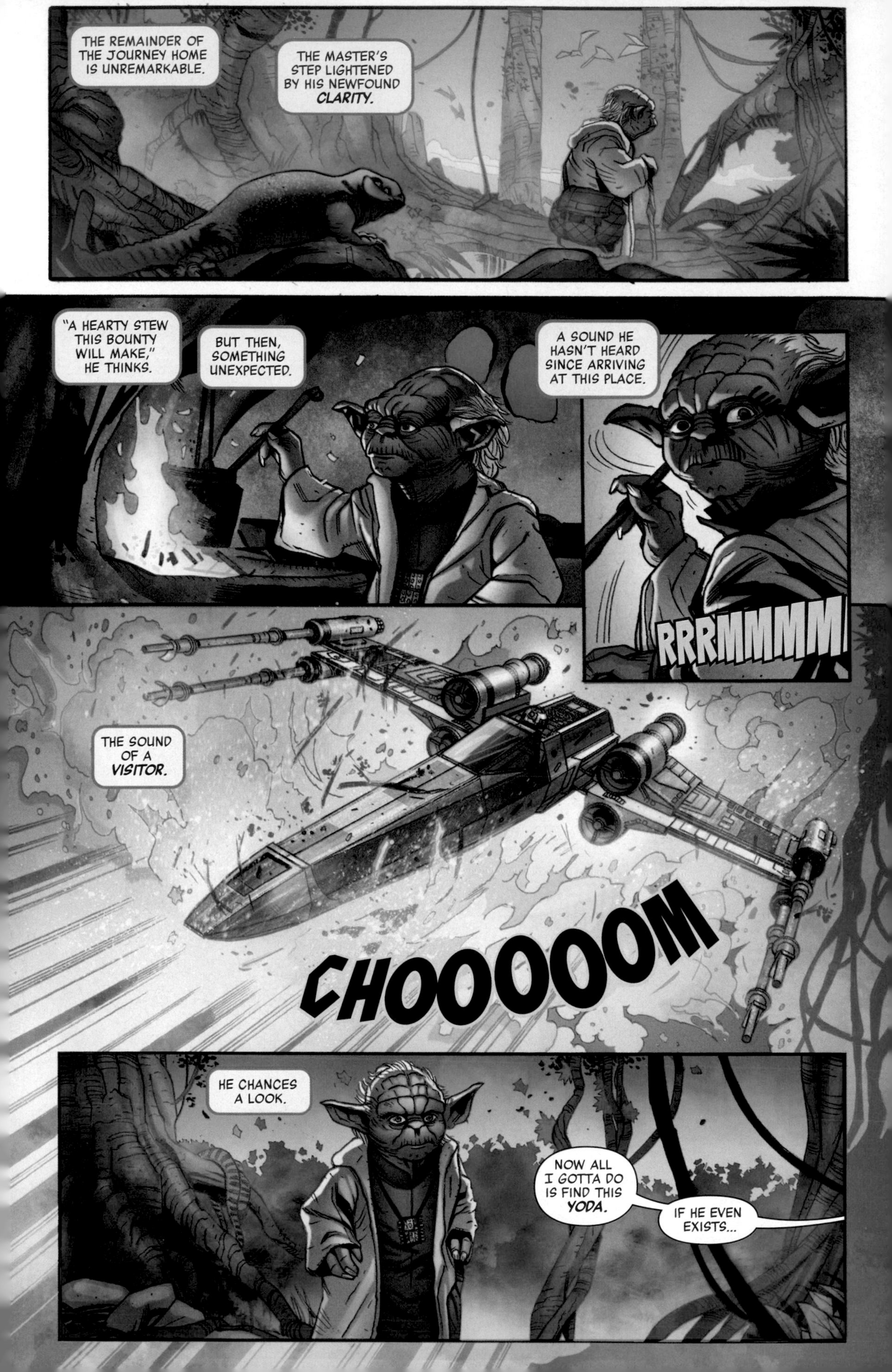
THE REMAINDER OF THE JOURNEY HOME IS UNREMARKABLE.
THE MASTER'S STEP LIGHTENED BY HIS NEWFOUND CLARITY.
"A HEARTY STEW THIS BOUNTY WILL MAKE," HE THINKS.
BUT THEN, SOMETHING UNEXPECTED.
A SOUND HE HASN'T HEARD SINCE ARRIVING AT THIS PLACE.
RRRMMMMM
THE SOUND OF A VISITOR.
CHOOOOOM
HE CHANCES A LOOK.
NOW ALL I GOTTA DO IS FIND THIS YODA.
IF HE EVEN EXISTS...

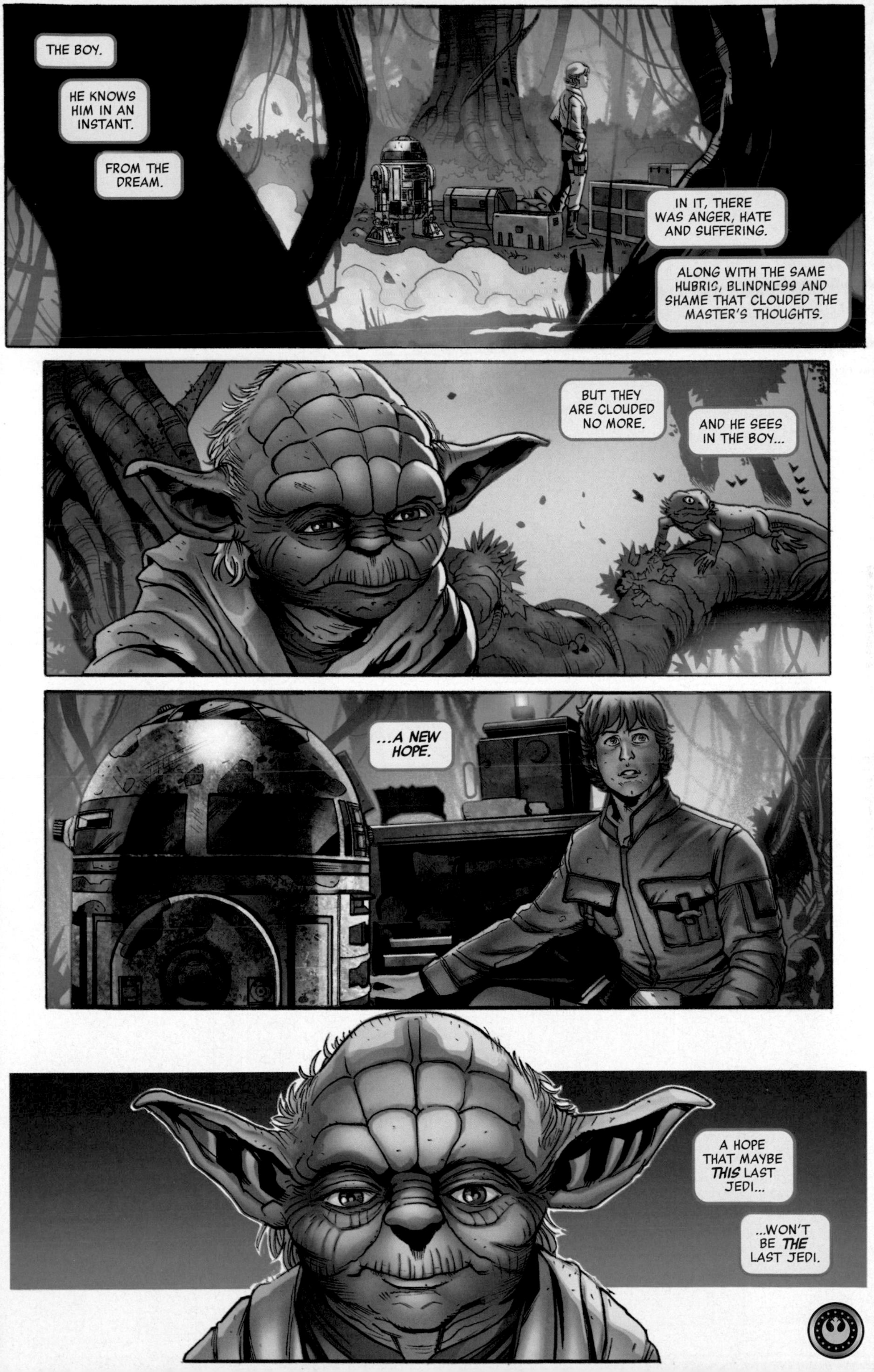
THE BOY.
HE KNOWS HIM IN AN INSTANT.
FROM THE DREAM.
IN IT, THERE WAS ANGER, HATE AND SUFFERING.
ALONG WITH THE SAME HUBRIS, BLINDNESS AND SHAME THAT CLOUDED THE MASTER'S THOUGHTS.
BUT THEY ARE CLOUDED NO MORE.
AND HE SEES IN THE BOY...
...A NEW HOPE.
A HOPE THAT MAYBE *THIS* LAST JEDI...
...WON'T BE *THE* LAST JEDI.

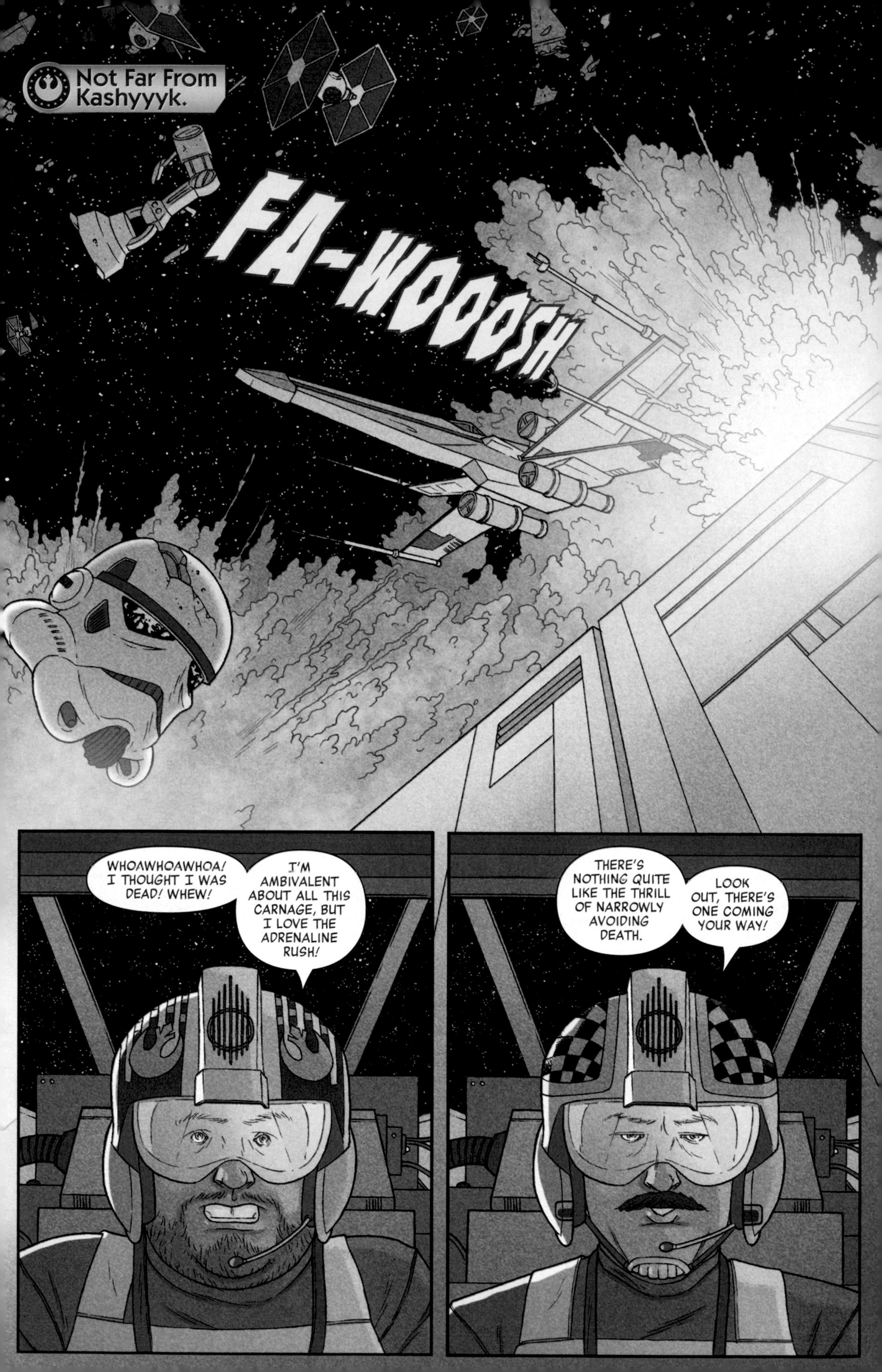

Not Far From Kashyyyk.
FA-WOOOSH
WHOAWHOAWHOA! I THOUGHT I WAS DEAD! WHEW!
I'M AMBIVALENT ABOUT ALL THIS CARNAGE, BUT I LOVE THE ADRENALINE RUSH!
THERE'S NOTHING QUITE LIKE THE THRILL OF NARROWLY AVOIDING DEATH.
LOOK OUT, THERE'S ONE COMING YOUR WAY!

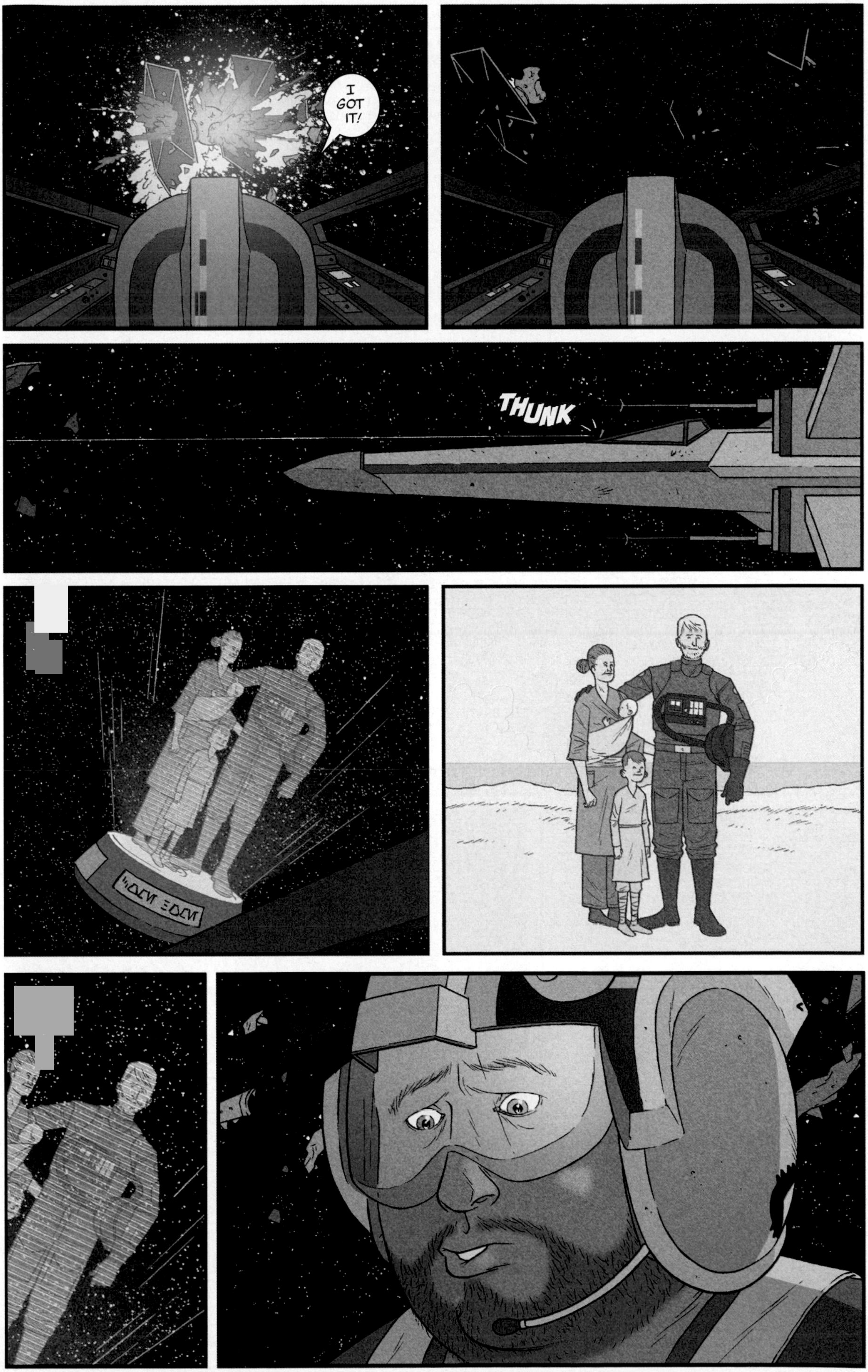
I GOT IT!
THUNK

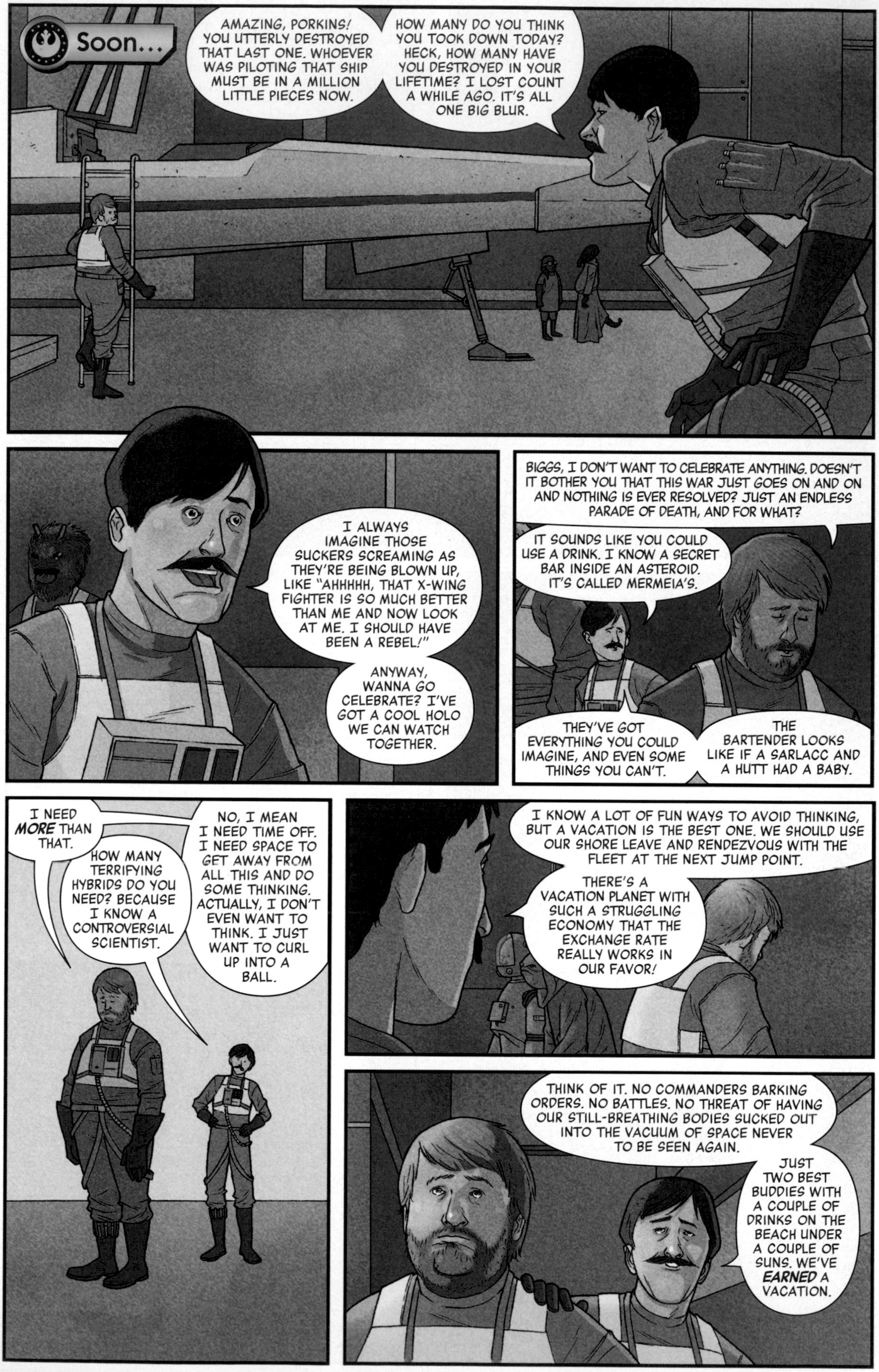
Soon...
AMAZING, PORKINS! YOU UTTERLY DESTROYED THAT LAST ONE. WHOEVER WAS PILOTING THAT SHIP MUST BE IN A MILLION LITTLE PIECES NOW.
HOW MANY DO YOU THINK YOU TOOK DOWN TODAY? HECK, HOW MANY HAVE YOU DESTROYED IN YOUR LIFETIME? I LOST COUNT A WHILE AGO. IT'S ALL ONE BIG BLUR.
I ALWAYS IMAGINE THOSE SUCKERS SCREAMING AS THEY'RE BEING BLOWN UP, LIKE "AHHHHH, THAT X-WING FIGHTER IS SO MUCH BETTER THAN ME AND NOW LOOK AT ME. I SHOULD HAVE BEEN A REBEL!"
ANYWAY, WANNA GO CELEBRATE? I'VE GOT A COOL HOLO WE CAN WATCH TOGETHER.
BIGGS, I DON'T WANT TO CELEBRATE ANYTHING. DOESN'T IT BOTHER YOU THAT THIS WAR JUST GOES ON AND ON AND NOTHING IS EVER RESOLVED? JUST AN ENDLESS PARADE OF DEATH, AND FOR WHAT?
IT SOUNDS LIKE YOU COULD USE A DRINK. I KNOW A SECRET BAR INSIDE AN ASTEROID. IT'S CALLED MERMEIA'S.
THEY'VE GOT EVERYTHING YOU COULD IMAGINE, AND EVEN SOME THINGS YOU CAN'T.
THE BARTENDER LOOKS LIKE IF A SARLACC AND A HUTT HAD A BABY.
I NEED **MORE** THAN THAT.
HOW MANY TERRIFYING HYBRIDS DO YOU NEED? BECAUSE I KNOW A CONTROVERSIAL SCIENTIST.
NO, I MEAN I NEED TIME OFF. I NEED SPACE TO GET AWAY FROM ALL THIS AND DO SOME THINKING. ACTUALLY, I DON'T EVEN WANT TO THINK. I JUST WANT TO CURL UP INTO A BALL.
I KNOW A LOT OF FUN WAYS TO AVOID THINKING, BUT A VACATION IS THE BEST ONE. WE SHOULD USE OUR SHORE LEAVE AND RENDEZVOUS WITH THE FLEET AT THE NEXT JUMP POINT.
THERE'S A VACATION PLANET WITH SUCH A STRUGGLING ECONOMY THAT THE EXCHANGE RATE REALLY WORKS IN OUR FAVOR!
THINK OF IT. NO COMMANDERS BARKING ORDERS. NO BATTLES. NO THREAT OF HAVING OUR STILL-BREATHING BODIES SUCKED OUT INTO THE VACUUM OF SPACE NEVER TO BE SEEN AGAIN.
JUST TWO BEST BUDDIES WITH A COUPLE OF DRINKS ON THE BEACH UNDER A COUPLE OF SUNS. WE'VE **EARNED** A VACATION.

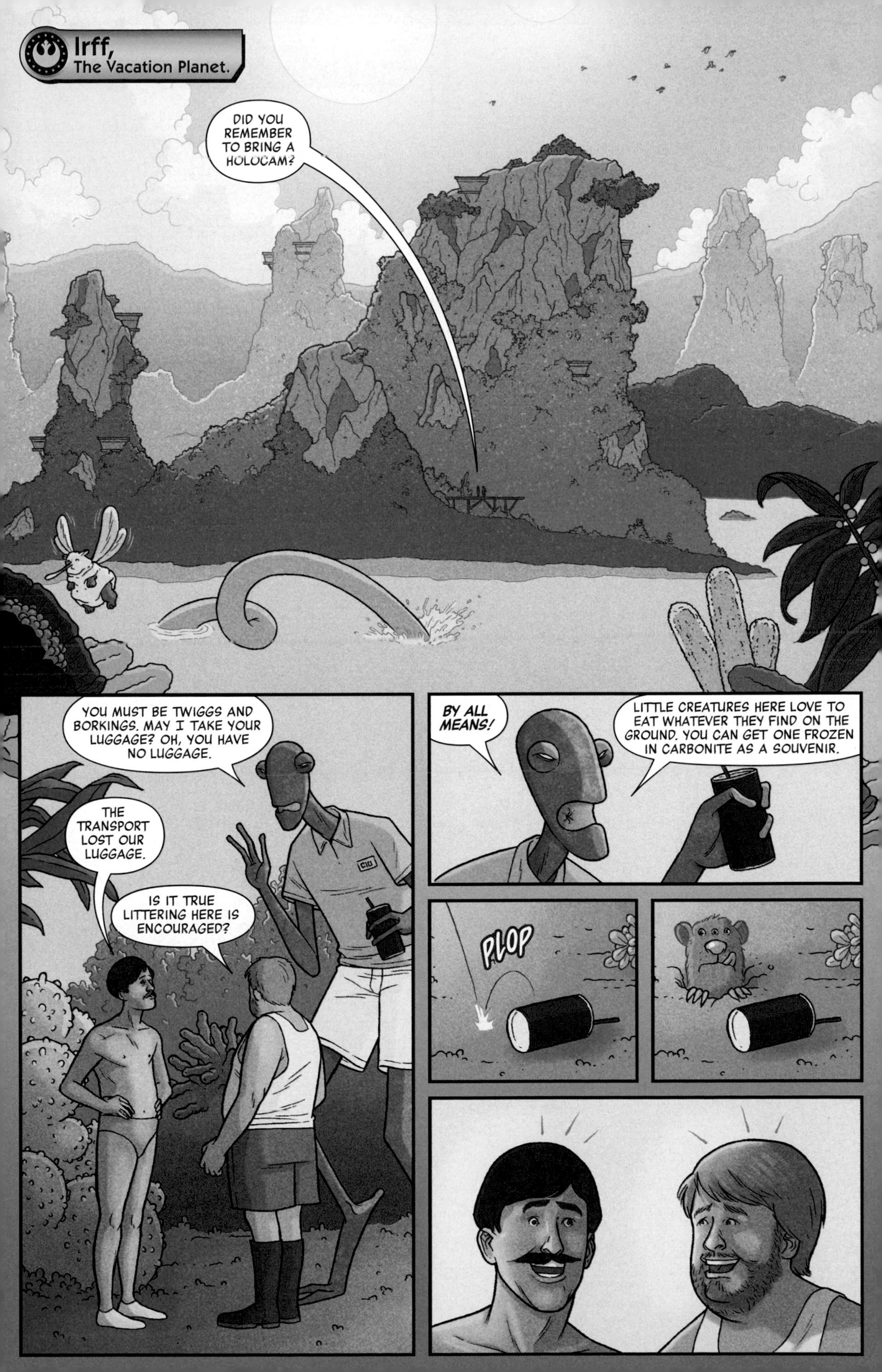
Irff,
The Vacation Planet.
DID YOU REMEMBER TO BRING A HOLOCAM?
YOU MUST BE TWIGGS AND BORKINGS. MAY I TAKE YOUR LUGGAGE? OH, YOU HAVE NO LUGGAGE.
THE TRANSPORT LOST OUR LUGGAGE.
IS IT TRUE LITTERING HERE IS ENCOURAGED?
BY ALL MEANS!
LITTLE CREATURES HERE LOVE TO EAT WHATEVER THEY FIND ON THE GROUND. YOU CAN GET ONE FROZEN IN CARBONITE AS A SOUVENIR.
PLOP

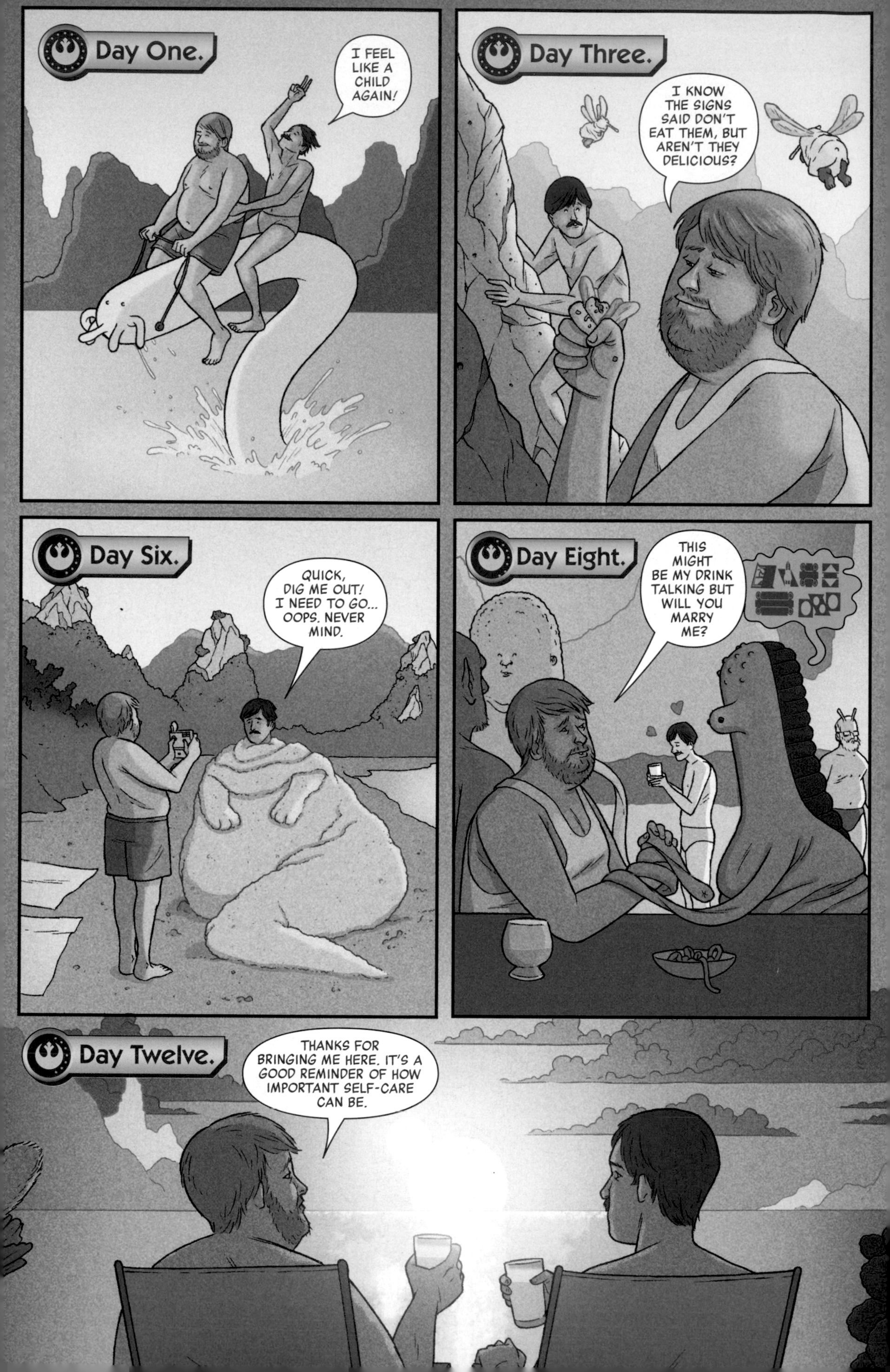
Day One.
I FEEL LIKE A CHILD AGAIN!
Day Three.
I KNOW THE SIGNS SAID DON'T EAT THEM, BUT AREN'T THEY DELICIOUS?
Day Six.
QUICK, DIG ME OUT! I NEED TO GO... OOPS. NEVER MIND.
Day Eight.
THIS MIGHT BE MY DRINK TALKING BUT WILL YOU MARRY ME?
Day Twelve.
THANKS FOR BRINGING ME HERE. IT'S A GOOD REMINDER OF HOW IMPORTANT SELF-CARE CAN BE.

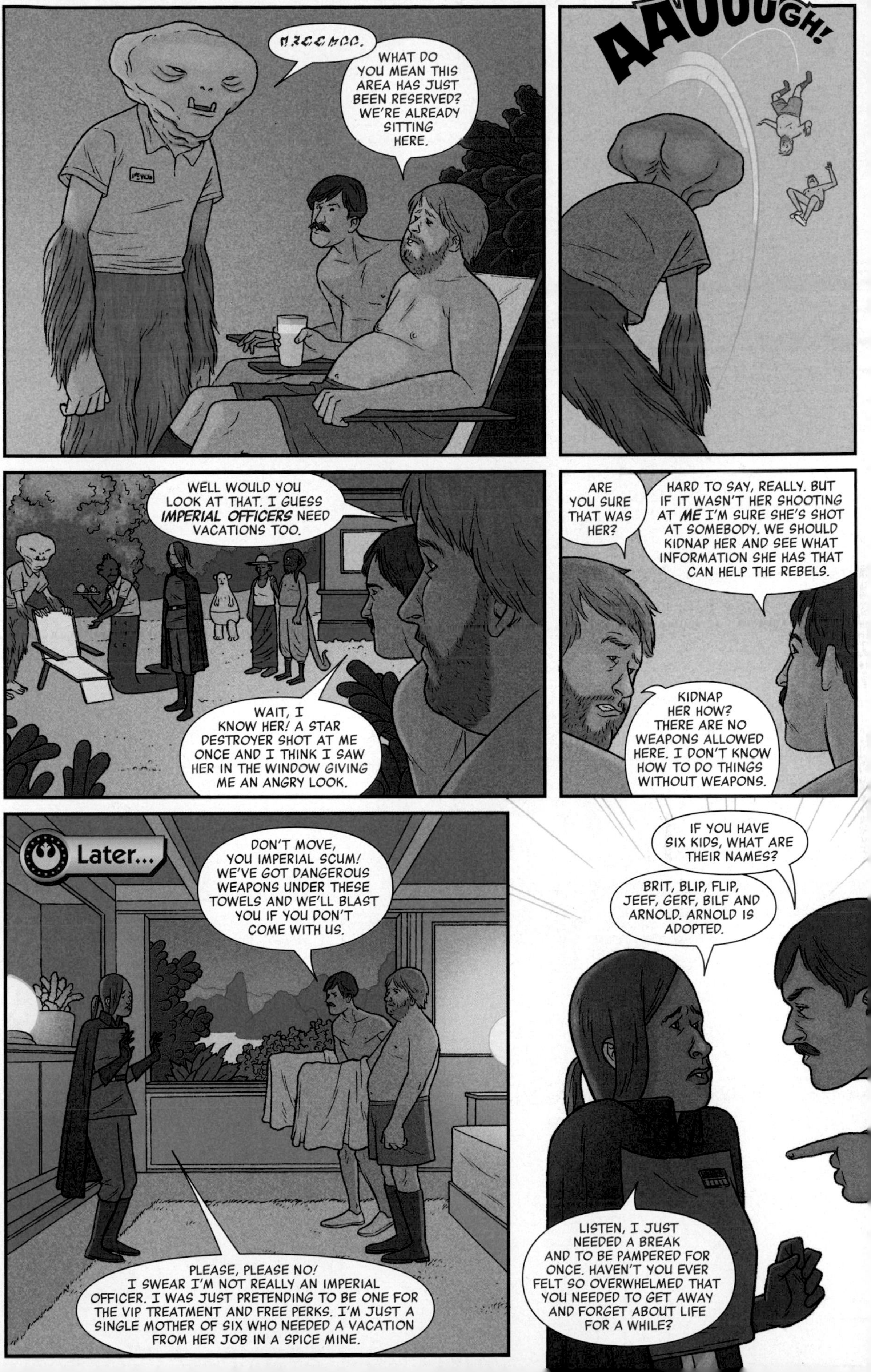
WHAT DO YOU MEAN THIS AREA HAS JUST BEEN RESERVED? WE'RE ALREADY SITTING HERE.
AAUUUGH!
WELL WOULD YOU LOOK AT THAT. I GUESS IMPERIAL OFFICERS NEED VACATIONS TOO.
WAIT, I KNOW HER! A STAR DESTROYER SHOT AT ME ONCE AND I THINK I SAW HER IN THE WINDOW GIVING ME AN ANGRY LOOK.
ARE YOU SURE THAT WAS HER?
HARD TO SAY, REALLY. BUT IF IT WASN'T HER SHOOTING AT ME I'M SURE SHE'S SHOT AT SOMEBODY. WE SHOULD KIDNAP HER AND SEE WHAT INFORMATION SHE HAS THAT CAN HELP THE REBELS.
KIDNAP HER HOW? THERE ARE NO WEAPONS ALLOWED HERE. I DON'T KNOW HOW TO DO THINGS WITHOUT WEAPONS.
Later...
DON'T MOVE, YOU IMPERIAL SCUM! WE'VE GOT DANGEROUS WEAPONS UNDER THESE TOWELS AND WE'LL BLAST YOU IF YOU DON'T COME WITH US.
PLEASE, PLEASE NO! I SWEAR I'M NOT REALLY AN IMPERIAL OFFICER. I WAS JUST PRETENDING TO BE ONE FOR THE VIP TREATMENT AND FREE PERKS. I'M JUST A SINGLE MOTHER OF SIX WHO NEEDED A VACATION FROM HER JOB IN A SPICE MINE.
IF YOU HAVE SIX KIDS, WHAT ARE THEIR NAMES?
BRIT, BLIP, FLIP, JEEF, GERF, BILF AND ARNOLD. ARNOLD IS ADOPTED.
LISTEN, I JUST NEEDED A BREAK AND TO BE PAMPERED FOR ONCE. HAVEN'T YOU EVER FELT SO OVERWHELMED THAT YOU NEEDED TO GET AWAY AND FORGET ABOUT LIFE FOR A WHILE?

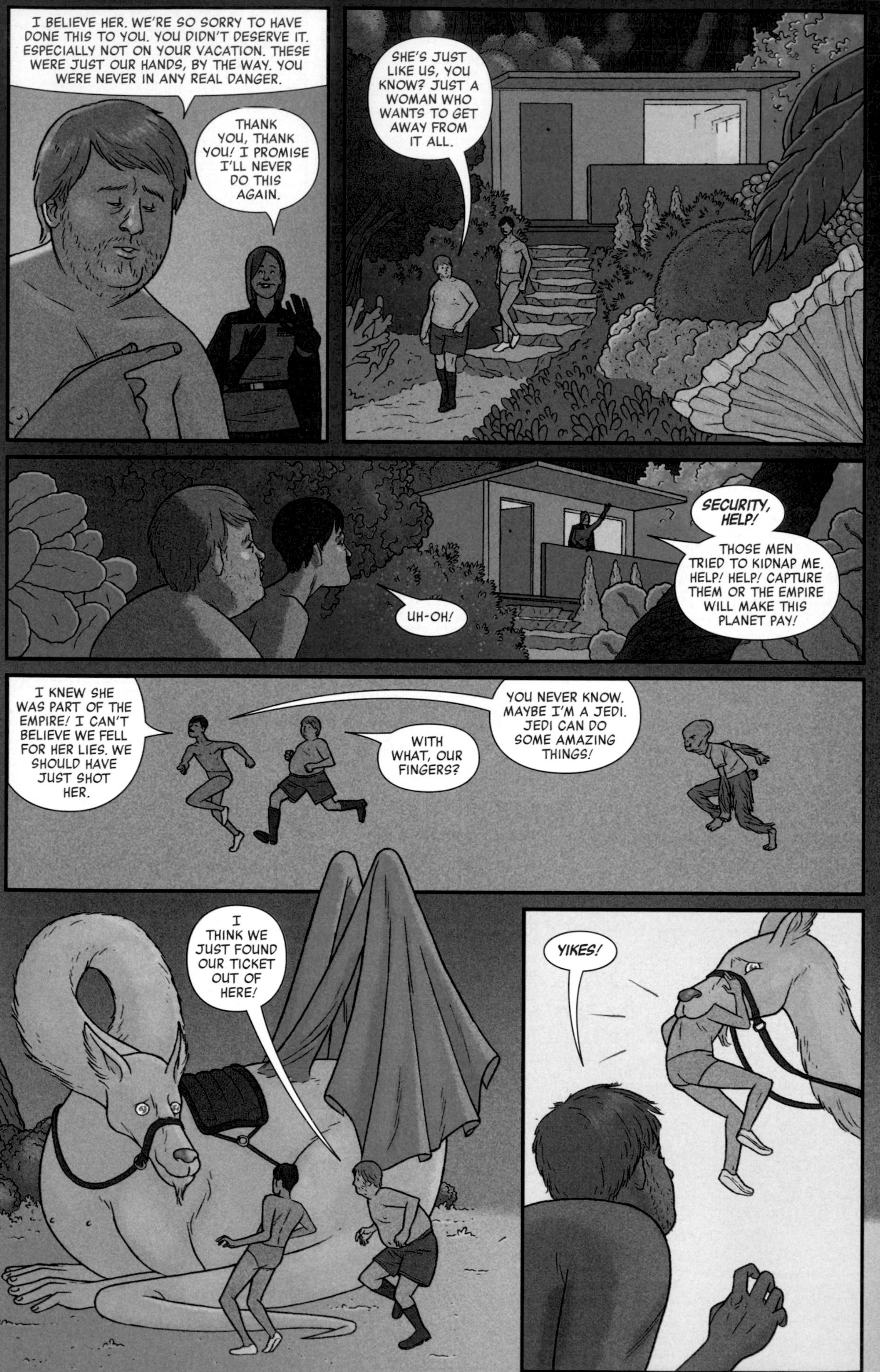
I BELIEVE HER. WE'RE SO SORRY TO HAVE DONE THIS TO YOU. YOU DIDN'T DESERVE IT. ESPECIALLY NOT ON YOUR VACATION. THESE WERE JUST OUR HANDS, BY THE WAY. YOU WERE NEVER IN ANY REAL DANGER.
THANK YOU, THANK YOU! I PROMISE I'LL NEVER DO THIS AGAIN.
SHE'S JUST LIKE US, YOU KNOW? JUST A WOMAN WHO WANTS TO GET AWAY FROM IT ALL.
SECURITY, HELP!
THOSE MEN TRIED TO KIDNAP ME. HELP! HELP! CAPTURE THEM OR THE EMPIRE WILL MAKE THIS PLANET PAY!
UH-OH!
I KNEW SHE WAS PART OF THE EMPIRE! I CAN'T BELIEVE WE FELL FOR HER LIES. WE SHOULD HAVE JUST SHOT HER.
WITH WHAT, OUR FINGERS?
YOU NEVER KNOW. MAYBE I'M A JEDI. JEDI CAN DO SOME AMAZING THINGS!
I THINK WE JUST FOUND OUR TICKET OUT OF HERE!
YIKES!

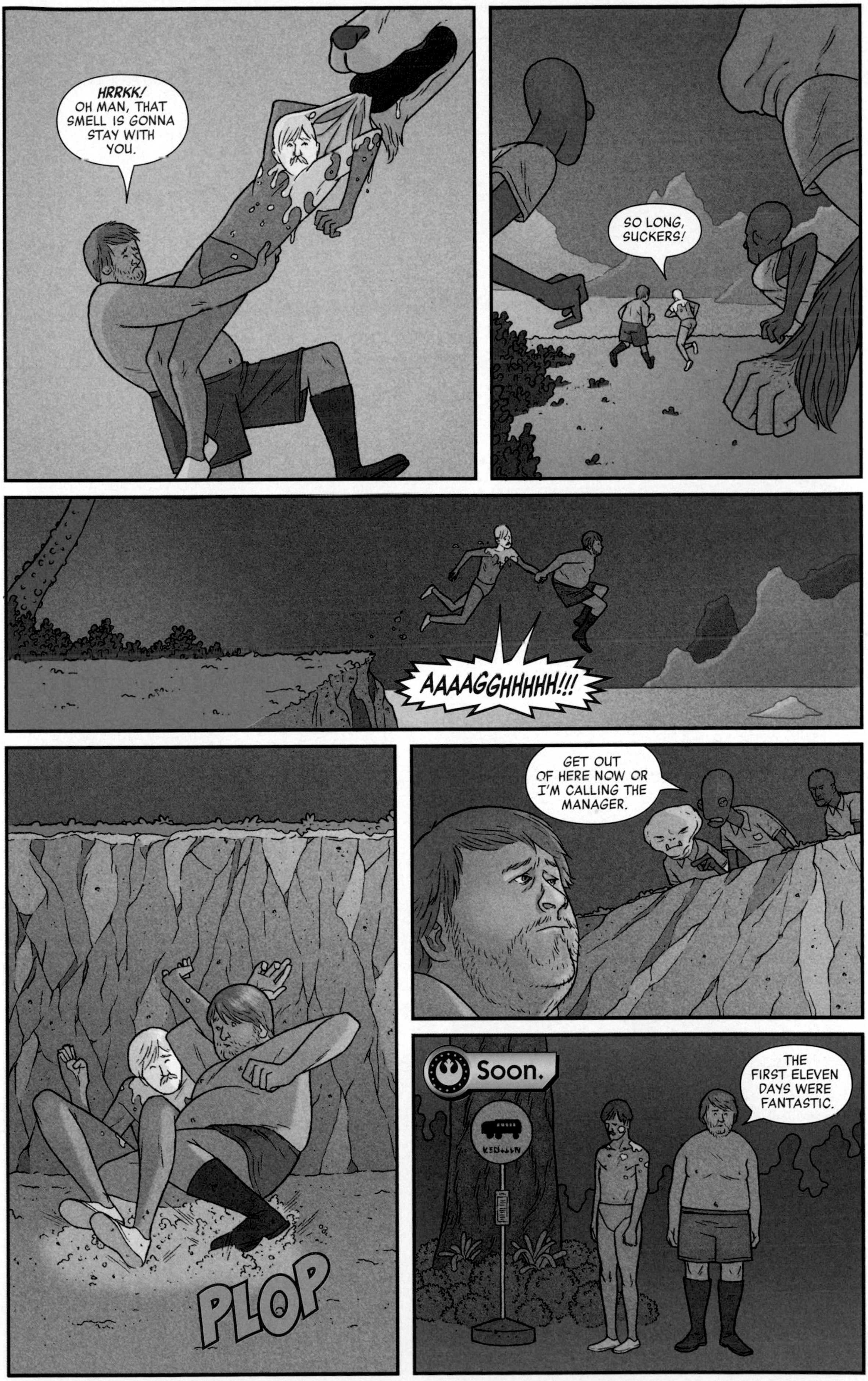
HRRKK! OH MAN, THAT SMELL IS GONNA STAY WITH YOU.
SO LONG, SUCKERS!
AAAAGGHHHHH!!!
PLOP
GET OUT OF HERE NOW OR I'M CALLING THE MANAGER.
Soon.
THE FIRST ELEVEN DAYS WERE FANTASTIC.

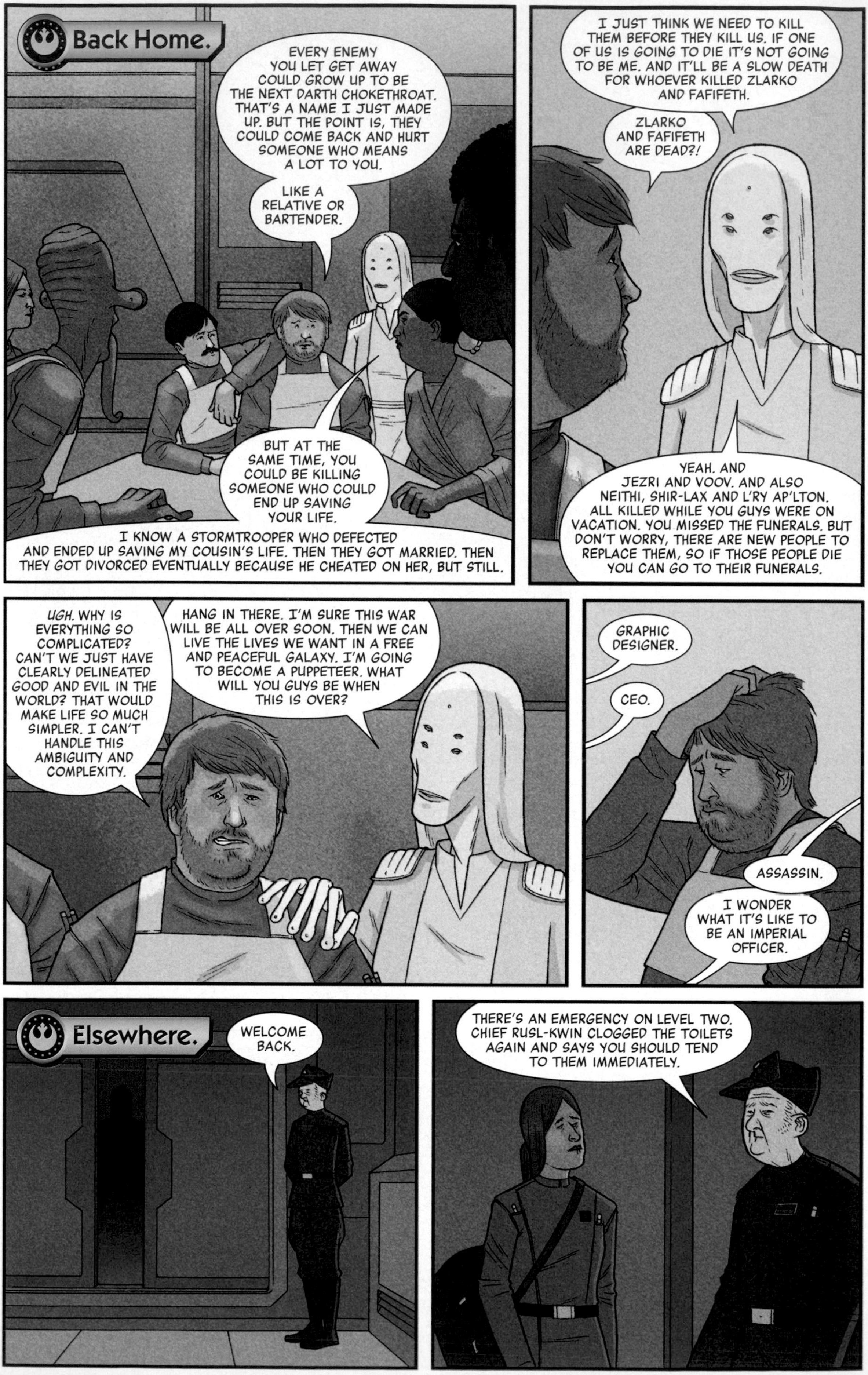
Back Home.
EVERY ENEMY YOU LET GET AWAY COULD GROW UP TO BE THE NEXT DARTH CHOKETHROAT. THAT'S A NAME I JUST MADE UP. BUT THE POINT IS, THEY COULD COME BACK AND HURT SOMEONE WHO MEANS A LOT TO YOU.
LIKE A RELATIVE OR BARTENDER.
BUT AT THE SAME TIME, YOU COULD BE KILLING SOMEONE WHO COULD END UP SAVING YOUR LIFE.
I KNOW A STORMTROOPER WHO DEFECTED AND ENDED UP SAVING MY COUSIN'S LIFE. THEN THEY GOT MARRIED. THEN THEY GOT DIVORCED EVENTUALLY BECAUSE HE CHEATED ON HER, BUT STILL.
I JUST THINK WE NEED TO KILL THEM BEFORE THEY KILL US. IF ONE OF US IS GOING TO DIE IT'S NOT GOING TO BE ME. AND IT'LL BE A SLOW DEATH FOR WHOEVER KILLED ZLARKO AND FAFIFETH.
ZLARKO AND FAFIFETH ARE DEAD?!
YEAH. AND JEZRI AND VOOV. AND ALSO NEITHI, SHIR-LAX AND L'RY AP'LTON. ALL KILLED WHILE YOU GUYS WERE ON VACATION. YOU MISSED THE FUNERALS. BUT DON'T WORRY, THERE ARE NEW PEOPLE TO REPLACE THEM, SO IF THOSE PEOPLE DIE YOU CAN GO TO THEIR FUNERALS.
UGH. WHY IS EVERYTHING SO COMPLICATED? CAN'T WE JUST HAVE CLEARLY DELINEATED GOOD AND EVIL IN THE WORLD? THAT WOULD MAKE LIFE SO MUCH SIMPLER. I CAN'T HANDLE THIS AMBIGUITY AND COMPLEXITY.
HANG IN THERE. I'M SURE THIS WAR WILL BE ALL OVER SOON. THEN WE CAN LIVE THE LIVES WE WANT IN A FREE AND PEACEFUL GALAXY. I'M GOING TO BECOME A PUPPETEER. WHAT WILL YOU GUYS BE WHEN THIS IS OVER?
GRAPHIC DESIGNER.
CEO.
ASSASSIN.
I WONDER WHAT IT'S LIKE TO BE AN IMPERIAL OFFICER.
Elsewhere.
WELCOME BACK.
THERE'S AN EMERGENCY ON LEVEL TWO. CHIEF RUSL-KWIN CLOGGED THE TOILETS AGAIN AND SAYS YOU SHOULD TEND TO THEM IMMEDIATELY.

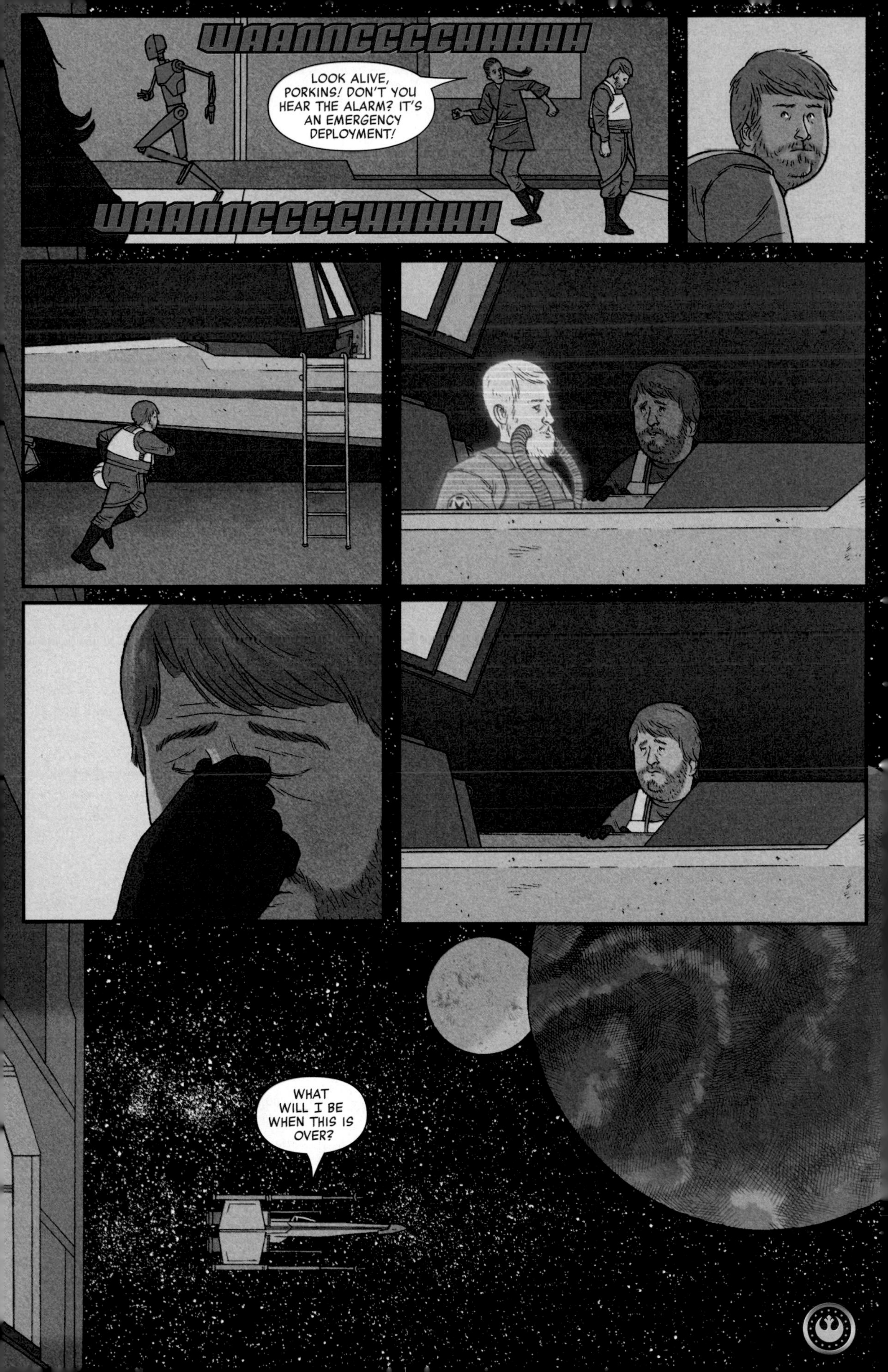
WAANNGGGCHHHHH
LOOK ALIVE, PORKINS! DON'T YOU HEAR THE ALARM? IT'S AN EMERGENCY DEPLOYMENT!
WAANNGGGCHHHHH
WHAT WILL I BE WHEN THIS IS OVER?

Concept art by Ralph McQuarrie and Joe Johnston

STORIES BEHIND THE STORIES:
The Heroes and Villains of the Age of Rebellion
By Bryan Young

One of the central attractions to the *Star Wars* saga is how "lived in" it feels. For many who were inspired by *Star Wars*, the feeling that it was a real place was one of the key things they homed in on. It was new and different when the films were originally released. In the 1970s, sci-fi tended to be very clean and polished, and the future was bright and happy. *Star Wars* gave us something more akin to a real world, set in the past and lived in.

Part of what made *Star Wars* feel so tangible was the wide array of humans, aliens, droids and creatures populating the universe. Every character, from the foreground to the background, seemed to have a story of their own. Everyone has their own path to follow, and the characters in the AGE OF REBELLION special are no exception. Would *The Empire Strikes Back* have worked as a film if Yoda didn't feel real? Would *A New Hope* have felt as endearing if the rebel pilots didn't all have personalities of their own? And what of the menace of the bounty hunters? Their stories made them feel real too, right?

Star Wars has so many stories to tell, but one of the most fascinating things about *Star Wars* is the stories *behind* the stories...

FROM BUFFY AND MINCH TO YODA

In George Lucas' original outlines for the *Star Wars* trilogy, Ben Kenobi was meant to train Luke through *The Empire Strikes Back*. This caused a bit of a problem when he decided to kill the wizened master in *A New Hope*. "So now I had to come up with another Jedi," Lucas said in an interview with StarWars.Com. "[One] who was older and wiser and shorter than Ben to train Luke. And that was the beginning premise of Yoda."

As Lucas began to explore what this character would become, Yoda had a very different name. In the earliest drafts of *The Empire Strikes Back*, "Buffy" was the name given to the diminutive, Yoda-like character. When Leigh Brackett wrote her version of the story, "Buffy" turned into "Minch Yoda." Lawrence Kasdan cut the whole thing down to just "Yoda."

As preproduction on the film ramped up and Lucas settled on the idea of having a puppet play the role, he went to Jim Henson, creator of the Muppets, and offered the part to him. In his THX interview with Leonard Maltin on the 1995 VHS release of *The Empire Strikes Back*, Lucas said, "I went to Jim and said, 'Do you want to do this?' And he said, 'Well, I'm busy, I'm doing this, and

doing that, I'm making a movie and all that. I really can't, but how about Frank [Oz]? You know, Frank's the other half of me.' And I said, 'Well, that'd be fantastic.'"

Frank Oz, the man behind Fozzie Bear and Grover, settled into the part with a puppet designed by the legendary Stuart Freeborn, and the rest was history. After the movie came out, the performance of Yoda was so believable and relatable that there was talk of Oz getting an Oscar nomination for the role.

Today, Yoda is viewed as one of the most iconic characters in *Star Wars*, and the wisdom he imparted in all of his appearances in the *Star Wars* films is quoted by fans on a daily basis.

DARKLIGHTER'S LIFE AND DEATH

Brought to life by Garrick Hagon, Biggs Darklighter was Luke Skywalker's closest friend on Tatooine. In some early drafts of the original screenplay, Biggs and Luke were even brothers, though their close friendship could be looked at as a brotherhood of a kind.

For fans in the early days of *Star Wars*, Biggs was merely a pilot we caught glimpses of. We saw pictures of Luke's time on Tatooine and heard stories of his defection (thanks to the NPR audio dramas and CD-ROM behind-the-scenes features), but it wasn't until the Special Edition of *A New Hope* was released that most audiences got their first real details about Luke's friend. Most modern audiences probably don't even remember a time before the scene of Biggs and Luke embracing before the battle of Yavin was in *Star Wars*. But, by adding back that one exchange into the film, the death of Biggs Darklighter during the trench run hits a whole lot harder.

Hagon would later tell StarWars.Com that he felt no ill will in having all of his early scenes cut. "Well, that was George's genius in cutting the film. He had this wonderful vision and story, and he didn't want to slow it down. He wanted just to drop the audience right in there and keep the action going. And he was right, of course."

WILLIAM HOOTKINS: PORKINS PERSONIFIED

Jek Porkins is another interesting character In a lot of ways. He was a member of the Tierfon Yellow Aces before joining Red Squadron prior to the battle of Yavin. In *The Force Awakens*, you can see Rey don a helmet left over from the Battle of Jakku from those very same Yellow Aces. Porkins was played by William Hootkins, a notable character actor who appeared in many of your favorite franchises; he played a crooked cop in *Batman* (1989) and one of the government stooges in *Raiders of the Lost Ark*.

His life was endlessly fascinating in its own right, but one of Hootkins' most bizarre experiences might have been being questioned, at age 15, in connection to the assassination of John F. Kennedy. Hootkins was just a student taking private lessons in Russian at the time of the president's death. But his tutor happened to be Ruth Paine, a Russian immigrant closely connected to Lee Harvey Oswald and his wife, Marina. After the president was killed, the FBI left no stone unturned in their investigation, and Hootkins got caught up in that net.

Not long after that, he joined his school's theater group, alongside Tommy Lee Jones, and went on to become one of the great supporting actors of the '70s and '80s.

STORIES OF *STAR WARS*

It doesn't matter if the stories are in the universe or behind the scenes, *Star Wars* is a playground for stories and art. Whether that's an artist kitbashing a Rolls-Royce to make a droid puppet or an actor who was questioned by the FBI in connection with the murder of a president, there's always a story behind the story waiting to be told.

Research and quotes sourced from StarWars.Com *and* HowStuffWorks.

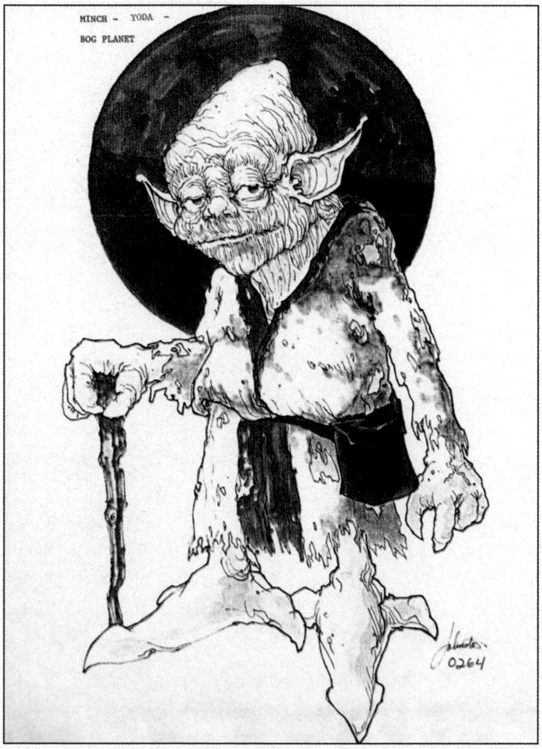
MINCH - YODA -
BOG PLANET
0264

Concept art by Joe Johnston

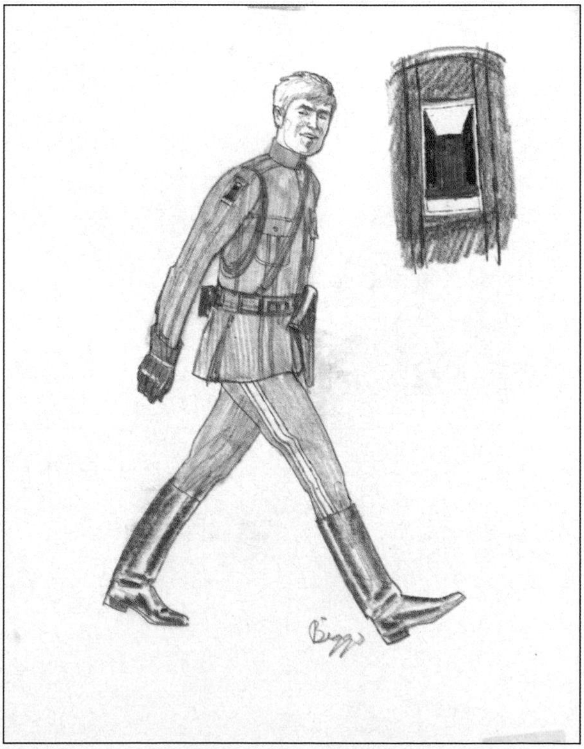
Biggs

Concept art by Ralph McQuarrie

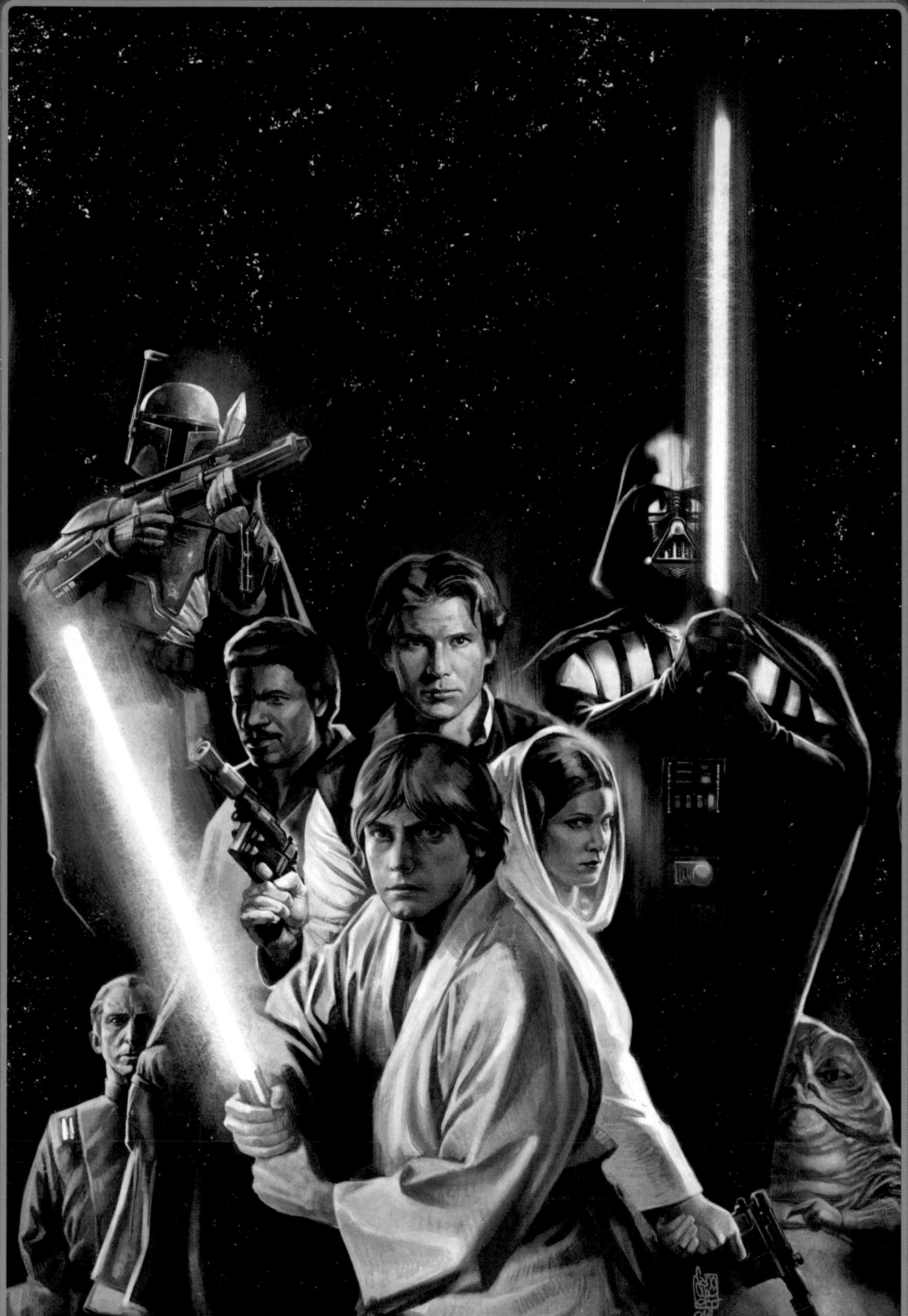

STAR WARS: AGE OF REBELLION – PRINCESS LEIA Variant by
GIUSEPPE CAMUNCOLI & ELIA BONETTI

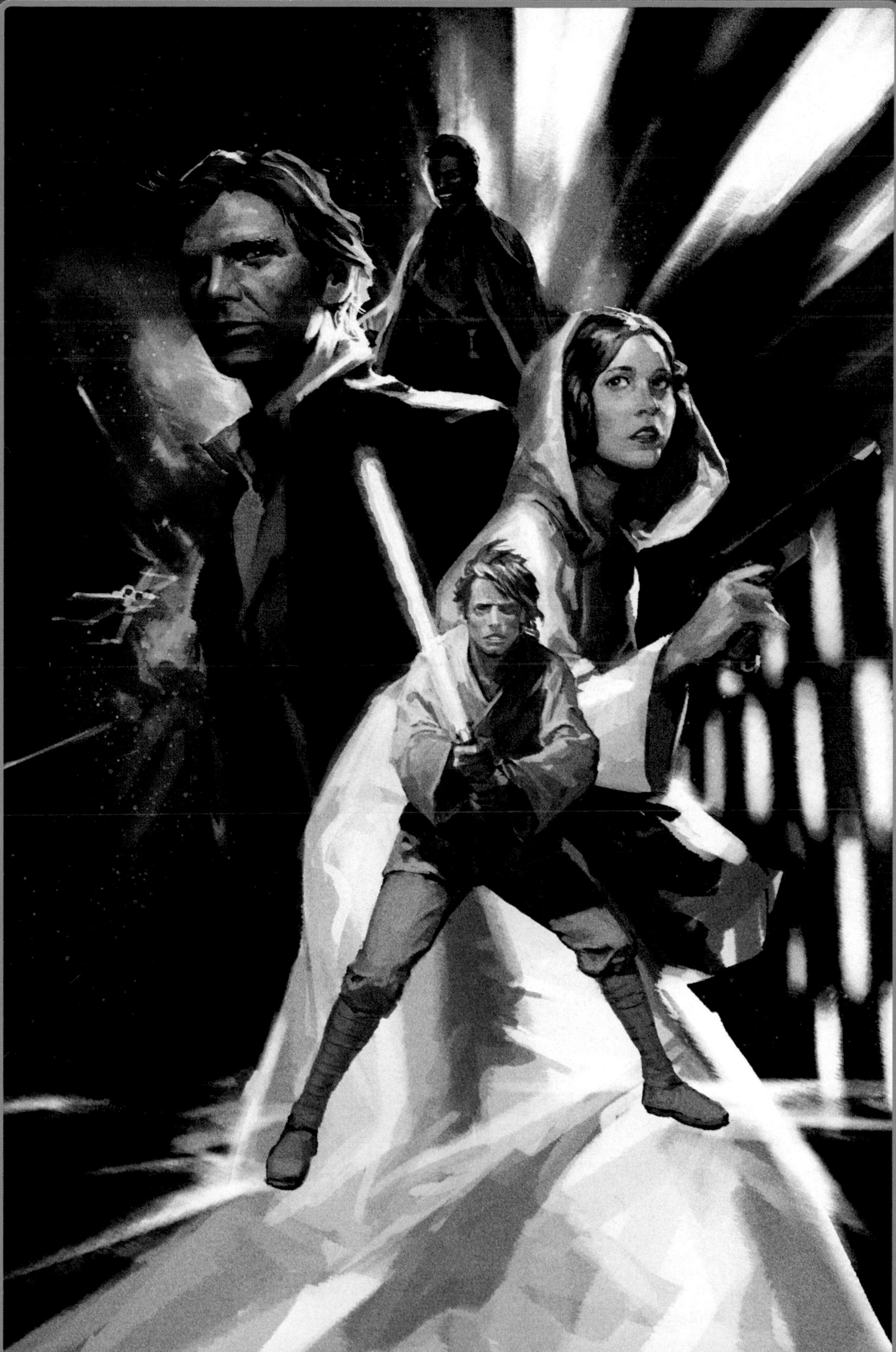

STAR WARS: AGE OF REBELLION – HAN SOLO **Variant by**
GERALD PAREL

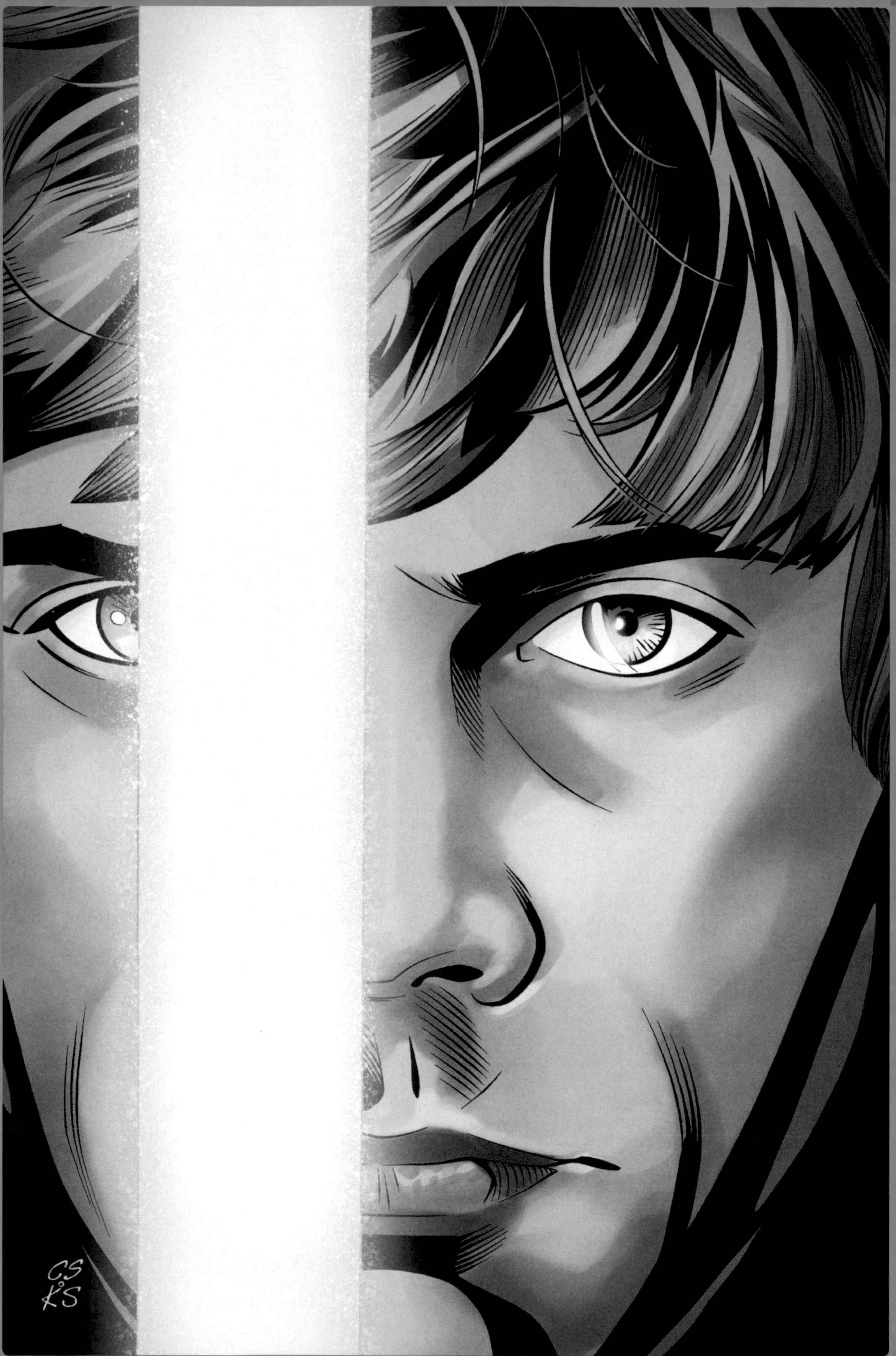

***STAR WARS: AGE OF REBELLION – LUKE SKYWALKER* Variant by**
CHRIS SPROUSE, KARL STORY & NEERAJ MENON

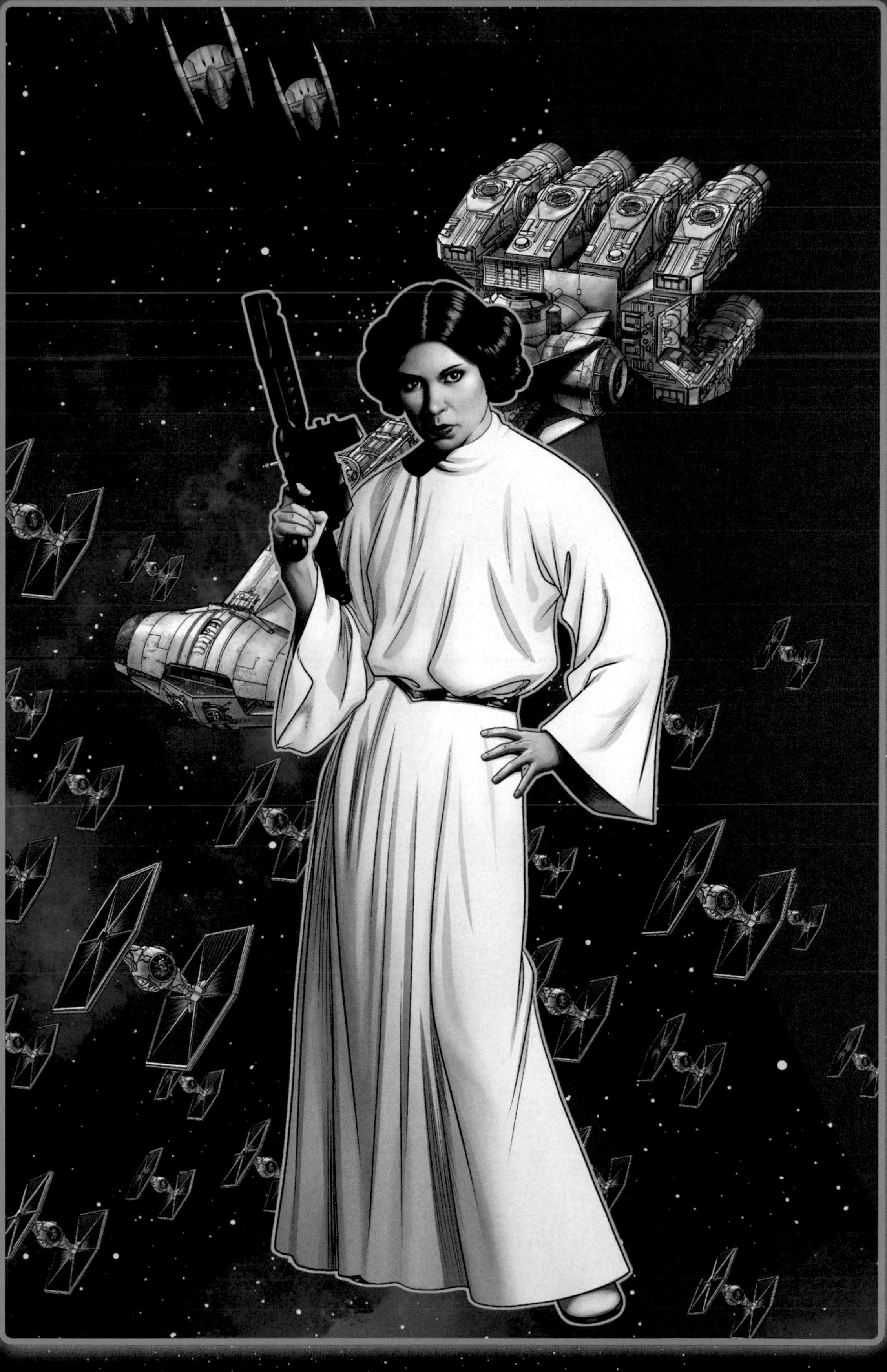

STAR WARS: AGE OF REBELLION – PRINCESS LEIA **Puzzle Piece Variant by**
MIKE McKONE & GURU-eFX

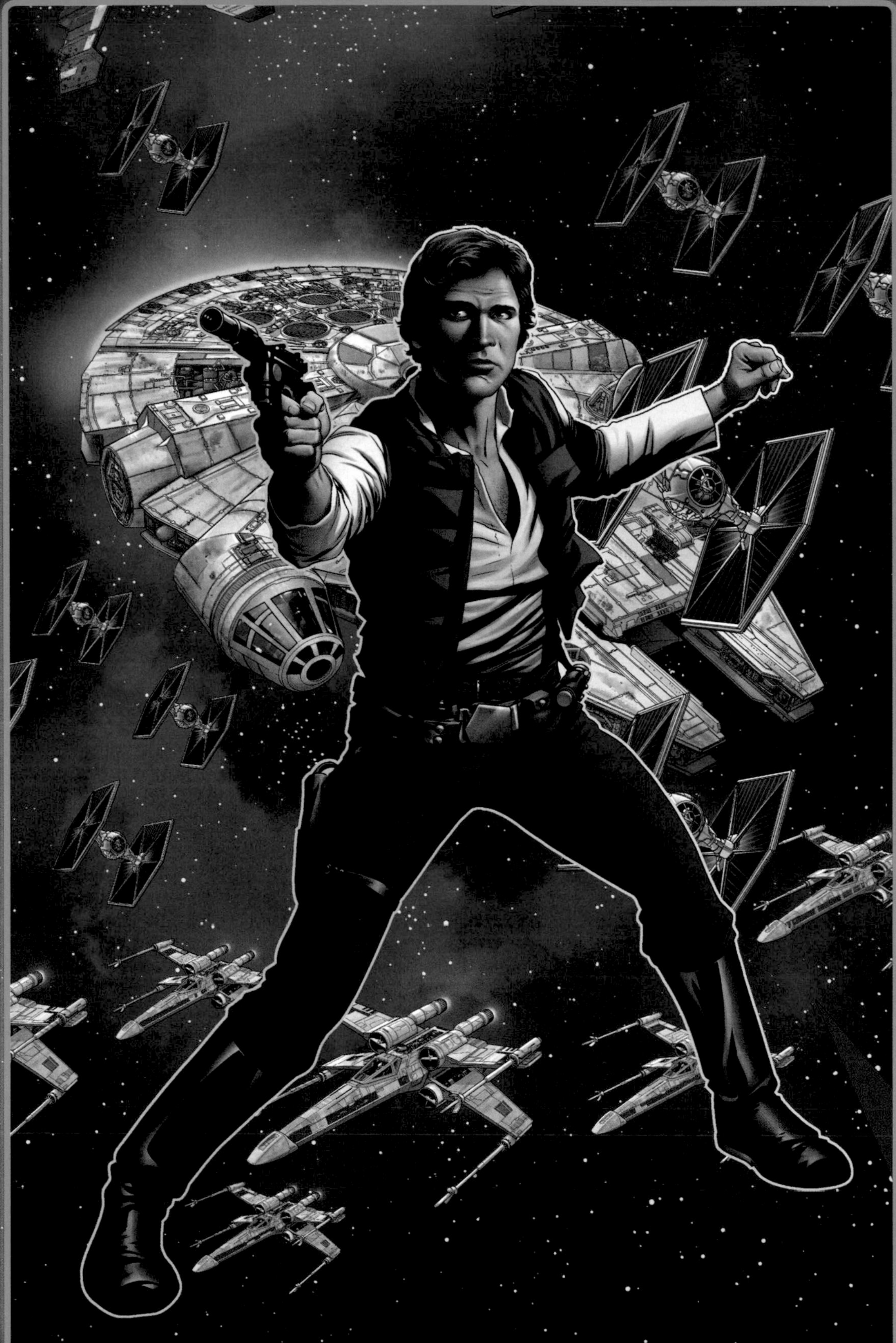

STAR WARS: AGE OF REBELLION – HAN SOLO **Puzzle Piece Variant by**
MIKE McKONE & GURU-eFX

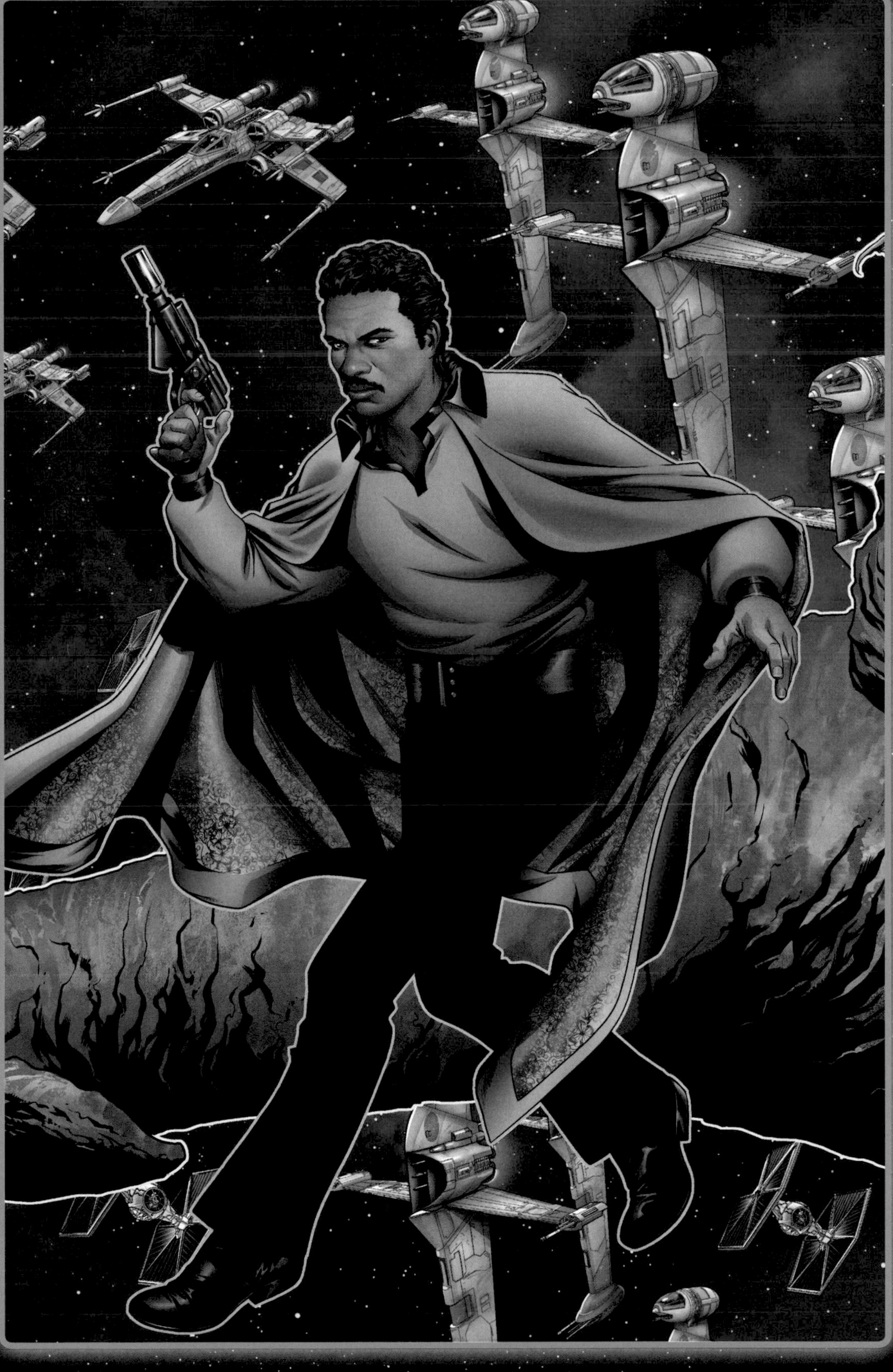

STAR WARS: AGE OF REBELLION – LANDO CALRISSIAN **Puzzle Piece Variant by**

MIKE McKONE & GURU-eFX

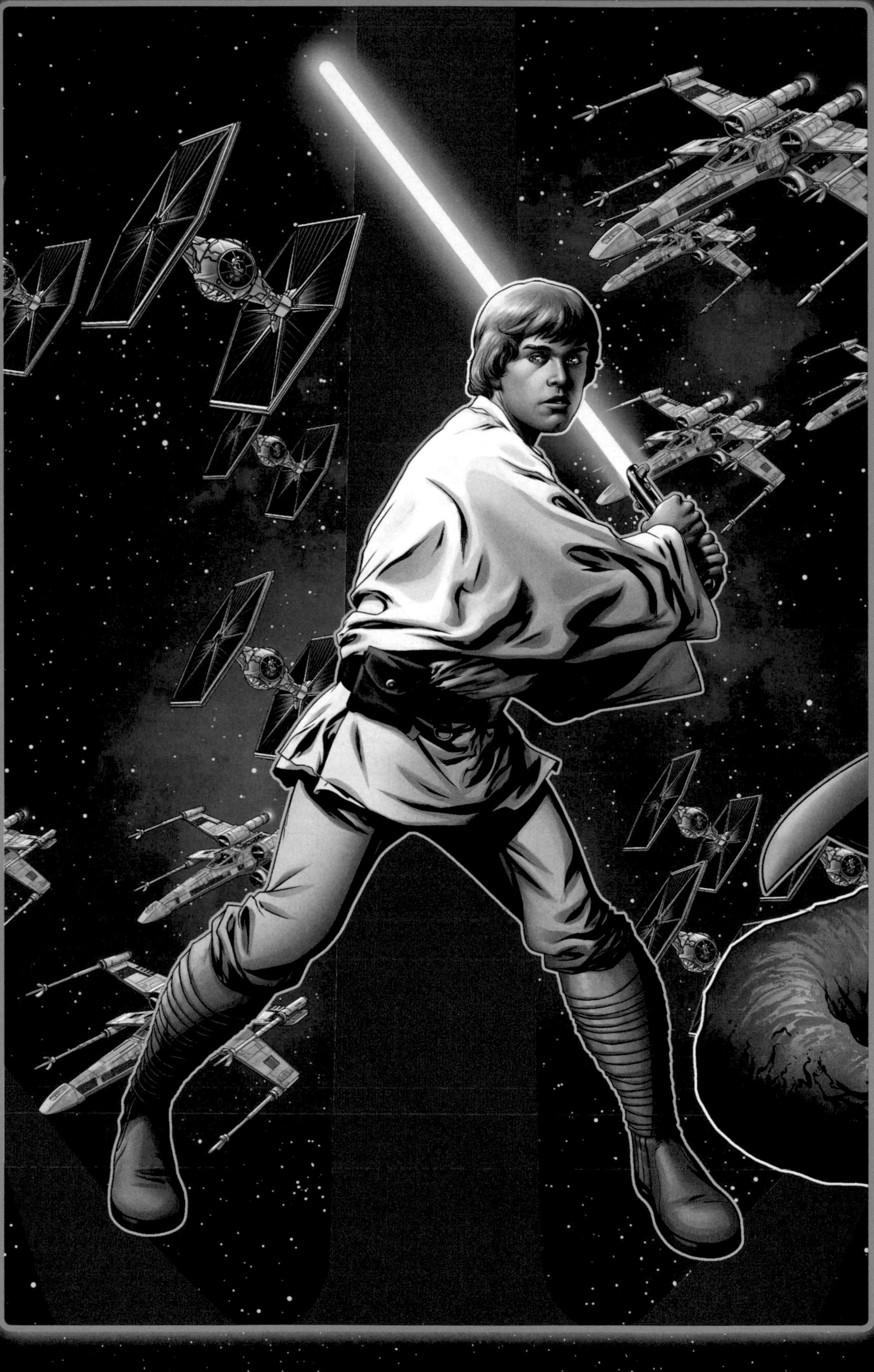

STAR WARS: AGE OF REBELLION – LUKE SKYWALKER Puzzle Piece Variant by

MIKE McKONE & GURU-FX

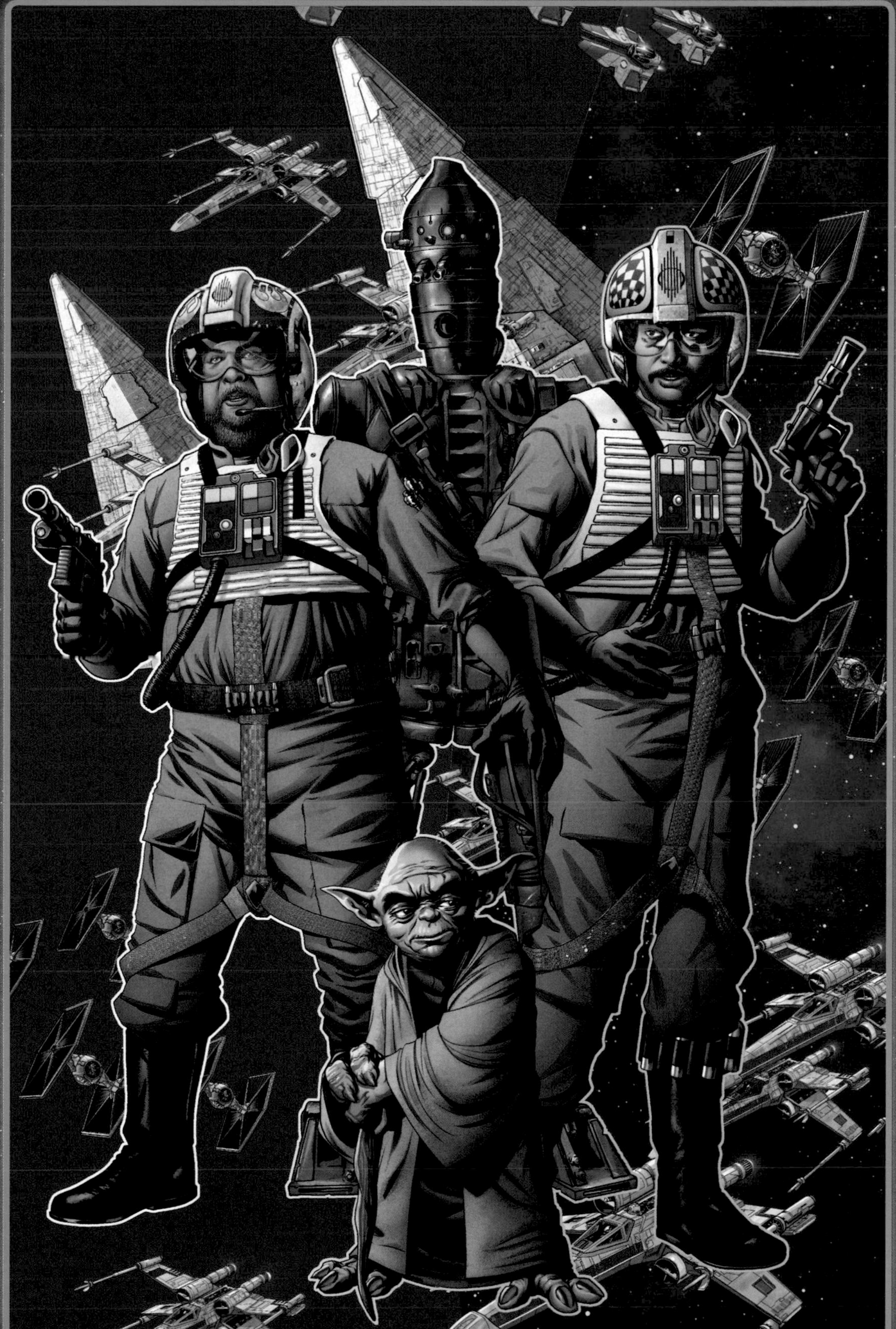

STAR WARS: AGE OF REBELLION SPECIAL Puzzle Piece Variant by
MIKE McKONE & GURU-eFX

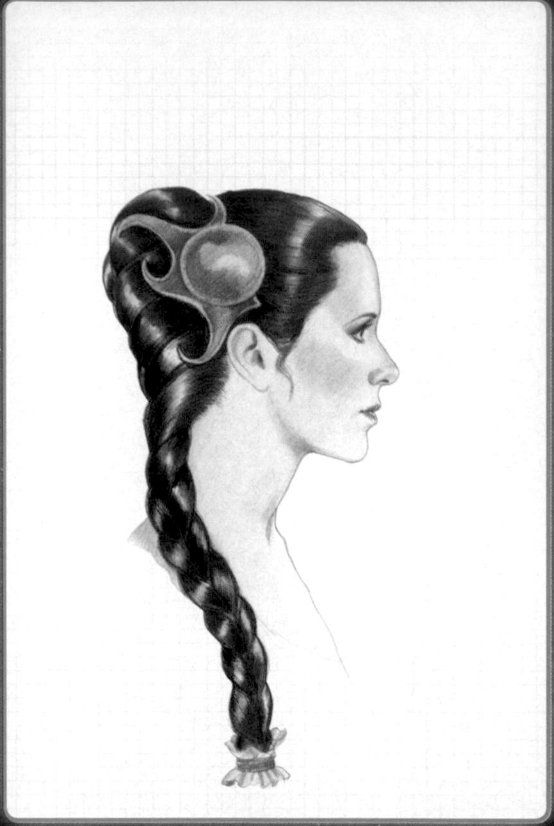

STAR WARS: AGE OF REBELLION – PRINCESS LEIA
Concept Variant by PAUL LEBLANC

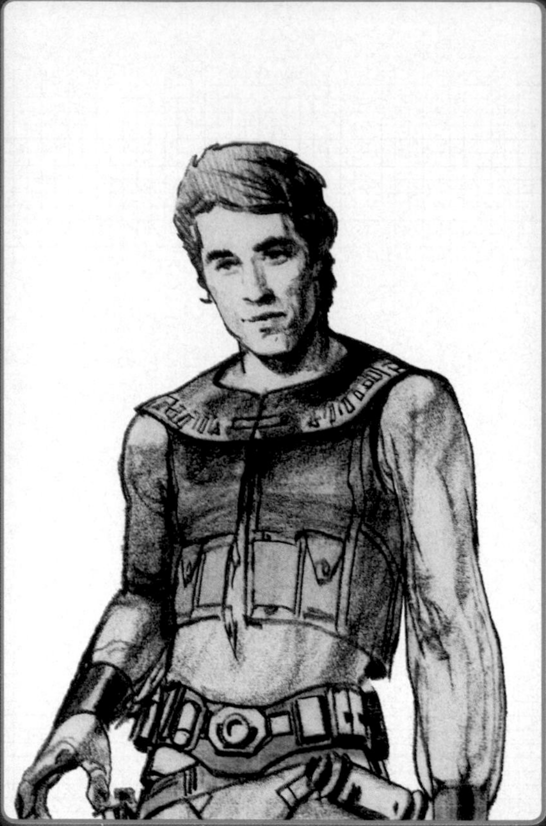

STAR WARS: AGE OF REBELLION – HAN SOLO
Concept Variant by RALPH McQUARRIE

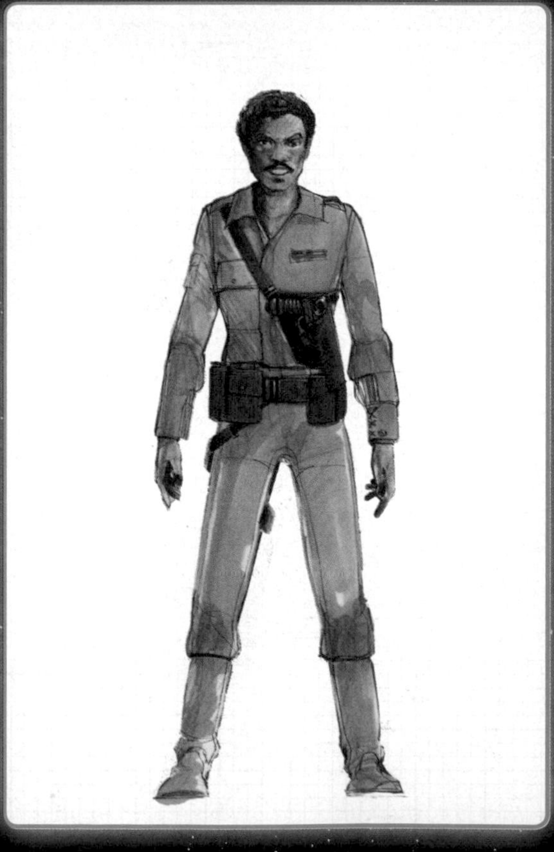

STAR WARS: AGE OF REBELLION – LANDO CALRISSIAN
Concept Variant by NILO RODIS-JAMERO

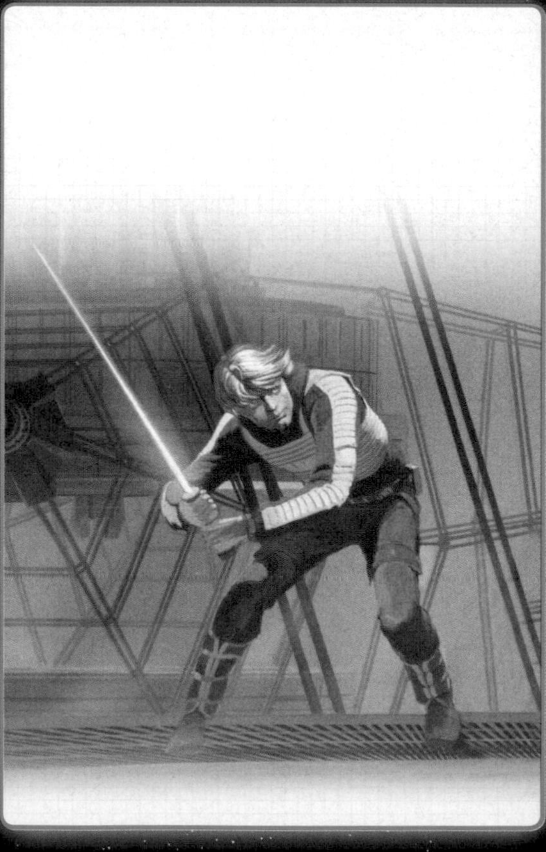

STAR WARS: AGE OF REBELLION – LUKE SKYWALKER
Concept Variant by RALPH McQUARRIE

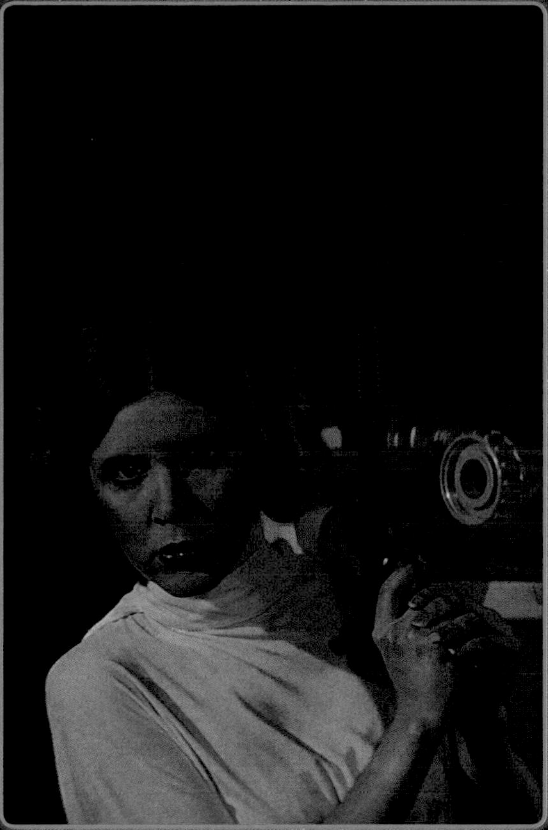

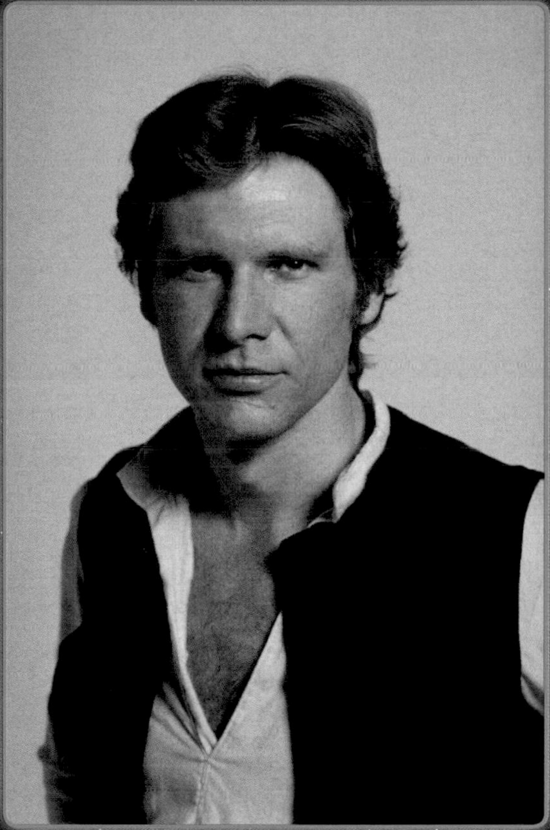

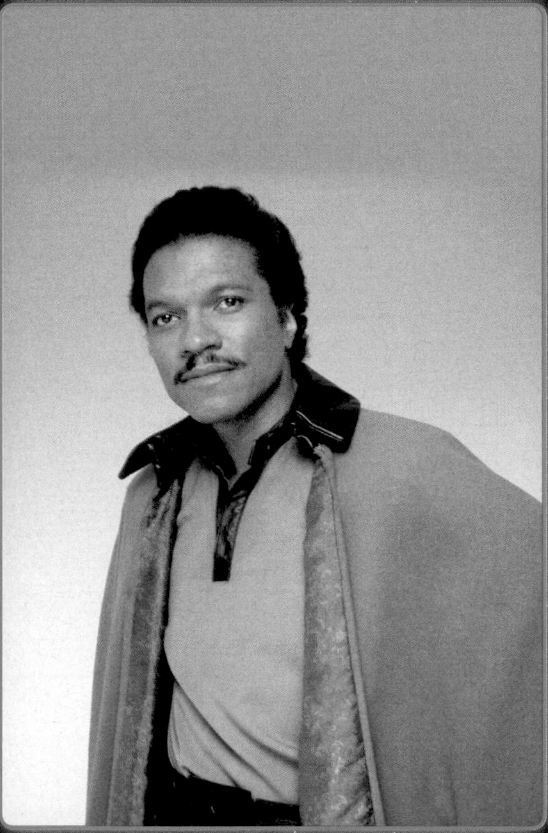

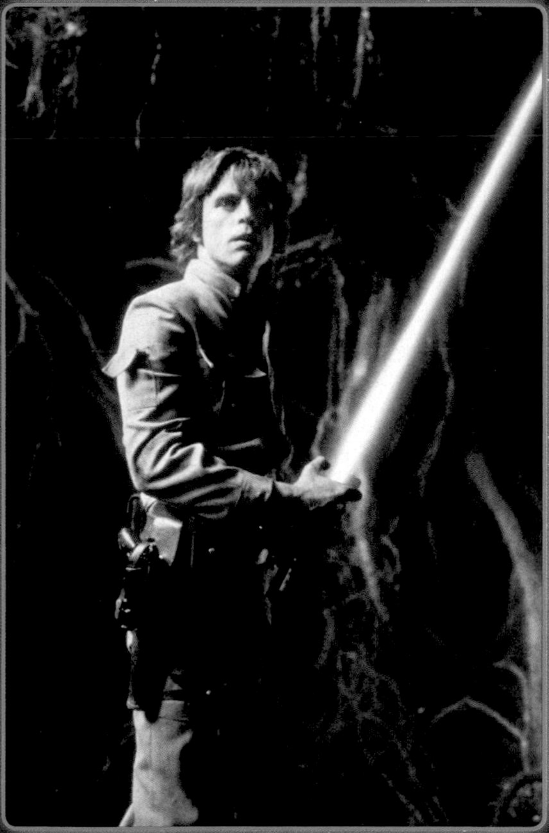

STAR WARS: AGE OF REBELLION – PRINCESS LEIA, HAN SOLO, LANDO CALRISSIAN & LUKE SKYWALKER **Movie Variants**

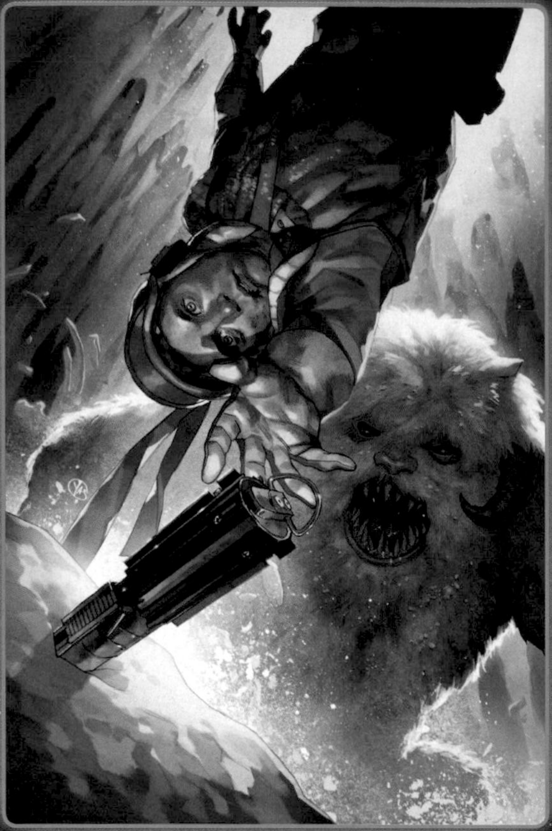

STAR WARS: AGE OF REBELLION – HAN SOLO
Star Wars Greatest Moments Variant by YASMINE PUTRI

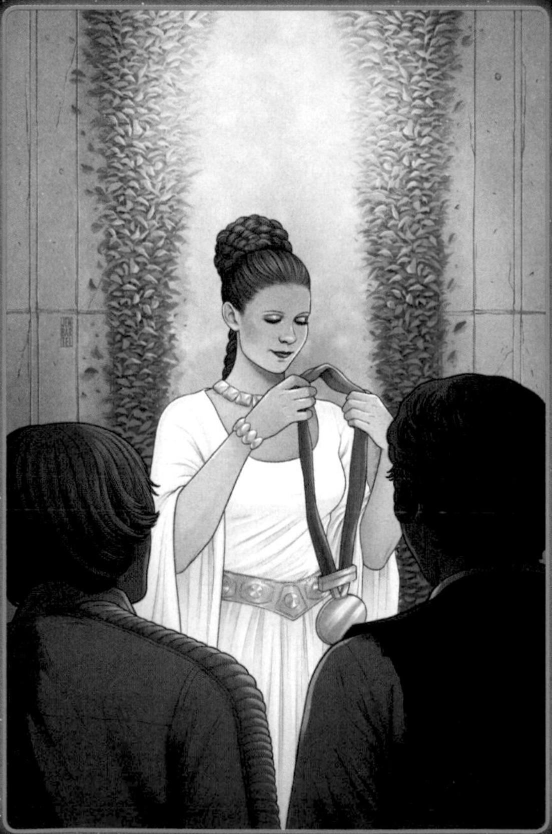

STAR WARS: AGE OF REBELLION SPECIAL #1
Star Wars Greatest Moments Variant by JEN BARTEL

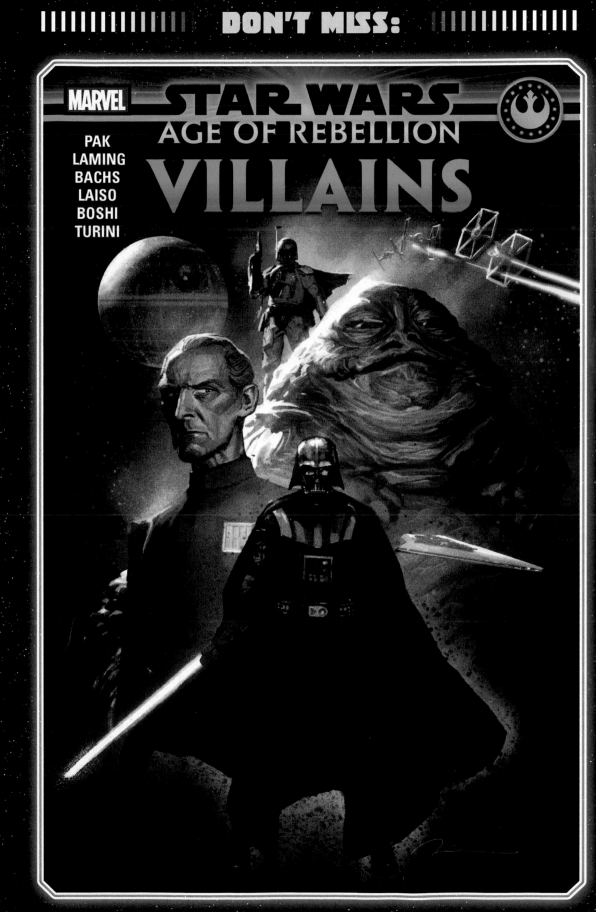

ALSO AVAILABLE:

MARVEL
STAR WARS
AGE OF REPUBLIC
HOUSER
SMITH
SANTOS
WONG
HEROES

MARVEL
STAR WARS
AGE OF REPUBLIC
HOUSER
ROSS
TARTAGLIA
VILLAINS

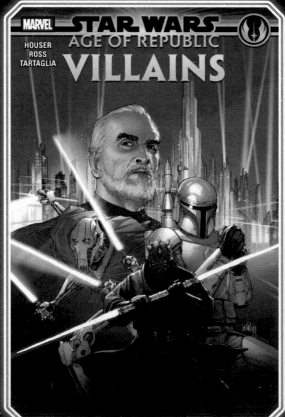